# LISTENING FOR GOD

"Peter Brown's *Listening for God* speaks directly to a time like our own so deeply divided between the seductions of believing too much, as William James once called them, and those of believing too little. In the face of such absolutist religious alternatives, he has found in the narratives of four modern American writers—Bernard Malamud, Flannery O'Connor, John Updike, and Toni Morrison—new resonances of the sacred that defamiliarize the spiritual by making it once again strange, mysterious, other, and unavoidable."

— Giles Gunn, preeminent Americanist and cultural critic;
and distinguished professor emeritus
of English and of Global Studies,
University of California Santa Barbara

"In *Listening for God*, Peter Brown embarks on a daring quest pursuing the sacred in modern American literature. Deeply versed in philosophy and theology, as well as the complexities of narrative, Brown deftly explores the imaginative work of four important writers—Bernard Malamud, Flannery O'Connor, John Updike, and Toni Morrison—finding in all a 'seam of radical responsibility' propelling their fiction toward ultimate meaning and the spirit. Brown's forceful and passionate analysis signals his own radical responsibility at locating the transcendent, making the significance of *Listening for God* extend far beyond the literary. Read it and start listening."

—Robert H. Brinkmeyer, Jr., Claude Henry Neuffer
Professor of Southern Studies,
University of South Carolina

MERCER UNIVERSITY

MERCER UNIVERSITY PRESS

*Endowed by*

TOM WATSON BROWN
*and*
THE WATSON-BROWN FOUNDATION, INC.

# LISTENING FOR GOD

*Malamud, O'Connor, Updike, & Morrison*

PETER C. BROWN

MERCER UNIVERSITY PRESS
*Macon, Georgia*

MUP/ H999


Published by Mercer University Press
1501 Mercer University Drive
Macon, Georgia 31207


25 24 23 22 21 20   5 4 3 2 1

Books published by Mercer University Press are printed on acid-free paper that meets the requirements of the American National Standard for Information Sciences—Permanence of Paper for Printed Library Materials.

Printed and bound in the United States.

This book is set in Adobe Garamond Pro.

Cover/jacket design by Burt&Burt.

ISBN 978-0-88146-7680
Library of Congress Cataloging-in-Publication Data

Names: Brown, Peter C., 1942- author.
Title: Listening for God : Malamud, O'Connor, Updike, & Morrison / Peter C. Brown.
Description: 1st. | Macon : Mercer University Press, 2020. | Includes bibliographical references and index. |
Identifiers: LCCN 2020015005 | ISBN 9780881467680 (hardback)
Subjects: LCSH: Malamud, Bernard. | O'Connor, Flannery. | Updike, John. | Morrison, Toni. | Holy, The, in literature. | Holy, The.
Classification: LCC PN56.H555 B76 2020 | DDC 813/.509382—dc23
LC record available at https://lccn.loc.gov/2020015005

## Contents

*For Will, Benedicte, and Charlotte Alyce*

# Acknowledgments

I owe a general note of thanks to Dr. Theodore Nordenhaug and other chairs and deans over four decades at Mercer University who let me teach pretty much whatever I wanted—in or out of the field of Philosophy. Over the long run, following my nose has turned out to be a rewarding intellectual strategy. Dr. Stephen Bluestone, poet and scholar, was the longtime provocative collaborator at Mercer who most helped me take advantage of that freedom of inquiry. Dr. Giles Gunn, distinguished Americanist and cultural critic, generously gave me the opportunity to begin the work reflected in this volume in a long-ago NEH Summer Seminar at the University of Florida. Crucially, Dr. Robert Detweiler at the Institute of the Liberal Arts at Emory University supported me with great tact and wisdom as I formally made the shift from epistemology and the philosophy of science to religion and literature—and resumed long-delayed Ph.D. studies. And, finally, a special thanks to my wife, Bette-Lou O'Connor Brown, who has stood by me for over half a century through all the twists and turns of my professional life.

[The critic] can be defined as the one that still has something to say

when everything has been said.

*Emmanuel Levinas*
*"Reality and Its Shadow"*

# Preface in Lieu of a Sermon

*After all these things God tested Abraham, and said to him, "Abraham!" And he said, "Here am I."—Genesis 22.1*

*And when the sixth hour had come, there was darkness over the whole land until the ninth hour. And at the ninth hour Jesus cried with a loud voice, "El'-oi, El'-oi, la'ma sabach-tha'ni?" which means, "My God, my God, why hast thou forsaken me?"—Mark 15.33–34*

Listening for God? At this late moment in Western modernity, how do we make such a project plausible—and why is it important?

*Secularization and Its Aftermath.* The moment is not propitious. We are forced to fight a rearguard battle against the atheist presumptions of brilliantly successful modern science.[1] At the opposite remove, we must somehow reconcile the omnipotent and just God of Christianity and Judaism with the singular horror of the Nazi Holocaust, with its Jewish genocide and its millennial Christian Anti-Semitic roots and multitudes of contemporary Christian bystanders and enablers. The whole project of listening for God may seem suspect as the West struggles with murderous Muslim jihadists martyring themselves in the name of Allah.

The notion that *we* may be the infidels seems to dumfound us. Aren't we past the point where religion is something to fight over? Has not tolerance become our secular faith? Live and let live. Indeed, over the past two centuries the traditional faiths of the West seem largely to have degraded into a cultural overlay on bourgeois motives, on getting and consuming as fundamental spiritual purposes. As Nietzsche famously proclaimed over a century ago, "God is Dead"; the spiritual energies of Europe were, he thought, exhausted. The Great Awakenings of the Eighteenth, Nineteenth, and Twentieth centuries in Protestant Europe and especially America—and eventually in world-wide

[1] Such defensive apologetics as (a) creationism (or supposedly "scientific" schemes for preserving Biblical literalism), (b) segregating provisional truths in the realm of facts (science) from absolute truth in the realm of values (religion), (c) the theistic argument from design for a "watchmaker" God, (d) the supposed cosmic teleological implications of the Anthropic Principle, and (e) the reasonableness of Pascal's wager on God's existence increasingly strike me as tired *ex post facto* rationalizations.

charismatic evangelism (Pentecostal and Anglican/Catholic)—were repeated attempts to substitute "enthusiasm" (literally, possession by the Holy Spirit) for fading doctrine and ritual, for the attenuated liturgies of communal belief. The prevailing enthusiasm of contemporary American evangelism comes in several questionable flavors—from the quasi-therapeutic array of feel-good and self-help activities in nondenominational megachurches to televangelist prayers (and donations) for blessings and prosperity to quasi-political calls to restore Christian values in our national institutions through the power of prayer, protest, and worship heavy on contemporary Christian music punctuated with cultic commitment. In spite of these revivals, young people in America increasingly express no religious affiliation at all.[2] This trend may in part reflect what the sociologist Grace Davie called "believing without belonging," which she saw in Britain as the effect of replacing the presumptive state church with a wide-open "market" in religious/spiritual expression or "implicit religion."[3] As many have since pointed out, "belonging without believing" is also a strong phenomenon,[4] ranging from "tribal Christianity" (loyalty to institutions and cultural forms shaped by Western Christianity) to "Christian Atheism" (prizing the death of supernatural theism as liberating Christians to follow Jesus as reformer and healer).

The sources of this nuanced disaffiliation are deeply embedded in our culture, seemingly a product of modernity itself. Modernity isn't just the latest "new"; it is an historically unique and radical break from all preceding civilizations, with their oppressive hierarchies of priests and warriors dominating society's producers. As Ernest Gellner brilliantly argues, historical modernity was a miracle: "How can it happen…that the whole organization and ethos of society changes, that Production replaces Predation as the central theme and value of life? Everything in the standard condition of agrarian society militates against such a miracle. Yet it did happen. In consequence, the

[2] According to Pew Research Center surveys, "As the Millennial generation enters adulthood, its members display much lower levels of religious affiliation, including less connection with Christian churches, than older generations. Fully 36% of young Millennials (those between the ages of 18 and 24) are religiously unaffiliated, as are 34% of older Millennials (ages 25-33)." Pew Research Center, "America's Changing Religious Landscape," 12 May 2015.

[3] Grace Davie, "Believing without Belonging," *Social Compass* 37.4 (1990): 455–469.

[4] See for example, Roberto Marchisio and Maurizo Pisati, "Belonging without Believing: Catholics in Contemporary Italy," *Journal of Modern Italian Studies* 4.2 (1999): 236–255.

world became transformed out of all recognition."[5] Gellner observes that there was no ontological or epistemic or social or cultural mandate for this transformation. He delineates fifteen historical factors in Western Europe and Great Britain that possibly—in some combination—explain this momentous sea change.[6] What was this transformation and what are its consequences—where does it put God? Empirical, impersonal science (and a Universe open to endless rational inquiry) replaced emotionally rich, logically incoherent magic and myth (and a multi-leveled Cosmos revealed in esoterica). Technological innovation, urbanization, and market capitalism (highly dynamic) displaced immemorial agrarian hierarchies with their mixture of coercion and sanctification (mostly static, except for periodic changes of regime). Citizenship in notional "nation states" (superficial *Gesellschaft*) supplanted ascribed identities rooted in local communal practices (deep *Gemeinschaft*). And, to our point, society in the West secularized.[7]

Charles Taylor in his magisterial study *A Secular Age* (based on his Gifford lectures of 1999) discerns three dimensions of secularization in the modern West. The most obvious is the withdrawal of religion from public life: "If we go back a few centuries in our civilization, we see that God was present...in a whole host of social practices—not just the political—and at all levels of society....These have been allegedly emptied of God, or of any reference to ultimate reality. Or taken from another side, as we function within various spheres of activity—economic, political, cultural, educational, professional, recreational—the norms and principles we follow, the deliberations we engage in, generally don't refer us to God or to any religious beliefs."[8] Of course, individuals remain largely free to believe or not, worship or not,

---

[5] Ernest Gellner, *Plough, Sword and Book: The Structure of Human History* (Chicago: University of Chicago Press, 1988) 158.

[6] Ibid., 158–171.

[7] The twentieth century scholarly consensus that modernity inevitably produces secularization has been largely overthrown (the United States and developing economies in the Third World seem to be exceptions, of a sort). Instead, secularization in Europe can be seen as one of the preconditions of the development of modernity. An interesting introduction to the question is to be found in the dedicated 2006 Spring & Summer issue of *The Hedgehog Review*: *After Secularization,* (8:1/2). The question of priority is a live one as the modernization/reform of Islam and the assimilation of Islamic immigrants into secular European nation states roils contemporary European politics and provokes the fear of a global clash of civilizations.

[8] Charles Taylor, *A Secular Age* (Cambridge: Harvard University Press, 2007) 1–2.

evangelize or not, propagandize or not. But, and this is Taylor's second point, the withdrawal from public spheres of practice is matched by "the falling off of religious belief and practice,...people turning away from God, and no longer going to Church. In this sense, the countries of Western Europe have mainly become secular—even those who retain the vestigial public reference to God in public space."[9] However, the third dimension of secularization is the one that interests Taylor the most. It is the loss of a sense of transcendence, so that for many good and intelligent people any value beyond human flourishing is inconceivable—and a self-sufficient, exclusive humanism *is* conceivable. Faith has become a reflective option, an aspiration for something more, a seeking for those who "[haven't] yet fully conquered the nostalgia for something transcendent."[10] As John Prine laments in "Angel from Montgomery,"[11]

> Just give me one thing that I can hold on to
> To believe in this living is just a hard way to go.

Since Max Weber, it has been more or less accepted that "disenchantment" was the tectonic shift that propelled this tsunami of unbelief.[12] Our ancestors of ten centuries ago, even the elites, lived naively in a world that was spirit-full, whose moral and social meanings were inherent in higher spiritual orders, where God's goodness was the necessary assurance of deliverance in the battle with demonic forces. The scientific revolution and the Protestant Reformation destroyed the remnants of this naïve enchanted cosmos,[13]

---

[9] Ibid.

[10] Ibid., 7.

[11] John Prine, *"Angel from Montgomery,"* www.lyrics.com/lyric/2853521 (1971).

[12] "The fate of our times is characterized by rationalization and intellectualization and, above all, by the disenchantment of the world. Precisely the ultimate and most sublime values have retreated from public life either into the transcendental realm of mystic life or into the brotherliness of direct and personal human relations." Max Weber, "Science as a Vocation," *Max Weber: Essays in Sociology*, eds. Hans Gerth and C. Wright Mills (London: Routledge & Kegan Paul, 1948), 155. Originally published in 1917.

[13] Gellner describes this disenchantment as having two phases: the pagan world of demons, demi-gods, household spirits, and nature deities first gave way in—what Karl Jaspers called—the Axial Age "when a unified and demanding Transcendent appears in human history, and partly replaces the communally oriented cults," then

collapsing us into ourselves and into our inner lives within a materialistic and meaningless universe—with anomie and nihilism and materialism as consequences.

Where does this leave us? At this moment in time, listening for God may seem a slender hope at best or, worse, an opening to atavistic fundamentalism (whether Christian, Judaic, or Muslim). But, this is also the moment when the rationalist dreams of the European Enlightenment are fading. The Holocaust was no less a rupture in reason than in faith. It was lawfully executed (at least in a *pro forma* sense) by a conscientious bureaucracy in the most scientifically, artistically, theologically, technologically, and philosophically advanced nation in the world. At the same time, postmodern thought has dismantled the idea of a rational foundation for democracy and the rule of law—and the respect for individual differences that underpins it. As Richard Rorty, for example, explains, our values of tolerance for private belief and public solidarity with those who suffer are fragile cultural accidents that may well not survive in the long term.[14] Cultural conservatives have long suspicioned that confidence in Enlightenment rationalism actually reflected the sentimental residue left from a decaying Christendom. In his recent book, *The Suicide of the West*, Jonah Goldberg persuasively argues that the emergent "bourgeois" virtues (reason, tolerance, individual self-reliance) that made possible "the Miracle" of modernity (democracy, free markets, innovation) have undermined the very structures that originally formed those virtues (family, church, communal norms).[15] Political modernity and the West that evolved from singular beginnings in Eighteenth Century England and Scotland may be self-limiting, "suicidal" in killing the goose that laid the golden egg. Modern democracy may turn out to be a relatively short-lived phenomenon—in part, because we grew to expect too much from it. (The last messianic/utopian gasp of Christianity?) Who knows where the current nativist and

in turn the monotheistic world of one true God becomes a precursor to the atheistic world of a uniform, empirically given, rationally knowable Nature: "A single, exclusive, jealous and iconoclastic deity, averse to magic and graven images, was perhaps one of the most decisive, formative influences in the education of the human race." Gellner, *Plough, Sword and Book*, 81–82. For Jaspers's notion of a world-wide shift in religious consciousness from 800 to 300 BCE (Zarathustra, Buddha, Confucius, Lao Tzu, Vardhamana, Elijah, Isaiah, Parmenides, Thucydides, Plato) see Karl Jaspers, *The Origin and Goal of History* (New Haven CN: Yale University Press, 1953).

[14] See Richard Rorty, "Pragmatism, Pluralism and Postmodernism," *Philosophy and Social Hope* (London: Penguin Books, 1999), 262–277.

[15] Jonah Goldberg, *The Suicide of the West* (New York: Random House, 2018).

ethnocentric turn of European and American politics will lead under the pressure of rapid social and economic change in the newly global, increasingly automated marketplace? Unfortunately, science for all its successes cannot tell us how to live—as Weber insisted.

So, we have begun this meditation—dear reader—with a jaundiced sketch of contemporary life in the Western world, a record of spiritual disenchantment, social anomie, scientific hubris, consumerist technocracy, political folly, religious decay, civic utopianism (political correctness), philosophic nihilism, and—consequently (à la Goldberg)—cultural revanchism (President Trump's *Make America Great Again*!!). In the words of Jackson Browne's song, "Running on Empty": "Everyone I know, everywhere I go, People are looking for a reason to believe, Running on—running on empty, Running on—running blind."[16] This is, I believe, exactly why the project of listening for God is important for us now. As Mircea Eliade has insightfully argued, in both traditional and Abrahamic religions the holy or sacred is the reference point that gives profane time and space a meaning and direction.[17] Historical time, without a hierophany at its mythic beginning or as its Messianic valorization, is terror. How can modern man, Eliade asks, "tolerate the catastrophes and horrors of history—from collective deportations and massacres to atomic bombings—if beyond them he can glimpse no sign, no transhistorical meaning?"[18] All modern attempts to replace the sacred with secular ideologies have been failures or worse. The secular messianism of Marxist communism produced one kind of murderous totalitarian state. The Fascist atavism of nation, blood, and soil produced another. Neoliberalism in the West and market-oriented authoritarian regimes in the East embrace greed and power as the only human virtues as our new billionaire masters emerge in global plutocracies and kleptocracies with their unprecedented digital means of social control. As a last gasp, the nihilistic, resigned aestheticism of existentialism becomes the only authentic response to the angst and nausea of radical human freedom in an absurd universe. That or sleepwalking into oblivion.

*Contemporary Sacred Stories.* But, if we are truly running on empty, what chance is there that God is addressing us here and now? Is the project of

---

[16] Jackson Browne, "Running on Empty," Asylum Records (1977).

[17] See Mircea Eliade, *The Sacred and the Profane,* trans. Willard R. Trask (New York: Harper Torchbooks, 1961).

[18] Mircea Eliade, *The Myth of the Eternal Return,* trans. Willard R. Trask (Princeton: Princeton UP, 1971), 151.

listening for God even plausible anymore? What is there to hear that we haven't already heard?

> Then His disciples asked Him what this parable meant. He replied, "The knowledge of the mysteries of the kingdom of God has been given to you, but to others I speak in parables, so that, 'Though seeing, they may not see; though hearing, they may not understand.'" (Luke 8:9–10)

We are now the "others" and need ears to hear—not a new Word—but a newly heard Word. The parable of God and man, the story of the sacred in human life, is *the* human story, the story that makes the human humane and not just a vector of desire. Narratives are more important to who we are as human beings than any ideas or habits or beliefs. Narratives place us in a world, a history, a society, a community, a family, a life. They generate and empower our goals, hopes, fears, and regrets. As Peter Brooks beautifully encapsulates it, "Narrative is one of the large categories or systems of understanding that we use in our negotiations with reality, specifically, in the case of narrative, with the problem of temporality: man's time-boundedness, his consciousness of existence within the limits of mortality. And plot is the principal ordering force of those meanings that we try to wrest from human temporality."[19]

But, without the story of the sacred, these formative narratives are hollow. As the fool confirms to the worldly wise Jacques in Shakespeare's *As You Like It*, "And so, from hour to hour, we ripe and ripe, / And then, from hour to hour, we rot and rot; / and thereby hangs a tale." We need more than the world's wisdom to play our part in a story that begins before we are on the stage and continues after we are shuffled off this mortal coil. Jacques's seven ages of man start too late and end too early: "Last scene of all, / that ends this strange eventual history, / Is second childishness and mere oblivion, / Sans teeth, sans eyes, sans taste, sans everything."[20] Human temporality advances by the synchronic clock of Being but is disrupted by an unaccountable—diachronic—surplus, by the sacred. As I argue below in "An Interpretative

[19] Peter Brooks, *Reading for the Plot* (Cambridge: Harvard University Press, 1992) xi.

[20] William Shakespeare, *As You Like It*, Act II, Scene VII (1598). As Jacques famously put it at the beginning of his oration, "All the world's a stage, / And all the men and women merely players."

Strategy," no plot is truly sufficient unto itself, and we shall see this demonstrated again and again in the narratives closely examined below.

The story of the sacred is still to be found in our most ancient literatures, buried in cultural and religious strangeness, recited most often by rote. In the "Philosophical Coda" to this meditation, I briefly explore an approach to reading the Old Testament that frees it from some of this strangeness and, perhaps, restores some of its essential meaning to us, to the disenchanted. But I am most interested in hearing this story in the literature written in our time for us. In our disenchantment, much of our contemporary literature alternates between cynical iconoclasm and wistful romanticism. But, exploring the role of the sacred in human life is still a deep motive for some of our most accomplished writers, who use cunning rhetorical means to cut through dead-end cultural and religious stereotypes. I have chosen four celebrated American writers for close reading and rereading to this purpose: Bernard Malamud, Flannery O'Connor, John Updike, and Toni Morrison. As I suggest below, I see them as representing in many ways the spectrum of serious American literature in the second half of the Twentieth Century. America's sense of destiny, its fascination with change, its democratic openness, its hustle and aggressive materialism, its melting pot of ethnicities, and its rather anomalous religiosity, all suggested there was a new kind of story waiting to be written exploring and celebrating its significance: "the Great American Novel," as John William DeForest denominated it in 1868.[21] After participating triumphantly in two barbarously murderous Great Wars and suffering through an intermediate decade of crushing worldwide economic Depression, resurgent post-WWII America underwent a spiritual sea change—one that still has us at sea. Voices from marginalized people and places emerged into full prominence. There were new stories to be told: stories of immigrant Jews and the two-edged sword of assimilation and stories of inassimilable Blacks and their invisible claim on America. There were old stories to be revived: stories by unapologetic Southerners insisting on the exceptionality of the defeated South (and its racism) and stories by resurgent Catholics inspired more by sin in a fallen world than by plaster saints in the sanctuary.[22] And fading

[21] It was to be "the picture of the ordinary emotions and manners of American existence." John William DeForest, "The Great American Novel," *The Nation* (9 January 1868) 28.

[22] In the last decades of the twentieth and the first decades of the twenty-first centuries, feminist, LGBT, Native American, and post-colonial writers have

remarkably rapidly from the cultural scene, the stories of the small-town boy or girl moving to the city—whose aspirations and frustrations were intended as a microcosm of the whole country—became passé.[23] In addition to representing these mid-century emergent, revived, or fading voices, our four authors' stories also have the added interest of coming out of significantly different, but related, faith traditions: Malamud/Jewish, O'Connor/Catholic, Updike/Protestant, and Morrison/syncretist.[24] More personally, long before I took a scholarly interest in these authors I read them as touchstones for a deeper existential meaning below their narrative surfaces. I believe a close reading of some of their most provocative stories now bears this out.

The subtly parabolic stories of authors like Malamud, O'Connor, Updike, and Morrison tune our ears to the voice of the sacred in human life. However, these stories are the farthest from being didactic tales that wear their message on their sleeves. Instead, they disrupt and confound any expectations of a takeaway moral. Thus, they must be read on many levels, and sacred presence will be a ground note more felt than heard. Our task in rereading them is to elicit this "peripheral" hearing of the sacred, recovering the profound in ordinary human life.

*Simply stated, the sacred is something set apart by a transcending presence, a presence that surpasses and confounds the natural order.* This can be given a psychological or phenomenological account, as does Rudolph Otto, for example, with the experience of natural awe or *mysterium tremendum et fascinans,* a sense of an uncanny Otherness that is simultaneously terrifying and

---

continued this amazing efflorescence of powerful new American voices. Having your own voice has almost become the same as having something to say.

[23] As a sophomore at Harvard University, John Updike wrote his parents back in Plowville, Pennsylvania, that "We need a writer who desires both to be great and to be popular, an author who can see America as clearly as Sinclair Lewis, but, unlike Lewis, is willing to take it to his bosom." Such a writer, he thought, could "produce an epic out of the Protestant ethic." Quoted in Adam Begley, *Updike* (New York: HarperCollins 2014) 82.

[24] Morrison is a lapsed Catholic convert incorporating elements of slave Christianity and African/Caribbean/Brazilian folkways in her novels, with an iconoclastic spirituality that seems suspicious of all merely inherited beliefs. Originally caught between deracinated pagan remnants and slave owners' Christianity, the African-American sense of the sacred continues to evolve, finding in *Exodus,* the Prophets, and the Gospels powerful narratives of deliverance and transfiguration while nevertheless experiencing the "benign" malignity of racist American life, including religious life.

fascinating.[25] Emile Durkheim gives the sacred an anthropological/sociological genesis as the totemic expression of the moral authority of the larger community, whether primitive clan or sophisticated Church.[26] Religious beliefs themselves typically invest sacred objects, places, people, and practices with supernatural power or authority. These attempts to make sense of the sacred, however, miss its truly primordial role in the emergence of human moral consciousness. Contra Otto, access to the sacred doesn't solely depend on the experience of religiously talented individuals attuned to the numinous. Whatever anthropological validity there is to Durkheim's totemism, modern commercial cultures successfully employ authoritative symbols of social identity that are entirely profane: political, athletic, and ethnic rivalries, shared habits of consumption and material display, institutional memberships, etc. And, at this distance from animism and warring gods, the supernatural is more scary than potent, the stuff of séances and poltergeists. The sacred, however, is present as the prelude to every moment of our ordinary, human lives.

What is this omnipresence that surpasses and confounds the natural order? The disruptive, eruptive sacred in our everyday lives is that by which we and our profane lives are judged. In our reading of these four authors we are already always under judgment. *We are already always under judgment.* We must follow an unaccountable trace of *radical responsibility* through the tangle of human religious speculation and the complexities of the narrative imagination. In itself, this trace is both mysterious (even God can be judged) and completely ordinary (our awareness of ourselves as agents and actors in our own lives). The presumption of *original sin*—stripped of its dubious theology—is at its core.[27] In the memorable lyric of Leonard Cohen, "There is a crack, a crack in everything, That's how the light gets in."[28] The fruit of the Tree of the Knowledge of Good and Evil in the Garden of Eden was the only

---

[25] Rudolph Otto, *The Idea of the Holy*, trans. John W. Harvey (Oxford: Oxford University Press, 1958).

[26] Emile Durkheim, *The Elementary Forms of Religious Life*, ed. Mark S. Cladis, trans. Carol Cosman (Oxford: Oxford University Press, 2001).

[27] Islam does not recognize an Adamic "original" sin somehow transmitted to his offspring (Allah forgave Adam). Judaism tends to believe that children are born without sin and subsequently freely choose sin. Christians, however—following Augustine—see sin everywhere, in an inherited wounded or sin nature ("concupiscence"), in a collective guilt for what was done in our name by Adam our "federal" head before the bar of divine justice, or in the total depravity of human nature outside of baptism and God's grace.

[28] Leonard Cohen, "Anthem," Columbia Records (1992).

element of God's Creation set apart as forbidden, as sacred. Adam and Eve's experience of its sacredness is their shame at their nakedness. This shame or self-judgment before the face of the Other comes directly from a new self-awareness, awareness of their capacity for evil—and for good. They are judged *before they sin* because they, like God when he created them, have brought the possibility of sin into the world.[29] This seam of radical responsibility is deeply embedded in the imaginations of the four authors we will reread together. Malamud, O'Connor, Updike, and Morrison explore the inevitability of moral failure in spite of—or even *because of*—our aspirations for the good. The temporal chaos and penultimate sense this makes of our lives is an experience of the sacred.

As the ethicist and Talmudist Emmanuel Levinas describes it, "Such a situation is the gleam of exteriority or of transcendence in the face of the Other."[30] This "infinity" or vertical dimension "beyond Being" reveals to us our unique human capacity for willful brutality, for war and rationalized cruelty. The face of the other transcends our mere creatureliness. In the momentary hesitation between the historical, social, psychological, and biological drives of the creature (Being as a given) and the free human act (*beyond Being* as a choice) lies the sacred: "It is this perpetual postponing of the hour of treason—infinitesimal difference between man and non-man—that implies

---

[29] Interpreting God's command not to eat of the fruit of the Tree as a test of their faithfulness and identifying their sin as disobedience gets it backwards. Their recognition of their capacity for evil is not in itself a sin. It is recognition of their radical responsibility before the Other, of their subjection to transcendent judgment. Only after they have tasted this sacred wisdom are they capable of disobedience and sin (or of obedience, for that matter).

[30] Emmanuel Levinas, *Totality and Infinity: An Essay on Exteriority*, trans. Alphonso Lingis (Pittsburgh: Duquesne UP, 1969), 24. Born in Russian Lithuania in 1906, Levinas was an early student of Husserl and Heidegger, a Jew who as a French citizen (since 1930) and soldier spent the Second World War in a German POW camp. His wife survived, hidden by friends. All of his Russian family were murdered by the Nazis. After the War, he studied Torah and Talmud with a mysterious polymath vagabond whose *nom de guerre* was M. Chouchani (also a teacher of Elie Wiesel) and for several decades thereafter he was the Director of the École Normale Israélite Orientale, continuing his Talmudic studies as well as his phenomenological investigations into "first philosophy." His publication of *Totalité et infiniti* in 1961 and *Autrement qu'être ou au-delà de l'essence* in 1974 [*Otherwise than Being or Beyond Essence*, trans. Alphonso Lingis (The Hague: Martinus Nijhoff Publishers, 1981)] made it clear that he was one of the major—and most difficult—philosophers of the twentieth century.

the disinterestedness of goodness, the desire of the absolutely other or nobility."[31] We are not quite running on empty—we can still recognize that looming hour of treason if we can listen carefully to some of the stories we tell ourselves about ourselves.

Listening for the sacred will require rhetorical disruption and deepening. Paradoxically, the sacred in a story only emerges as the story's narrative presumption and power—and our self-confidence—are disrupted. God cannot be caught in our net—we are caught in His. Finally, *we* do not judge; we are judged. The sacred is Albert Gans, a high school biology teacher seeking a miracle from a wonder-working Rabbi to deliver his father from death's door, who—in Malamud's "The Silver Crown"—finally manages to invoke God's will in a burst of patricidal fury. In O'Connor's "Everything That Rises Must Converge," a son's moral superiority and enlightenment is brutally revealed as inferior to his mother's genteel racism and Jim Crow condescension. Updike's "Rabbit" tetralogy remorselessly chops Harry "Rabbit" Angstrom's spiritual pretensions down to size and takes God's majesty down with them—with just enough left of both to offer *maybe* a glimpse of redemption for his feckless, messed-up son, Nelson. Morrison's *Paradise* turns triumph to ashes, as victims become their own oppressors in the name of self-pride and dignity—there are no fresh starts in history. These are storytellers in whose tales no one lives happily ever after. The sacred judges us from outside rather than exalts us from within. The result is not pretty. The power of these storytellers keeps us from averting our eyes—however much we might want to. Once glimpsed, their sacred visions cannot be unseen.

---

[31] Ibid., 35. See below "Philosophical Coda," especially 226–28 and 237–40, for further reflection on Levinas's key insight.

## An Interpretive Strategy: Briefly

*How will you look for it, Socrates, when you do not know at all what it is? How will you aim to search for something you do not know at all? If you should meet with it, how will you know that this is the thing that you did not know?—Plato Meno (80d)*

As writers, all four of our authors believe that stories and the rhythm of stories can be revelatory and transformative. Modernist irony pervades their writing but never gets the last word. This faithfulness to the word means they have something valuable to show us, but—as I've noted—it doesn't lie at the surface of their story-telling. They are all masters of riveting popular writing that points to deeper meanings, rewarding our sustained attention and touching on the prophetic mystery to which Levinas alludes. Thus, they all also struggle with the most profound and promising challenge embedded in their theological traditions: *how to make the sacred present through words?* In the light of this shared challenge, we will take the broad rhetorical genius of the Bible as a guide to an interpretive strategy for our reading of these contemporary writers. The rhetorical touchstones that will guide us in focusing and deepening our reading are, first, to pay close attention to "narrative amphiboly"[1] and, secondly, to cultivate an attitude of negative capability.

*Narrative Amphiboly.* Every telling has a beginning, middle, and end. But strictly speaking, no tale or story told has a narrative beginning or end, whether it is a historical narrative, personal memory, or case study—or a fable, mimetic fiction, or fantasy. There's always something imputed before the beginning and something implied beyond the end of a story, a context real or imaginable. Famously, Erich Auerbach distinguished mimetic fictions within the Western tradition by the degree to which they either disguised this fragmentary narrative character or exploited it.[2] Thus, Auerbach describes the

---

[1] Narrative amphiboly is a multiplicity of stories (not just of interpretations) within a single telling. There is one telling but many tolds, and the telling is not one of the tolds. We might call it the Scheherazade effect, narrative ambiguity that continues to surprise and gratify our readerly expectations while an unlikely tale of enchantment and transformation unfolds above or below the telling.

[2] Erich Auerbach, *Mimesis,* trans. Willard Trask (Princeton: Princeton University Press, 1953). I am here appropriating Auerbach's contrast as pointing to a

seminal Homeric texts as characterized by "fully externalized description, uniform illustration, uninterrupted connection, free expression, all events in the foreground, displaying unmistakable meanings, few elements of historical development and of psychological perspective."[3] The Homeric texts, like Odysseus' old nurse recognizing him in disguise by his scar, appear rhetorically complete, fulfilling the logic of an epic of return. By contrast, Biblical texts, like the binding of Isaac, are fraught with unexpressed background (Why Abram out of all the world?) and dimly adumbrated futures, epics of exodus and exile (Jacob? David? Jesus? Luther? Hitler? Golda Meir?). We are left wanting to know much, much more about the singular Abraham and his posterity—*as if there were indeed more to know.* According to Auerbach, these seminal Biblical texts are characterized by "certain parts brought into high relief, others left obscure, abruptness, suggestive influence of the unexpressed, 'background' quality, multiplicity of meanings and the need for interpretation, universal-historical claims, development of the concept of the historically becoming, and preoccupation with the problematic."[4] As Auerbach notes, it matters to us whether Abraham is real or not—the first question asked of the Biblical text is "Is it true?" *Is* there a covenant between God and the Jews? The history of the Bible and its influence is essential to this question—but only complicates our answer immeasurably. On the other hand, the more we think about Homer's epic and situate it in its cultural moment, the stronger the illusion becomes that we can understand "Odysseus" fully if not exhaustively as Homer knits together legend, story, and epithets. Whether or not there is some historical Troy and Ithaca behind the Homeric

---

semantic distinction in mode of reference rather than as marking the difference between stylized classical rhetoric and realist religious rhetoric.

[3] Ibid., 23.

[4] Ibid. Auerbach's distinction is obviously a matter of degree, and both categories of mimesis (sophisticated stylized or quotidian realist) require readers who will play along with the game. Postmodern critics have taken it upon themselves to debunk stylized fictions by exposing their submerged evasions, betrayals, gaps, and contradictions (as it were, "badly" written) and realist fictions by uncovering their *sub rosa* ideological agenda (as it were, "dishonestly" written). This "willful suspension of belief" erases distinctions: subject/object, expression/representation, criticism/literature, high/low, canonical/ephemeral, realist/stylized. Like taking care to catalogue all the faults of your friends, this seems to me—whatever its intellectual interest—finally to be a losing game. It forecloses much more than it reveals—the sour revenge of marginalized epigones.

tale matters hardly at all to the question why Odysseus rejects immortality on the island of Calypso in order to make his way home.

The stories that Malamud, O'Connor, Updike, and Morrison tell are multi-leveled. At a superficial level, they—like the Homeric epics—offer narrative suspense and striking resolutions, with vivid characterizations. We want to know what happens next and how will it end? With Heraclitus, in the end we grasp the way in which character was fate in the story, in spite of all the contingent twists and turns. All of which speaks to our fascination with storytelling and its many lessons. But at a deeper level, these stories—like the Biblical glimpses into an alienated reality—are fraught with potent disconnections and singular discontents. We are left not knowing what is really going on or what we are to make of it all. The more closely we read them, the harder it is to say where the story starts and where it ends—that is, the harder it is to say what amphibolous story is being told. And the more closely we read them, the more important it is to decide if they touch some buried truth—*the telling*—that we must accept or reject. *We will read these stories for everything that insinuates that the story is a fragment of something larger, deeper, higher.*

*Negative Capability*. Having reread for higher and deeper meanings, we still must resist the temptation to reach finally for a takeaway message or insight. The process of reading (and thinking) is what counts, not the product, much less the intellectual product.[5] So, the other touchstone that will guide these rereadings will be traces of a superlative rhetorical passivity, a passivity akin to the primordial rebuke that Levinas called the gleam of transcendence

[5] In this sense, these narratives—while "parabolic"—are not really parables, i.e., not homely stories or fables used to illustrate by analogy obscure moral or religious points. They function more like John Dominic Crossan's notion of Jesus' "challenge" parables: "Challenge parables *mean*—that is, intend—to make us probe and question, ponder and wonder, discuss and debate, and, above all else, practice that gift of the human spirit known as thinking. About what? About the absolutes of our religious faith, the certainties of our theological vision, the presuppositions, presumptions, and prejudices of our social, political, and economic tradition....Challenge parables foster not periodic doubting, but permanent questioning." John Dominic Crossan, *The Power of Parable,* (San Francisco: HarperOne, 2012), 111. "Riddle" parables and "example" parables make up the other two categories of parables that Crossan describes. Challenge parables are, according to Crossan, the subtle, esoteric pedagogical vehicles Jesus relied on to prepare the way for a transformative paradigm-shift in social relations, having seen and learned from John the Baptist's fatal fate unguardedly proclaiming the *eschaton*.

in the face of the other. The poet John Keats was the first to draw critical attention to this "negative capability," which he attributed in the highest degree to Shakespeare. In a letter to his brothers in 1817, he described it as "when a man is capable of being in uncertainties, mysteries, doubts, without any irritable reaching after fact and reason."[6] In the same letter, he disparaged Coleridge, for instance, as willing to "let go by a fine isolated verisimilitude caught from the Penetralium of mystery, from being incapable of remaining content with half-knowledge."[7] In a later letter to a friend, he asserted that "We hate poetry that has a palpable design upon us."[8] Trying to reconcile ourselves to reality by representing it in fiction as intelligible from some perspective or another betrays reality and trivializes fiction—just as it does Scripture. Keats prized rhetorical responsiveness to whatever presents itself to us, even though it makes little sense or violates propriety or escapes common notice: "With a great poet the sense of Beauty overcomes every other consideration, or rather obliterates all consideration."[9] Elsewhere he calls this "gusto" (borrowing from William Hazlitt): "The 'poetical Character' is not itself—it has no self—it is everything and nothing—It has no character—it enjoys light and shade; it lives in gusto, be it foul or fair, high or low, rich or poor, mean or elevated—It has as much delight in an Iago as an Imogen. What shocks the virtuous philosopher delights the camelion Poet."[10]

The legal theorist and political activist Roberto Unger has expanded this notion of negative capability to encompass the penumbra of human freedom that he believes escapes historical necessity and institutional structures by intuitively anticipating what's not there and working to modify given contexts in order to bring "it" into being. He describes negative capability as "the practical and spiritual, individual and collective empowerment made possible by the disentrenchment of formative structures."[11] Just so, we will look for this "disentrenchment of formative structures" in our re-readings of our four authors. In their disarming absence, we will relax our critical, analytical, and pragmatic impulses to find fault, neatly characterize, or draw out the

[6] John *Keats, The Complete Poetical Works and Letters of John Keats,* ed. Horace E. Scudder (Boston: Houghton, Mifflin and Company, 1899) 277.

[7] Ibid.

[8] Ibid., 314.

[9] Ibid., 277.

[10] John Keats, *The Letters of John Keats, 1814–1821*, ed. Hyder Edward Rollins, (Cambridge: Cambridge University Press, 1958) 386–87.

[11] Roberto Unger, "The Critical Legal Studies Movement," *Harvard Law Review* 96 (1983): 56.

significance. Instead, we will be alert to the incongruous verisimilitude that nevertheless strikes us as somehow indicative to the presence of something larger, deeper, higher. In this light, Nathan Scott compares negative capability to Heidegger's concept of *Gelassenheit* or "releasement," which Scott explains as "the spirit of *disponibilité* [availability] before What-Is which permits us simply to let things be in whatever may be their uncertainty and their mystery."[12] Updike's delicate, appreciative portrayal of a negligible jerk, O'Connor's generously sadistic story lines, Morrison's high-minded refusal to claim the high ground, and Malamud's triumphant self-stultification will each test—and, I hope, reward—our *Gelassenheit.*

[12] Nathan A. Scott, Jr. *Negative Capability* (New Haven CN: Yale University Press, 1969) xiii. Heidegger was deploying the concept of *Gelassenheit* from its original use by the fourteenth-century Christian mystic Meister Eckhart.

1

# Malamud's Imagined Jews

*"All men are Jews but few men know it."—Bernard Malamud*

Bernard Malamud resisted being classified as a "Jewish-American" writer. He was, he thought, an American writer who wrote about Jews. He claimed Hawthorne writing about the Puritans was his inspiration. As he insisted in his *Paris Review* interview in 1975, "I'm an American, I'm a Jew, and I write for all men. A novelist has to, or he's built himself a cage. I write about Jews, when I write about Jews, because they set my imagination going."[1] So, who were the Jews he wrote about, and how and why did he imagine them?

Malamud, born in 1914 in Brooklyn, began writing in his middle twenties, as Father Charles Coughlin's immensely popular radio broadcasts pushed the anti-Semitic agenda of the so-called Christian Front—and, in 1939, the German-American Bund convened a huge rally in Madison Square Garden in support of Hitler as a bulwark against anti-Christian Communism. When the Nazis smashed their way across Europe in the spring of 1940, Malamud wrote a non-fiction piece for the *Washington Post* about the fall of France. His short story "Armistice," written a few months later (but published only in 1989), offers us the first glimpse of Malamud's imagined Jews. We must remind ourselves that the story looks forward into an absolutely unknown future, as yet no Pearl Harbor, no Holocaust, no Nazi attack on the USSR, no partition of Germany, no Israel. Abram departing from Harran for an unknown bourne.

## "Armistice"

The resonance of the title already connects several stories. Armistice Day, celebrated on November 11, had become a national U.S. holiday in 1938 (now known as Veterans Day). This worldwide Day of Remembrance for the 20 million who died in World War I began in 1919 and from 1920 on was

[1] Daniel Stern, "The Art of Fiction, Bernard Malamud No. 52," *The Paris Review* 61 (1975) www.theparisreview.org/interviews/3869/bernard-malamud-the-art-of-fiction-no-52-bernard-malamud.

marked with a red poppy emblem worn in the lapel.[2] It commemorated the Armistice signed by Marshal Foch in the forest of Compiègne ending the Great War at 11:00 a.m. on November 11, 1918, the 11th hour of the 11th day of the 11th month. When two decades later Hitler received France's capitulation on June 22, 1940, it was by his orders at that exact same spot in the forest in the same railcar that had served as Foch's office in 1918, the *Wagon de Compiègne*. After the signing of this Second Armistice at Compiègne, the SS destroyed all traces of the original French memorial of the earlier German defeat, except for the statue of Foch, left overlooking the scene of France's new humiliation. Famously, Foch had warned that without ceding the Rhineland to France the Versailles peace treaty of 1919 would turn out to be merely a twenty-year armistice. He was exactly right. Just so, the Armistice of June 22, 1940, was only the start of another great war—whose outcome Malamud, or any of his contemporaries, could not have foreseen in those dark days, when England's capitulation was expected to follow shortly.

The conflict that engages Malamud's immediate interest, however, is much more intimate: "Leonard came into the store and heard the loud voices. He ran into the kitchen and saw the two men arguing. A feeling of nausea and shame overcame him. 'Pa,' he begged, 'don't fight.'" After this nasty confrontation between Morris Lieberman, a widowed grocer in Brooklyn, and Gus Wagner, who is a purveyor of delicatessen meats, Gus drives off thinking contemptuously about Morris and his fourteen-year-old son Leonard: "He thought of the boy crying and his father holding him. It was always like that with the Jews. Tears and people holding each other."

Morris's anxiety for his son, his feeling that Gus is some kind of threat to Leonard, has its roots in another story altogether. "Armistice" opens with one of the most brutal vignettes in all of Malamud's fictions: "When he was a boy, Morris Lieberman saw a burly Russian peasant seize a wagon wheel that was lying against the side of a blacksmith's shop, swing it around, and hurl it at a fleeing Jewish sexton. The wheel caught the Jew in the back, crushing his spine. In speechless terror, he lay on the ground before his burning house, waiting to die." The horror, the helplessness, and the immemorial incomprehensibility of this searing moment—an image of the frequent pogroms that drove Malamud's father and over 3 million other Russian Jews to

[2] The imagery was taken from John McCrea's popular poem "In Flanders Fields" ("In Flanders fields the poppies grow / Between the crosses row on row") written by Colonel McCrea, a poet and physician, during the Second Battle of Ypres after the battlefield funeral of a close friend.

immigrate to the U.S. between 1881 and 1914—has preyed on Morris's mind since the Nazis had come to power in Germany. He listens obsessively to the radio for reports of their persecution of the Jews. As the Nazis crashed through the French lines in May 1940, "his anxiety became intolerable." Between waiting on customers, he sits in the rear of the store listening, mourning, and hoping for a miracle: "The salesmen from the wholesale grocery houses and the drivers who served Morris were amazed at the way he suffered. They told him that the war had nothing to do with America and that he was taking it too seriously. Some of the others made him the object of their ridicule outside the store. One of them, Gus Wagner, who delivered the delicatessen meats and provisions, was not afraid to laugh at Morris to his face." Even Leonard, his son, "saw how overwrought his father became and tried to shut off the radio."[3]

What does it mean to take the war "too seriously?" Malamud was intimately familiar with mental illness and paranoia; his mother had her first psychotic break when he was three, after his brother Eugene was born. At thirteen, he saved her life when he came home from school to find her sitting on the kitchen floor foaming at the mouth from the disinfectant she had swallowed. She died immured in an insane asylum when he was fifteen. By 1940, his brother was beginning to falter and dropped out of high school. Eugene's schizophrenia emerged as "combat fatigue" while fighting in the Pacific in World War II. Malamud's youthful friends remembered Bernie as a high-spirited clown and expert mimic who read voraciously. As he himself confessed, however, he was often overwhelmed with shame at his mother and disappointment in his father and the narrow life he lived. Malamud's daughter Janna (a practicing psychotherapist) shares this insight in her memoir of her family: "His protective tenderness toward his parents existed side by side with his sense of having been gypped, his anger about it, and then his shame and guilt."[4] In later years, his guilt extended to Eugene, who he felt had needed support he wasn't in a position to give. Read through this screen, the story seems to support Gus's claim that "the Jews" are ridiculously

---

[3] Bernard Malamud, *The Complete Stories*, ed. Robert Giroux (New York: Farrar, Straus and Giroux, 1997) 3–8. All references to "Armistice" are to this edition.

[4] Janna Malamud Smith, *My Father Is A Book* (Boston: Houghton Mifflin Co., 2006) 10.

overwrought—indeed, that the story itself is overwrought.[5] We'll return to that question when we ask what Malamud is up to in the story.

The deeper issue is not Morris's nightmares of flight and falling as he awaits word of Marshal Pétain's capitulation. The deeper issue is Leonard. Leonard, a slight and studious boy, is worried for his father's health and pleads with him not to listen to so many news broadcasts. Every time he makes a delivery to the grocer, Gus Wagner pokes fun at Morris for wanting the French to win. Although he doesn't say so for fear of losing Morris' custom, he is deeply impressed by the German military prowess. He also resents Leonard checking his bills and sometimes finding errors. Gus is careless in arithmetic; Leonard is good at it. Gus and Morris have known each other for nine years. At one time, after the death of Morris's wife four years before, Gus and Morris "had nearly been friends." Leonard's dislike of the meat man, with his "nauseating cackle," and Leonard's careful scrutiny of Gus's bills had driven them apart. Once Morris mentioned a five-dollar prize in mathematics that Leonard had won and Gus said, "'You better watch out, Morris, He's a skinny kid. If he studies too much he'll get consumption.' Morris was frightened. He felt Gus was wishing harm upon Leonard. Their relations became cooler."

The day of the Armistice, Morris dreads Gus's arrival that afternoon. After a crack about Morris's "skinny kid," Morris snaps back:

> "He looks out for my interests," answered Morris. "He's a good mathematics student," he added. "That's the sixth time I heard that," said Gus. "You'll never hear it about your children." Gus lost his temper. "What's the hell's the matter with you Jews?" he asked. "Do you think you own all the brains in the world?" "Gus," Morris cried, "you talk like a Nazi."

In the midst of this shouting match, Leonard comes into the store from school. He begs his father not to fight. Gus shoves him aside: "Mind your own business, you little bastard." Morris holds his sobbing son "and kissed him again and again." Morris assures Leonard: "No. No more, Leonard.

---

[5] To go back to the story of the Garden, the Lord God himself may seem to have gotten a bit overwrought over a couple of bites of an apple, whose only immediate effect was to give Adam and Eve a conscience. Why does having a conscience put us at thundering risk of an unaccountable payback? Or, as Nietzsche puts it, "The bite of conscience, like the bite of a dog into a stone, is a stupidity." Friedrich Nietzsche, *The Wanderer and his Shadow*, trans. R.J. Hollingdale (Cambridge: Cambridge University Press, 1996) sec. 38.

Don't cry. I'm sorry. I give you my word. No more." The armistice is concluded: a cessation of combat, not a peace treaty. Gus, his face still red with anger—but afraid to lose Morris's business—pulls two liverwursts and a bologna from his basket: "'The meat's on the table,' he said. 'Pay me tomorrow.'" Everything is still to be resolved. This is just a pause—an armistice—in these multiple stories, as we will see more clearly in a moment.

On the surface, it appears that for Malamud the Jew represents a certain mode of imagination or feeling, which the *goyim*—represented here by the meaty Mr. Wagner—neither share nor comprehend. It is a mode conditioned—on both sides—by a long history of displacement or diaspora: the Jew as an alien in an alien land. As Morris muses into the night awaiting the signing of the Armistice the next day, "The Jews lived in an indeterminable exodus. Long lines trudged forever with their burdens on their shoulders." In outline, Malamud's issue seems clear. On the one hand, the Jews are perpetual refugees from persecution, with clannish pride and the fragile hope in the education of the next generation as their only compensation. On the other hand, the crude, ubiquitous oppressors have contempt for these very "weaknesses" in their victims. But even in this fledgling story, written while he was still a clerk in the Census Bureau, Malamud slyly knocks this contrast askew.

Gus, knowing he's gone too far, swallows his anger and leaves. Driving his truck on the avenue—his face grim—he thinks "Why feel sorry for them?" He thinks of the Armistice and imagines that he is in Paris driving a massive tank through the wide boulevards, "The French…overpowered with fear." Then Malamud ends the story (just six pages long) with what will become a rhetorical trademark of his stories, an oddly syncopated last sentence: "He drove tensely, his eyes unsmiling. He knew that if he relaxed the picture would fade." Seemingly out of nowhere, Gus betrays his vulnerability with a comic and compensatory fantasy whose fragility suggests an uneasiness about his own supposedly secure position in the world. It is only a half-heard hint, as much proleptic as historic, but Gus Wagner, American-born and a veteran of the American Expeditionary Force in World War I, has already lived through one round of virulent anti-German-American feeling in the U.S. following the sinking of the Lusitania and entry into World War I. And—at the tail end of the Great Depression—he must bite back his tongue when attacked as a Nazi for fear of losing Morris's business, all of two liverwursts and a bologna a day (Axis meats!). Unexpectedly, the contrast between suffering Jew and brutal goyim is blurred, put under an odd tension, both humanized and in a sense dehumanized. The archetypical distance between victim and oppressor is mediated by a common vulnerability, but the particularity of

Jewish alienation is also shifted toward the Jew as everyman caught in the maw of history and its inevitable conflicts—Compiègne the scene both of French triumph and twenty years later German revenge.

We can already see that something doesn't add up here. Where are these several stories going? We are left hanging, knowing that there must be more to come: the larger war, the long history of diaspora and persecution, the overwrought, isolated father and son. Everything is possible, but nothing is yet determined; it's left to the imagination. At the same time, the seemingly obvious theme of a moral contrast between Jew and goy is knocked askew. What makes this a specifically Jewish theme at all? A sorrowing Old Country refugee confronts a successfully Americanized second-generation immigrant, who laughs at his tears. It is Gus who insists on personalizing the confrontation as Jew versus goy. As Morris exclaims, Gus thinks like a Nazi, both despising and resenting "the Jews."

How Jewish is this story? Malamud was himself unobservant and admitted that what he knew about Judaism he learned mainly from reading. Against both families' wishes he married Ann de Chiara, a Gentile and a Catholic. As Harold Bloom writes in his "Introduction" to *Malamud, Modern Critical Views*, "The Jewishness of Malamud's fiction has been a puzzle from the start, as the better critics always indicated. Malamud's vision is personal, original, and almost wholly unrelated to the most characteristic or normative Jewish thought and tradition."[6] Yet, Mark Shechner in his review of *The Stories of Bernard Malamud*, declares that "Malamud is quintessentially a Jewish writer, though there is nothing of religious belief and only shards of ritual to be found in his writing and only *shmatas* of Jewish culture or history. Yet, for all of that, his writing is so impregnated with Jewishness—as distinct from Judaism—that there can be no mistaking it." Shechner describes this Jewishness in a phrase from Matthew Arnold's definition of Hebraism, "strictness of conscience": "strictness of conscience is as much his abiding theme as sorrow is his abiding disposition."[7] Philip Roth in his highly controversial "Imagining Jews" makes the point more pungently, remarking "how fierce and

---

[6] Harold Bloom, "Introduction," *Bernard Malamud, Modern Critical Views*, ed. Harold Bloom (New York: Chelsea House Publishers, 1986) 1. Ruth Wisse takes this criticism a step further and reads Malamud out of the Jewish canon altogether, claiming that Malamud identifies the Jewish capacity for suffering as "the paradigm of Christianity." Ruth R. Wisse, *The Modern Jewish Canon* (New York: The Free Press, 2000) 291.

[7] Mark Shechner, "Sad Music," *Critical Essays on Bernard Malamud*, ed. Joel Salzberg (Boston: G.K. Hall & Co 1987) 71.

reflexive is the identification in Malamud's imagination between renunciation and Jew and appetite and goy."[8] Comparing Malamud to Saul Bellow in this respect, Roth (not exempting himself from the comparison) finds that

> In the work of Bernard Malamud these tendencies are so sharply and schematically present as to give Malamud's novels the lineaments of moral allegory. For Malamud, generally speaking, the Jew is innocent, passive, virtuous, and this to the degree that he defines himself or is defined by others as a Jew; the Gentile, on the other hand, is characteristically corrupt, violent, and lustful, particularly when he enters a room or a store or a cell with a Jew in it.[9]

Roth's libidinous Portnoy (*Portnoy's Complaint*) acts as much against and within this constraint of conscience as does the resentful son, Albert Gans in Malamud's "The Silver Crown": They are "nightmares of bondage, each informed in its way by a mood of baffled, claustrophobic struggle"[10]—or original sin, we might suggest. You are damned if you do, damned if you don't. (To which Roth replies, "In that case, I choose to *do*!")

At the end of his diatribe against his critics and former mentors, Roth in fact brilliantly reconceives the cultural challenge to the mid-century Jewish-American writer. The twentieth century had seen the unprecedented Americanization of millions of Jews and their successful immigrant offspring, as well as the genocidal extermination of millions of Europeanized Jews and the flight of Jewish-European intellectual and artistic elite to the security of the United States and Great Britain, followed by the establishment of millions of refugee Jews as a defiant and improbable Jewish state in ancient Palestine. For well over a century, reimagining what Jews are and ought to be has been a central cultural, moral, and political preoccupation of Jews and their friends and enemies in the West. Therefore, the mid-century Jewish-American writers' enterprise, Roth suggests, is "imagining Jews being imagined, by themselves and by others."[11] The reach and limitation of that re-

---

[8] Philip Roth, "Imagining Jews," *Critical Essays on Bernard Malamud*, ed. Joel Salzberg (Boston: G.K. Hall & Co 1987) 103. Originally published in the *New York Review of Books* in 1974.

[9] Ibid., 98. Roth tore apart Malamud's work and made it personal, accusing Malamud of a dissimulating, deeply repressed rage, expressed in *The Fixer* (1966) at least, as a violent pornography. Malamud bitterly resented Roth's critique, feeling betrayed by his onetime admirer. It caused a rupture that lasted many years.

[10] Ibid., 107.

[11] Ibid.

imagination is Malamud's deepest theme, much deeper than the superficial moral allegory that Roth sees in him.

"Armistice," early as it is, provides a template for Malamud's Jewish problem, the problem that sets his imagination going. Morris and Gus are disastrously entangled, almost friends once, vendor and customer, bitterly divided over the War, attacking each other's children, both "Americans" *malgré lui*. Again and again, Malamud reimagines the Jew as tending toward this kind of *mésalliance*, that is, *as being shaped by intimate relations against type, interest, or desire.* Jews are strangers in a strange world. In "Armistice," it is the tense "American" engagement of a refugee Jew with a Nazi manqué. But, it can be the mésalliance of traditional Polish emigrants undone by American dynamism in "The Cost of Living" (1949)—or the mésalliance of a Holocaust survivor's dogged devotion and a shoemaker's dreams of a better life for his daughter in "The First Seven Years" (1950)—or the mésalliance of a *yiddishe kop* fascinated by the image of a matchmaker's streetwalker daughter in "The Magic Barrel" (1953)—or, more fantastically, the mésalliance of a "romantic" Jewish-American floorwalker misconceiving both himself and the mysterious Italian Holocaust "princess" he woos in "The Lady of the Lake" (1958)—or, at the outer limits of fable, the savage mésalliance of a Yiddisher raven done in by an "anti-Semeets" Jewish paterfamilias in "The Jewbird" (1963)—or, at a Freudian depth, the mésalliance of guilt and hate, realism and hope, in the soul of a son with a dying father in "The Silver Crown" (1972). In these and many other stories, being a Jew is a failure of imagination, an inability either to embrace or to escape who you are, a Jew-in-spite-of-yourself—chosen, not choosing.

Ultimately, Malamud's Jews live in a world not made for them, discovering their limits—not in service to their ideals—but in rebuke for their aspirations. Their failure is witness to their encounter with transcendence, with the unmasterable sacred—in the face of which imagination must fail. This, of course, also encapsulates Malamud's challenge as a writer. His literary imagination, anyone's literary imagination, will be unequal to this task. What cannot be said, what skewers the imaginary, what becomes at best bitter-sweet comedy are Malamud's defining literary limits—and the paradoxical indications in his writing of something beyond literature and the imagined to which we are accountable.

## "The Cost of Living"

"Winter had fled the city streets but Sam Tomashevsky's face, when he stumbled into the back room of his grocery store, was a blizzard." His wife Sura is sitting at a table eating bread and a salted tomato. One look at him and she socks her chest in a gesture of mourning and to make the bite go down. The tomato turns a deeper red. "'My God,' Sam croaked. She screamed, making him shudder, and he fell wearily into a chair. Sura was standing, enraged and frightened. 'Speak for God's sake.' 'Next door,' Sam muttered....'Oi.' She bit her knuckle and sank down moaning. It could not have been worse."[12] The cause of this crisis and despair, the cost of living as it were, seems comically disproportionate and overwrought: "A grocery comes next door." Typically, Malamud's use of free indirect discourse blurs the point of view we are to take. "It could not have been worse" is not the narrator's sentiment but the character's, yet framed in the narrator's voice we don't know whether to read it as a sympathetic or a satiric observation of her feeling.[13] In "The Cost of Living," Sam Tomashevsky and his wife Sura have invested themselves deeply in their small grocery store and the neighbors who were their customers. After twenty-seven years of back-breaking sixteen-hour days, "insults, petty thievery, doling of credit to the impoverished by the poor," the emptiness of the store next door becomes within months a glittering chain grocery, keeping a manager and two clerks busy. Sura tears her cheeks in mourning and Sam engages an auction house: "The money they got was not a quarter of the sum needed to pay the creditors....So long as he lived he would not return to the old neighborhood, afraid his store was standing empty, and he dreaded to look through the window." What would he see—or not see? More deeply, what does he think? Is this hard won self-insight—or the narrator's superior judgment? The theme is straight out of John Galsworthy's famous narrative essay "Quality": the stubborn and hopeless inability to compete in a progressive milieu where convenience trumps the personal and devalues the humane.[14] Sam's increasingly futile attempts to

---

[12] "The Cost of Living," *The Complete Stories* 55–62. All references to "The Cost of Living" are from this edition. This was Malamud's first professionally published story, accepted by *Harper's Bazaar* in 1949.

[13] The nineteenth-century novelist Gustave Flaubert, a meticulous "*le mot juste*" writer after Malamud's own heart, was the first to identify *discours indirect libre* as a style.

[14] John Galsworthy, "Quality," originally published in 1912 and reprinted in *Scribner's Magazine* Fiftieth Anniversary issue (January 1937) describes the decline

accommodate to soulless modern commerce illustrate his limited imagination, just enough imagination to get him to America, not enough to sustain him there—a definition of diaspora or cultural mésalliance. On the other hand, does Sam himself come to realize this? Is this a superannuated *Bildungsroman*? Are we meant to identify with Sam and Sura? Yes, of course. And, of course, *we* would not have handled it like they did, which is to say *we* would not have been them and lived their lives. And what then are their lives, what is their story—and how does it connect to us? "Sura, who had all their married life nagged him, now sat silent in the back." This is narrator and character finely fused by free indirect discourse, and it cuts deep. Malamud refuses to sum it up for us—or allow us to dismiss it. There *is* aspiration, endurance, suffering, crisis, and despair here, in a minor key to be sure, an inarticulate judgment on a life a long time coming. The only way Sam could have escaped his fate would have been to be someone else some time else. Now, it is up to us to find the imagination to sense these hints of moral dignity in this pitiful and negligible tale. This *is* the cost of living—and somewhere somehow this is quite a different tale from Galsworthy.[15] Where and how this whisper of transcendence? It will nag at us even if Sura doesn't.

## "The First Seven Years"

With "The First Seven Years" Malamud created, in Sidney Richman's words, "what many writers, and even better ones, must struggle for years to attain: a voice that is distinctively his own."[16] Yet, this voice was, according to many

---

and death of a skilled German boot maker in London done in by the lazy new-fashioned preference for readymade—inferior—shoes. Galsworthy received the Nobel Prize for Literature in 1932 when Malamud was 18. In "The Cost of Living," the looming empty storefront next to the Tomashevsky's had housed an Italian shoemaker forced out of business by more modern competition, a version of Galsworthy's failed boot maker.

[15] We can take it as given that this story, like many others, is also a working out of Malamud's ambivalent attitude toward his father and an expression of his overwhelming desire to escape that dreary life into the world of literary imagination and recognition. There were *no* books in his father's house.

[16]. Sidney Richman, *Bernard Malamud* (New York: Twayne, 1966) 100. "The First Seven Years," *The Complete Stories* 69–78. All references to "The First Seven Years" are to this edition. "The First Seven Years," originally published in the *Partisan Review* in 1950, was the lead story in Malamud's first collection, *The Magic Barrel* (1959).

critics, "gratingly inappropriate," as Samuel Bellman wrote.[17] Malamud's mixed diction and self-parody are meant to tell a story and at the same time to undermine its narrative and thematic unities to open the reader to mystery.[18] How do you listen for something that is not there, something not to be given through representation? You listen for what is missing: failed connections, elusive endings, preemptive defeats, displaced hopes, unaccountable responsibilities. But you know it is missing only because conventional narrative themes of challenge, hope, transformation, and fulfillment somehow undermine and discredit themselves. Dorothy Seidman Bilik identifies it as Malamud's "unique brand of negative capability."[19]

To begin with, the story's title does not fit its ending. The title and the story allude to the biblical tale of Jacob and his seven years of labor for his uncle Laban to earn his bride, Laban's daughter Rachel. Feld, a shoemaker, has a daughter Miriam now nineteen, for whom he had high hopes that she would go to college or at least "marry an educated man and live a better life." For five years, his helper Sobel has worked for him, quickly learning the trade and, after Feld's heart attack, expertly running the business for him. Sobel, bald and stocky, "old before his time," his "soft blue eyes prone to tears over the sad books he read," asks for very little. He puzzles Feld, why he stays when he could earn much more elsewhere? "He finally answered it that the man, no doubt because of his terrible experiences as a refugee, was afraid of the world." When Feld seizes a chance opportunity to suggest a meeting between Miriam and Max "the college boy" studying for years to be an accountant, he reenters the shop to find Sobel furiously pounding on the naked iron last. When it breaks, Sobel rushes out. A week later, having let Sobel stew in his rooming house, he goes to ask his "temperamental" assistant to come back—

---

[17] "Style, surely, it cannot be, for Malamud's diction is not seldom gratingly inappropriate." Samuel Bellman, "Women, Children, and Idiot's First: Transformation Psychology," *Bernard Malamud and the Critics*, eds. Leslie A Field and Joyce W. Field (New York: New York University Press, 1970) 12.

[18] See Peter C. Brown, "Negative Capability and the Mystery of Hope in Malamud's 'The First Seven Years,'" *Religion & Literature* 29.1 (1997): 63–94 for a more comprehensive analysis of the critical and cultural context for these tropes.

[19] Dorothy Seidman Bilik, *Immigrant-Survivors: Post-Holocaust Consciousness in Recent Jewish American Fiction* (Middletown: Wesleyan University Press, 1981) 59. Commenting on critics' inability to analyze the meaning of the striking last image in "The Magic Barrel," she comments that "no explication suffices or seems really called for. . . . Malamud's critics may not have recognized his unique brand of negative capability."

and is rebuffed by the landlady. He hires a new assistant, who steals from him. On discovering this, he has another mild heart attack and, finally, three weeks later painfully makes his way up the stairs to Sobel's poor room, "with a narrow cot, a low table, and several stacks of books piled haphazardly on the floor along the wall, which made him think how queer Sobel was, to be uneducated and read so much." From the age of fourteen, Miriam always had a book in her hand, recommended by Sobel together with his elaborate written commentaries.

What do you want from me, Feld asks? As he had somehow sensed, but never allowed himself to think, Sobel wants Miriam: "Feld has a sudden insight. In some devious way, with his books and commentary, Sobel had given Miriam to understand that he loved her." Not Max, the college boy, who was in Miriam's words a materialist: "He has no soul. He's only interested in things," but Sobel who "read, he said, to know." His dreams for Miriam dead—after all she would have no more in life than her mother—Feld brokenly agrees that in two years, when Miriam is twenty-one, Sobel can speak to her about marriage. Unaccountably, he walks back home in crisp, falling snow "with a stronger stride," and the next morning arriving at the store with a heavy heart "he saw he needn't have come, for his assistant was already seated at the last, pounding leather for his love." The seven years of labor will be accomplished—and Rachel/Miriam will be the payoff.

But no: the title tells us that it is the *first* seven years. After seven years of labor, Laban deceived Jacob and sent Rachel's older sister Leah with her "weak eyes" veiled in to Jacob. In the morning, behold it was Leah. After Laban insisted that the older must be married before the younger, Jacob agrees to labor another, *second* seven years for Rachel—and, when Leah's bridal week is accomplished, he goes in to Rachel, whom he loves. Seeing that Leah is hated by her husband, the Lord opens her womb and closes Rachel's. And Jacob grows richer and richer outwitting his uncle with God's connivance. Finally, Jacob finesses his older brother's wrath over having been tricked out of his birthright to return—after twenty years—to the land of his father's sojourns, the Promised Land.

Malamud's story appears to be a modest triumph of love over loss, soul over materialism, loyalty over calculation. But the title suggests not just delay but disappointment—and barrenness. Malamud's story ends before any consequences can be foreseen, but the biblical allusion thoroughly ironizes its theme of fulfillment. On every count, the allusion fails to cohere. Sobel is no wily Jacob and has no homeland to which to return—he's the sinned against, not the sinner. Feld is no prosperous and powerful opponent; he is virtually

Sobel's dependent. Nor is there exceeding prosperity to be earned in the shoemaker's store. And standing behind all of it, the abiding covenantal promise to the patriarch Jacob-become-Israel, a refugee from his brother's wrath, bitterly contrasts with Sobel "bald and old with his miseries, who had by the skin of his teeth escaped Hitler's incinerators." But beyond this there is an even more profound displacement. The story isn't about Sobel, it's about Feld. The story begins with Feld lost in reverie, old regrets, and daydreams peering "through the partly frosted window at the near-sighted haze of falling February snow." By the end of the story, Feld will see much more clearly who his daughter is, who Sobel is, who he himself is, and what life can be. As Robert Solotaroff concludes: "Having confronted some of the truth in his heart, Feld is now free to confront as well the compassion and moral intelligence that also lie there.... For once, Malamud quickly rewards ethical behavior in material terms."[20]

We might like to think it turns out that way. The reality, as Malamud insinuates, is much more equivocal. Feld offers to pay him more: "Who cares for your wages!" Then Sobel explodes in anger: "So why you look for strange boys in the street they should go out with Miriam? Why you don't think of me?" Feld frozen in place and speechless croaks out his distaste and distain: "'So what has my daughter got to do with a shoemaker thirty-five years old who works for me?' 'Why do you think I worked so long for you?...For the stingy wages I sacrificed five years of my life?'" Then for what, shouts Feld? For Miriam, Sobel blurts. Finally, Feld manages to say, "I pay wages in cash, Sobel." Contrary to what Solotaroff and others have concluded,[21] Feld's incipient nobility goes to mush at just this point. Feld had long ago sensed Sobel's attentions to his daughter (all those books!) and out of instinctive self-interest hidden this realization from himself. Now, forced to confront his subtle exploitation of the refugee (afraid of the world, he had rationalized), out of self-interest he makes the bargain explicit. He will pimp out his daughter and get at least two more years of dutiful work out of Sobel. (He certainly does not tell him to go away and come back in two years.) The narrator tells us in the first few sentences of the story that "Feld, if anything, was a practical man." The story here tracks Jacob and Laban's transaction precisely. After a

---

[20] Robert Solotaroff, *Bernard Malamud: A Study of the Short Fiction* (Boston: Twayne, 1989) 25.

[21] Richman, for example, argues that "for Feld there is an instant of real though muted triumph, a gesture which...stamps the story with the spectral promise of salvation through love." Richman, *Bernard Malamud,* 103.

month in Laban's home, Laban approaches him to make a deal. Just because you are my kinsman you should not serve me for nothing: "Tell me, what should your wages be?" Seven years in exchange for Rachel. Of course, Laban has something up his sleeve, a second seven years and another daughter off his hands. It's hard to see how Feld will get a second seven years out of Sobel, having only one daughter whose life he has tried to stage manage into the ground (from college to college boy to Sobel/shoemaker).

Where does this leave us? Indeed. Miriam's future is stretched like a tightrope between father and husband-to-be. There couldn't be a worse alliance for her future. Not only is Feld a limited person, whose world is defined by worn-out shoes and degraded notions of education; he is not even what the narrator assured us he was: practical. The scene of the story opens with Feld peering into the falling snow, lost in reverie, with bitter memories of his snowy Polish childhood, old disappointments and wishes for a son, his chagrin that Miriam refused his offer to support her in college, musing by contrast on Max the college boy who had trudged past in the snow. He is so deep in these dreams and regrets that when Max himself opens the door and enters with a pair of shoes to be repaired, Feld does not at first recognize him and then is so deafened by the opportunity to match-make he can't even hear a word Max says. A practical man does not badly misread who Max, Miriam, and Sobel are. He does not jeopardize the two things that matter most to him, his daughter's happiness and his own livelihood, by failing to grasp their basis. Feld, far from being a practical man, is lost in his hopeless dreams. Sobel, if anything, is even more feckless. He bursts into sobs when Feld calls him old and ugly. This poor man fleeing war-torn Europe fell in love with a fourteen-year-old girl "less than half his age" and for five years (and two more to go) had no way to tell her so except in his obsessive reading and writing—and his dogged service at the last. Feld is all vaporous imaginations and Sobel, in spite of all his sad reading of the classics and perhaps because of his even sadder experience of Poland and the war and the death camps, seems to have no imagination at all. This is a classic mésalliance between a *shlemiel* or moral bungler and a *shlimazl* or born loser.[22] This will take us—and Miriam—nowhere.

Malamud has cunningly misled us with multiple story lines while hiding the real—but irresolvable—plot in plain sight. At first, it appears that it is all

[22] As Leo Rosten illustrates, "A *shlemiel* is a man who is always spilling hot soup—down the neck of a *shlimazl*." Leo Rosten, *The Joys of Yiddish* (New York: Washington Square Press, 1968) 349.

comedy. After fumbling through matchmaker and suitors, the promise of a marriage of true minds is held out to us: Miriam and Sobel laboring at meaningless jobs and reading sad books together in the twilight. But shortly a very different tale emerges, the tragicomedy of love and identity across immigrant generations in a dynamic America, a favorite Jewish-American theme. Feld loves his daughter for whom he thinks she should be. Miriam loves her father, but feels no need to sacrifice her independence to make his dreams come true. And then there is the story the critics want to hear, how Feld—in spite of his cultural limitations and lack of self-knowledge—at the very end reaches out to Sobel: "His teeth were on edge with pity for the man, and his eyes grew moist.... 'Ugly I didn't mean,' he said half aloud." This is straight out of a soap opera; a natural for Oprah's Book Club. Unfortunately, this is Laban and Jacob all over again, as Rachel stole even the household gods from her father as Jacob lights out with all his spotted and striped sheep carefully culled and cultivated from his father-in-law's diminishing herds. This is the expected unexpected. We have unaccountably strayed far from our structuring allusion. Or has the allusion wandered away from the story and its staccato ending, "pounding leather for his love?"

Is this story about desire or destiny? About choosing or being chosen? The question at the end—*what comes next?*—is inescapable and unanswerable.[23] Malamud has taken us exactly nowhere with this story. Its first sentence introduces Sobel's "fanatic pounding at the other bench." Its last sentence has him still pounding. The story's turning point is Sobel's infuriated pounding at the naked iron last. The story has the structural symmetry of a chiasmus, ending where it began. But the title still hovers over this static resolution, the *first* seven years. There's more to it; we just don't know what. But this is, indeed, the force of the larger allusion. At every step, from gulling his brother and abusing his father's trust, to courting Rachel at the well, to agreeing to the bargains with his father-in-law, to cheating him, to escaping from him and winning a detente, to wrestling the night long at the ford of the Jabbok with an angel, to offering his brother bribes to let him return, to fleeing beyond his brother's reach, Jacob has temporized his future. To what purpose? To get what he could get, while the getting was good? No—that is what Jacob

[23] Frank Kermode precisely identifies the rhetorical trick Malamud uses again and again to close a story without truly ending it: "In the broadest terms Malamud's method is to conduct his characters through a more or less plausible series of events to a climax by which they are frozen into ritual attitudes, and to allow this tableau to close the work." Frank Kermode, *Continuities* (London: Routledge, 1968) 217.

thought he was doing (we never get a clue how he justified to himself his aggressions against almost all those closest to him, excepting only his mother and Rachel). But a very different plot was unfolding through these distasteful slitherings. It is Leah the despised wife, gotten by crooked accident, who is fertile. She bears the son Judah, who is the line of David, the promise to Abraham. Rachel dying in childbirth is buried along the road. Leah is buried with her husband and Isaac and Abraham.

The covenantal relationship is fulfilled, not because of desire and strategy—yet not despite them either. The irony that messianic hope rests with a trimmer like Jacob is the same irony that Feld's improvident and delusive matchmaking "works": Sobel gets Miriam—maybe! The irony expands to include author and reader. The author is reliable, but not to be trusted to have the final word as it turns out. The reader's narrative anticipations are led astray at the very moment they become self-conscious. The story confounds us with something that has the capacity to force us toward the limits of storytelling. Sobel's superb patience, his unlimited devotion (the *first* seven years), his endless pounding, are figures for an openness beyond fulfillment or closure, an inscrutable expectation that transcends desire. As Levinas might say, "a thought which at every moment thinks more than it thinks."[24]

## "The Magic Barrel"

Out of naiveté and arrogance, Leo Finkle, the rabbinical student in "The Magic Barrel,"[25] runs to embrace mésalliance:

> Violins and lit candles revolved in the sky. Leo ran forward with flowers outthrust.
>
> Around the corner, Salzman, leaning against a wall, chanted prayers for the dead.[26]

---

[24] Emmanuel Levinas, "Philosophy and the Idea of Infinity," *Collected Philosophical Papers*, trans. Alphonso Lingis (Dordrecht: Nijhoff, 1987) 56.

[25] "The Magic Barrel" is the concluding story in the 1959 National Book Award winning collection of the same name, Malamud's literary breakthrough to national recognition by critics and other writers. Flannery O'Connor, writing to Father James H. McCown in 1958, recommends that he read *The Magic Barrel*: "The stories deal with Jews and they are the real thing. Really spiritual and very funny."

[26] "The Magic Barrel," *The Complete Stories* 134–156. All references to "The Magic Barrel" are to this edition.

Nearing the end of his six years of study at Yeshiva University ("Not long ago," the narrator tells us in a classic fairy-tale opening), Leo was advised by an acquaintance to marry in order to more easily "win himself a congregation." Living in "a small, almost meager room, though crowded with books" on the fourth-floor of an uptown rooming house, Leo—speaking through the narrator's voice—acknowledges "he had no present prospects of marriage." From a two-line ad in the *Forward*, he requests the services of one Pinye Salzman, marriage broker. Salzman arrives one evening, smelling of fish, shabbily dressed, animated but with "mild blue eyes [that] revealed a depth of sadness." Leo immediately takes charge with a detailed explanation of his situation: alone in the world except for elderly parents, devoted entirely to his studies, respecting—by the way—the "ancient and honorable" function of the marriage broker (his own parents brought together by a matchmaker), desirous of a wife, and concluding "he thought it the better part of trial and error—of embarrassing fumbling—to call in an experienced person to advise him on these matters." "Embarrassing fumbling" being perhaps the narrator's wry *sotto voce* comment on Leo's real motivation concealed behind his rationalizing euphemism of "the better part of trial and error." Salzman is at first embarrassed by Leo's apparent need to defend his decision to consult him, but later "he experienced a glow of pride in his work, an emotion that had left him years ago, and he heartily approved of Finkle." (And so, we get another take on matchmaking and its unintended, inscrutable outcomes. What *are* we trying to match up?)

Salzman flips through the packet of cards he withdraws from a well-used black portfolio while Leo pretends not to notice and Salzman sizes him up, "the long, severe scholar's nose, brown eyes heavy with learning." When Leo sees that Salzman has only six cards to show him, he's disappointed. Salzman assures him that he has many, many cards, his drawers so full that he keeps them now in a barrel, "but is every girl good for a new rabbi?" Leo blushes, realizing that in the curriculum vitae he had sent Salzman he had revealed more of himself than necessary trying "[to acquaint] him with his strict standards and specifications." His first question is to ask for photographs—so much for standards and specifications. First family, then dowry, then promises—*then* pictures, Salzman reproves him. Each card conceals a flaw, one a widow, another a teacher already thirty-two years old. When he presses Salzman on the third card—which seems too good to be true—he says "'I don't understand why an American girl her age should go to a marriage broker.'...'So for the same reason you went, she comes.'" When Ruth K., nineteen, an honor student, pretty, her father a medical doctor, turns out to be lame from a car accident when she was twelve, Leo feeling "curiously bitter" dismisses Salzman. The next night, however, Salzman reappears, cadges a cup of tea, and reveals that the high school teacher, Lily H. is really only twenty-nine—a mistake in his notation. She speaks four languages, has a new car and $10,000 in the bank, her father a dentist guarantees another $12,000. "She will give you a first-class home and children. How near do we come in our life to paradise?" Leo objects that if she is truly so wonderful, why wasn't she married ten years ago? "'Why?' said Salzman with a heavy laugh. '—Why? Because she is *partikiler*. That is why. She wants the best.'" Just like Leo.

His walk along Riverside Drive with Lily Hirschorn is an unpleasant revelation to him. Petite and "not unpretty," au courant and animated, she impresses him with her honesty. She asks his permission to speak more personally and inquires after his "calling," how he became "enamored of God?" Outraged, he realizes that Salzman, the trickster, had sold her a bill of goods too—Lily looked to him "past thirty-five and aging rapidly" and *he* was certainly no "semi-mystical Wonder Rabbi."

> "I am not," he said gravely, "a talented religious person," and, in seeking words to go on, found himself possessed by shame and fear. "I think," he said in a strained manner, "that I came to God not because I loved Him but because I did not."

This unexpected confession plunges him into despair. What else has he not known about himself? "It seemed to Leo that his whole life stood starkly revealed and he saw himself for the first time as he truly was—unloved and loveless."

After a week of agonizing ("he drew the consolation that he was a Jew and that a Jew suffered"), he flips his seeking on its head. First must come love and then marriage: "for this sanctified seeking who needed a Salzman?" However, Salzman shows up that very night, "How did you like her?" Leo's anger is soon dissipated. He explains his new found "necessity of premarital love." Salzman is astounded. Living and worshipping as a male Jew is its own end, love a mere byproduct (it is different for the ladies, he thinks). Leo agrees, but "for myself I find it necessary to establish the level of my need and fulfill it." So, if Leo wants love, he will get "love." Salzman pulls out a packet of pictures for him: "such beautiful clients that you will love them the minute your eyes will see them." Though Leo tries to get Salzman to take them away as he hurriedly leaves, the packet remains behind unopened. Spring arrives but "no social life to speak of developed with a member of the opposite sex." In a funk, Leo tears the packet open and stares excitedly at the six photographs. But finally they all look like Lily Hirschorn, "past their prime, all starved behind bright smiles, not a true personality in the lot." As he slips them back into the packet, he discovers another snapshot ("of the type taken by a machine for a quarter").

Her face and eyes "leaped forth to his heart." She had suffered; there was an impression of evil: "Only such a one could understand him and help him seek whatever he was seeking. She might, perhaps, love him." He rushes to Salzman's one-room tenement apartment. Salzman's asthmatic wife turns him away: "So who knows where he is? Every time he thinks a new thought he runs to a different place. Go home, he will find you." To Leo's joy, Salzman is miraculously waiting at his door when he returns home. He shows him the snapshot. Salzman groans and frantically flees down the stairs with the pictures and the snapshot. Leo corners him in the vestibule and shakes him. Ashamed, Leo begs Salzman to tell him who she is. Not for you, a wild one, "without shame," like an animal. "For her to be poor was a sin. This is why she is dead to me now." Bewildered, Leo asks "'Why are you so excited?' 'Why he asks,' Salzman said, bursting into tears. 'This is my baby, my Stella, she should burn in hell.'"

Through days of torment, Leo struggles not to love her—"fearing success, he escaped it," the narrator interpolates this deeper impulse. Finally he "concluded to convert her to goodness, himself to God. The idea alternately nauseated and exalted him." Encountering Salzman sucking on a bony fish in a cafeteria, Leo confesses that "love has at last come to my heart." The meeting is arranged. On a spring night, Stella stands smoking under a lamppost, wearing a white dress with red shoes. "From afar he saw that her eyes—clearly her father's—were filled with desperate innocence. He pictured, in her, his own redemption." The narrator generously lends his rhetorical weight to this fantasy. Perhaps he would like it to be true as much as Leo would, but Salzman gets the last word, "[chanting] prayers for the dead." It is a last word in lieu of a fairy tale ending—and they lived happily ever after. We have no idea how this tale would/should conclude in the real world. Malamud's drumbeat last sentence, as in many of his stories, terminates without concluding—a faux, merely rhetorical ending. What the narrator has set in motion has its conclusion somewhere else, perhaps in the very beginning of it all.

Leo doesn't know himself, but seeks to create himself as a rabbi, as a Jew, as a husband, as a man of the Law, as someone with strict standards and specifications, but also, it seems, as a romantic, a lover, redeemer, beseecher, and penitent. Lily Hirschorn imagines him as "enamored of God," Pinye Salzman as "weighted with wisdom." His is a character both grandiose and jejune, childish. Running to meet Stella, both evil and innocent, he is like a seven-year-old arsonist who has been told over and over again not to play with matches. He has enough imagination to get into big trouble, but is not mature enough to imagine how much trouble waits for him. It is hard not to see this as Adam and Eve in the Garden. You'll be as gods, says the Serpent. The next thing they know is they are East of Eden, the way back into Paradise barred by a cherubim with a flaming sword—and God is definitely harder to get in touch with. Who would have thought it?! As Leo leaves the cafeteria after arranging with Salzman to meet Stella, "he was, however, afflicted by a tormenting suspicion that Salzman had planned it all to happen this way." Was God surprised that Eve ate the apple? God and man—and woman—what kind of a relationship is possible? Leo is no Moses, in spite of "I was always interested in the Law." To be an ordinary Jew—"not a talented religious person"—is already to be a kind of mésalliance, chosen and disappointing on the one hand (exaltation?) and choosing and regretting on the other (exile?), none of it working out too well for any One/anyone—so far. Original sin is responsibility without being responsible for it.

## "The Lady of the Lake"

"The Lady of the Lake," with its Arthurian overtones, presents Henry Levin as a Coney Island Galahad incognito, abroad in Italy as a Lancelot *du lac*—newly styled *Henry R. Freeman*—seeking "love, adventure, freedom." [27] Henry Levin—a former floorwalker in Macy's book department—is a Jew re-imagining himself as a knight errant living by a code of chivalry in service to an idealized romantic love—instead of by the Mosaic Law whose first commandment is: "I am the LORD your God, who brought you out of Egypt, out of the land of slavery. You shall have no other gods before me." What is freedom? Trying to escape his vaguely unsatisfactory history (handsome but a bit short, girlfriends who "had come to less than he had expected"), feeling life slipping through his fingers somehow, willing to sacrifice his nominal Jewishness for romance ("what had it brought him but headaches, inferiorities, unhappy memories?"), Freeman—like Don Quixote before him—is trying to imagine the imaginary as a way of life, with all the illusions (and literary *allusions*) the imaginative attempt brings in its train. His nag, an aquatic Rocinante, is a cumbrous rowboat ("like pulling a hearse") that takes him to

[27] "The Lady of the Lake," *The Complete Stories*, 221–240. All references to "The Lady of the Lake" are to this edition.

the evanescent, magical Isola del Dongo of his Lady of the Lake.[28] But the aristocratic Isabella del Dongo—a vision of dark, medieval grace—turns out to be Isabella della Seta, a caretaker and tour guide of the palazzo with her father and brother. It also turns out that Isabella, meaning "pledged to God" in Hebrew, is a survivor of Buchenwald. Amidst "the moonlit statuary: stags, tigers, and unicorns, poets and painters, shepherds with pipes, and playful shepherdesses," misunderstanding her concern that he might be a Jew, posed to ask her to marry him, he denies for the third time being a Jew: "How many no's make never? Why do you persist with such foolish questions?" In answer, she reveals to him her breasts with concentration camp numbers tattooed across them, arousing and then horrifying Levin and declares "I can't marry you. We are Jews. My past is meaningful to me. I treasure what I suffered for." As Levin/Freeman fumbles for words to make himself known to her, she slips away among the statuary: "when he vainly sought her in the veiled mist that had arisen from the lake, still calling her name, Freeman embraced only moonlit stone." Once again the staccato last sentence terminates rather than concludes the story.

The story is tricked-up and tongue-in-cheek, with abundant easy—if amusing—ironies. It turns mésalliance on its head, intimacy is thwarted by the misperception of mésalliance where none existed. Guessing at who you are and who someone else is, by denying yourself and idealizing the other, is a formula for disappointment. But the real interest of the story is what we see along the way, the "fine isolated verisimilitude." As Isabella reveals herself through an indelible mark in the flesh, Freeman is unable to even find words to speak. Instead, "He groped for her breasts, to clutch, kiss, or suckle them." We are repulsed. This ending is wrong literarily *and* morally—an adolescent sensuality intruding on the horror, betrayal, and mass murder of the Holocaust. But, it is discouragingly authentic—a romantic sensibility (the world is splendid) and collective shame (the world is debased) can co-exist in the same soul. As we look again at the story, we see in fact that Levin's dignity and the romantic power of his quest are undermined again and again. There is some deep psychic disturbance acknowledged by the narrator, if not the character. Finding his initial adventure in Paris a bit disappointing, he flees

---

[28] Isola del Dongo alludes to Stendhal's great "realist romance" *The Charterhouse of Parma*, an epic tale of personal betrayals, religious bad faith, thwarted love, and fecklessness. The padrona of Freeman's pensione warns him not to have anything to do with anyone on the Isola del Dongo: "The family had a perfidious history and was known for its deceit and trickery."

by train to Milan but after Dijon "developed a painful, palpitating anxiety." At the sight of Lake Maggiore, he makes an instant decision to alight there ("He at once felt better."). Later, seeking another glimpse of the girl in white, suffused by flowers and fragrances, he is intoxicated by beauty, but "At the same time, though it was an 'underground' reaction, he experienced a painful, contracting remembrance—more like a warning—of personal poverty." Invited back to the island, he finds her—Celtic water spirit—waiting beside a fountain. She brushes back her hair, "a gesture so beautiful it saddened him, because it was gone in the doing;...he could not help thinking as he dwelt upon her lost gesture that she might be as elusive as it, as evanescent; and so might this island be, and so, despite all the days he had lived through, good, bad, and boring, that too often sneaked into his thoughts—so, indeed, might he today, tomorrow." Lost, all lost, before it is even gained, "a deep sense of the transience of things." Touring through the ancient palazzo with Isabella, surrounded now by beautiful, artistic fakes (including the girl), they enter a room hung with genuine and valuable tapestries illustrating scenes from the *Inferno*. They pause before one of a writhing leper, tearing at his sores.

> "What did he do to deserve his fate?" Freeman inquired. "He falsely said he could fly." "For that you go to hell?" She did not reply. The hall had become gloomily dark, so they left.

Griffolino de Arezzo was burnt at the stake by Albert of Siena for claiming he could fly while nevertheless failing to teach Albert how to do it, evidence, Dante tells us, of the vanity and stupidity of the Sienese. However, Griffolino's eternal and foul torment is actually punishment for practicing the false art of alchemy, trying to turn base metal into gold, fooling others and perhaps himself. For this sin, his body is transmuted into rotting flesh. The morning after their first kiss, Freeman is filled with restless memories "enormously potent, many satisfying, some burdensome; they ate him, he ate them." The thought that worried him the most "was the lie he had told her, that he wasn't a Jew....At first sight love and a lie; it lay on his heart like a sore."[29] Like Griffolino, Levin has fooled himself and others that he can transmute Jew

---

[29] Wounded, perhaps, like the Fisher King "in the thigh" for a lack of chastity. On the first night, swimming nude in the Lake, Levin worries that Isabella may have seen his mutilated/circumcised penis. Like the Fisher King, Levin will be deprived of his patrimony until cured of his wounded, leprous heart/penis by being asked the right question. Unlike the Christian Fisher King (Guardian of the Grail) Jewish Levin is asked the right question but gives the wrong answer: mésalliance (Betrayer of the Shoah).

into Christian knight, Shylock into Parsifal. When Isabella gives him one last chance to admit he is a Jew, he tries again to put his past behind him, which has been his whole project of travel, new identity, new chance, redeeming love, freedom. "I hoped you were.... We are Jews. My past is meaningful to me."

Isabella's declaration is an implicit rebuke, certainly of Levin/Freeman, but more tellingly, of our narrator. Against the backdrop of the Holocaust, it is easy to parody Levin's vague dissatisfactions, casual apostasy, and fatuous imaginings. And the author seems to have little of the affection for his hero that Cervantes had for his noble and addled quester, perhaps because Levin/Freeman has so much of the author in him.[30] The narrator, however, is a different and more elusive target of scorn. The persistent slide into free indirect discourse means that narrator takes on some of the coloration of his protagonist—the opening sentence of the story puts "him" firmly on Levin's side: "Henry Levin, an ambitious, handsome thirty,..." But his ironic distance also increases his responsibility. It is the narrator who gets a rise out of Freeman—and us—by displaying Isabella's succulent breasts: "When she revealed her breasts—he could have wept at their beauty (now recalling a former invitation to gaze at them, but he had arrived too late on the raft)—to his horror he discerned tattooed on the soft and tender flesh a bluish line of distorted numbers." The delectation of "soft and tender flesh" is all the narrator's. So, we have a narrator, who should and does know better, living vicariously through his character, slyly displaying his sophisticated literary allusions, using the Holocaust as a plot ploy, and leaving poor Levin/Freeman clutching moonlit stone. From whence come these judgments? The question is easy to answer for our protagonist. The narrator picks at every disingenuous, befuddled, and subterranean motive that has launched Levin on the lake of love. Not so easy for the narrator. The author is not the narrator's alter ego. The "chameleon poet" revels in the dark as much as in the light, in evil as much as in good. The judgment on the narrator is not the author's judgment. Whose is it? Does the reader have nothing but her/his own disgusted

[30] Malamud and his family sojourned in Italy on sabbatical for nine months in 1956, following the publication of *The Assistant*. Ann Malamud was fluent in Italian, with extended family living there. Many of Malamud's stories are set in Italy, including the picaresque novel, *Pictures of Fidelman*. The failure of art to redeem life is a persistent theme of the Italian stories. The desire to escape, first from New York City and a cramped life, then from philistine Cascadia (Oregon) State College is the subject of Malamud's highly autobiographical *A New Life: A Novel* (1961) whose protagonist is one S. Levin.

or cynical amusement to draw on? From whence come these judgments beyond the story? A transcendent viewpoint—but not an ideology—subtly emerges like mist on a lake, almost evanescent.

We are also left with an apparent conundrum. If history can be dismissed à la Levin/Freeman, then nothing matters—we are left only with fantasies where failure and success are ultimately indistinguishable and life is evanescent indeed. But, if history is indelible à la Isabella, then no genuine future is possible and we inherit a Waste Land. Here Malamud takes advantage of the "end" of his story, which will be just the beginning of something utterly unlike what Levin/Freeman thought he was about. As Jessie Weston famously first recognized, "the [Arthurian] Grail Quest should be viewed primarily as an initiation story, as a search into the secret and mystery of life; it is the record of an initiation *manqué*. The Quest properly speaking, begins only when the hero, having failed at his first unpremeditated visit to the Castle to fulfill the tests to which he has been subjected, sets out with the deliberate intention of finding the vanished Temple of the Grail, and fulfilling the conditions which shall qualify him to obtain full knowledge of the marvels he has beheld."[31] How will Freeman redress this lost opportunity? How will he incorporate his Jewish fate into his desire for love? How will he learn to face the world as it is, good and bad, not as he wants to imagine it? The invitation is already implicit in the lost opportunity.

> "Welcome," Isabella said, blushing....Although he felt in her presence a fulfillment, as if they had already confessed love for each other, at the same time Freeman sensed an uneasiness in her which made him think, though he fought the idea, that they were far away from love; or at least were approaching it through opaque mystery. But that's what happened, Freeman, who had often been in love, told himself. Until you were lovers you were strangers.

A tour of the palace and its treasures, a naked moonlit swim, and Isabella sets a lavish picnic supper before him—straight out of a scene by Chrétien de Troyes. The missed opportunity includes the promise—or points the direction toward a different kind of love—or at least leaves him searching for something deeper. Neither history nor future, but a deeper connection to life

[31] Jessie Laidlay Weston, *The Quest of the Holy Grail* (London: G. Bell, 1913) 95. Malamud had taken Weston's 1920 *From Ritual to Romance* as a guide to Arthurian legend as he wrote *The Natural*, imitating T.S. Eliot for whom her work played a similar role in his writing *The Waste Land* in 1921.

and love—*beyond imagination*—to countenance an opaque mystery, the stranger Other.

## "The Jewbird"

"The window was open so the skinny bird flew in. Flappity-flap with its frazzled black wings. That's how it goes. It's open, you're in. Closed, you're out, and that's your fate."[32] In this case, Mr. Schwartz is both in and out. He's a Jew; he dovens and speaks Yiddish. But, he's also a bird, a "Jewbird," once removed from a Jewfish he responds when challenged. Jews are not a race or a nation—they are a tribe, the sons of Jacob or a tribe of tribes originally, first twelve, then after exile two: Judah and Levi. On the wing from anti-Semites and also eagles, vultures, hawks, and crows, Mr. Schwartz flappity-flaps into the kitchen of one Cohen, a "heavy man with hairy chest and beefy shorts," a frozen-foods salesman. Cohen is a descendent of the tribe of Levi, heir to the exclusive role of kohen or priest by way of Moses' brother Aaron. Sacrifice, blessing, purity, and teaching are his ancestral calling. Flappity-flap into a family, Edie "in skinny yellow shorts and a red halter" and Maurie ("after her father") "a nice kid though not overly bright," the narrator tells us. Bedraggled, eyes slightly crossed, smelling of herring, Schwartz the Jewbird becomes a part of the family, in spite of Cohen's objections:

> "What do you have against the poor bird?" "Poor bird, my ass, He's a foxy bastard. He thinks he's a Jew." "What difference does it make what he thinks?" "A Jewbird, what a chutzpah. One false move and he's out on his drumsticks."

Cohen's mother is ill, dying. Schwartz plays the role of a wise and witty grandfather, helping Maurie with his homework (his grades improve), keeping Edie company while Cohen is at work. But he's the wrong kind of old Jew. Or Cohen is the wrong kind of young Jew—he's certainly no kohen, dispensing blessings and modeling devotion. In one confrontation, Schwartz calls him a "Grubber yung," a coarse young man, a punk. It's not the mésalliance of human and beast occupying the same cultural territory—the bird is more of a mensch than the man. Cohen's imagination is too tribal, the clannishness that often made Jews suspect subjects throughout Christendom: imagined as bloodsuckers, Christ-killers, parasites, conspirators. The

[32] "The Jewbird," *The Complete Stories* 322-330. All references to "The Jewbird" are to this edition.

mésalliance is in Cohen's tribal mind, but that's enough. He begins a campaign of hidden harassment, including bringing home a murderous cat. The day after Cohen's mother finally dies (and Maurie comes home with a zero on an arithmetic test) Cohen attacks the bird. He drags him out of his birdhouse on the balcony. He whirls him around by his legs as Schwartz manages to catch Cohen's nose in his beak. Finally, he punches him loose and flings him into the street—and his birdhouse after him—Cohen's nose swollen to three times its size:

> "Where is he now," Edie asked, frightened. "I threw him out and he flew away. Good riddance." Nobody said no, though Edie touched a handkerchief to her eyes and Maurie rapidly tried the nine-times table and found he knew approximately half.

In the spring Maurie went looking for him. He found a dead bird, wings broken, neck twisted, and eyes plucked out: "'Who did it to you, Mr. Schwarz?' Maurie wept. 'Anti-Semeets,' Edie said later." Being a Jew is not enough to make you a Jew—in Malamud's imagination.

However, a subtle questioning of the power of literary imagination is also secreted in this fable. As J. Gerald Kennedy first argued, "The Jewbird" is a parody of America's most famous narrative poem, Edgar Allan Poe's "The Raven."[33] This wildly popular poem (translated by Mallarme and illustrated by Manet, for example) was subsequently parodied many, many times—and itself borrowed the mechanism of a talking raven from Charles Dickens's *Barnaby Rudge: A Tale of the Riots of Eighty*. Poe had reviewed *Barnaby Rudge* in series and on completion and opined that the raven could play a much more prophetic role.[34] Remarkably, Poe himself wrote a kind of parody of his poem, a critical dissection of it explaining the rationale behind every element of the text and its effects on the reader. His "The Philosophy of Composition" was published a year later and was so overdone that it has often been suspected as being itself a satire or critical spoof. Needless to say, its effect is rather the opposite of the effect of the original poem. Where the poem was

---

[33] J. Gerald Kennedy, "Parody as Exorcism: 'The Raven' and 'The Jewbird,'" *Critical Essays on Bernard Malamud*, ed. Joel Salzberg (Boston: G.K. Hall & Co, 1987) 108–115.

[34]In the satiric verse by James Russell Lowell (*A Fable for Critics*, 1848) "Here comes Poe with his Raven, like Barnaby Rudge,/Three fifths of him genius, two fifths sheer fudge." "Grip," the loquacious companion of the half-wit Barnaby, was itself modeled on Dickens's garrulous pet raven, which rather ruled the household—and can be seen today (stuffed) in the Free Library of Philadelphia.

eerie and seemed to plunge deep into a twisted soul, the critical theory showed instead that "the work proceeded, step by step, to its completion with the precision and rigid consequence of a mathematical problem," beginning with how long it should be: 100 lines more or less.[35] Poe was one of America's first literary critics and known for his vitriolic takedowns. Here he may be mocking the authors who "prefer having it understood that they compose by a species of fine frenzy—an ecstatic intuition—and would positively shudder at letting the public take a peep behind the scenes, at the elaborate and vacillating crudities of thought, [etc.]... ."[36] Or it may be mockery of the reader, so easily manipulated by the author's bag of tricks. Or he may only be making it clear that he himself was not moved or undone by his poem, which when he read publicly he would do in an irritating sing-song voice.[37] Parody is often mockery, but as "The Philosophy of Composition" reveals it is not always easy to see what is being mocked.

The purpose and effect of Malamud's parody in "The Jewbird" is, in Kennedy's words, "unclear": "simultaneously overt and discreet, unmistakably present yet playfully elusive." Kennedy sees the parody as Malamud's attempt to break the spell of Poe, to exorcize and subordinate obsessive material: "Only through this arcane ritual, it would seem, can he free himself from the literary influence which haunts him like an ominous bird of yore."[38] Poe was, of course, also one of the inventors of the short story, Malamud's inimitable province. Arguably, the detective story, science fiction, and the horror story are all creations (at least partially) of Poe's genius. Baudelaire, Mallarme, and Valery praised his critical perspective[39]—in contradistinction to very mixed American and British judgments. What could have gotten under Malamud's skin enough to parody Poe? Kevin Jackson reviewing the 2012 film

---

[35] Edgar Allan Poe, "The Philosophy of Composition," *Graham's Magazine* 28.4 (1846): 163.

[36] Ibid.

[37] Although he made almost no money from it, the poem was so well known that urchins on the streets of Baltimore would run up to Poe cawing and flapping their arms. He might well have regretted its spell, which has been persistent. Who would have thought that almost 200 years later Baltimore's National Football League team would take the field as the Ravens?

[38] J. Gerald Kennedy, "Parody as Exorcism: 'The Raven' and 'The Jewbird,'" 110, 115.

[39] At the end of his life, Baudelaire addressed his morning prayers to God...and to the spirit of Edgar Allan Poe.

*The Raven* nicely identifies the source of Poe's staying power: "One of the gifts Poe had was the creation of small, imperishable images that have wormed their way into our collective psyche. Just as there are millions of people who know something about Oliver Twist and Fagin without having read a word of Dickens, so there are millions who have at least some memory of a sinister raven, a man buried prematurely, a dead heart that will not stop beating, a pit and a pendulum, a house owned by the Ushers that falls."[40] Harold Bloom had a similar insight in his response to the publication in 1984 by The Library of America of two large volumes of Poe's poetry, tales, essays, and reviews. Condemning (with Henry James, T.S. Eliot, Aldous Huxley, D.H. Lawrence, and George Orwell) Poe's style, taste, and ideas as tone-deaf, vulgar, narcissistic fantasies, Bloom concedes that, nevertheless, "he has a mythical power that makes him inescapable, even though his tales contrast weakly with Hawthorne's, his poems scarcely bear reading, and his speculative discourses fade away in juxtaposition to Emerson's, his despised northern rival.... Whatever his actual failures as poet and critic, whatever the gap between style and idea in his tales, Poe is central to the American canon, both for us and for the rest of the world."[41] Through parody, Malamud insinuates a different why and how for fiction—and a different interest in reading what is written.

As we juxtapose "The Raven" and its theory of composition with "The Jewbird," we see Malamud recognizing Poe's genius while disowning it in order to distinguish his own mythologizing from Poe's.[42] The most salient distinction between Poe and Malamud is their approaches to composition.

---

[40] Kevin Jackson, "The Great Bad Writer," *Prospect: The Leading Magazine of Ideas* (March 2012). "The Raven" was the focus of two earlier films, one in 1935 starring Boris Karloff and Béla Lugosi and one in 1963 starring Vincent Price, Peter Lorre, Boris Karloff, and a young Jack Nicholson—played as farce. The 1963 film was one of seven films directed by Roger Cormon in the 1960s that were based on Poe's stories.

[41] Harold Bloom, "Inescapable Poe," *New York Review of Books* 31.15 (1984) www.nybooks.com/articles/1984/10/11/inescapable-poe/

[42] Similarly, we might recognize nuclear bombs as the acme of warfare while disowning them as weapons. Or, we might admire Leni Riefenstahl's incomparable ability to stage rousing communal spectacles for the Nazis while disowning them as destructive of genuine community. Moral revulsion can trump creative triumph, in spite of Keats's amoralism.

Poe insisted that writing must begin with a clear view of the effect to be accomplished, with all matters of composition controlled by this end-in-view, like a proof in mathematics: "I say to myself, in the first place, 'Of the innumerable effects, or impressions, of which the heart, the intellect, or (more generally) the soul is susceptible, what one shall I, on the present occasion, select?' Having chosen a novel, first, and secondly a vivid effect, I consider whether it can be best wrought by incident or tone—whether by ordinary incidents and peculiar tone, or the converse, or by peculiarity both of incident and tone—afterward looking about me (or rather within) for such combinations of event, or tone, as shall best aid me in the construction of the effect."[43] By contrast, Malamud's writing is often autobiographical, sparked by an experience or a memory, or else is suggested by an historical situation, whatever sets his imagination going, as he said. His greatest pleasure in writing was rewriting, with many drafts, obsessively reworking turns of phrase.[44] The effect emerges from these details, but—as we have already seen—the end of the story is rarely an end-in-view. Malamud cannot conclude his stories because he himself doesn't know where they are going. He can more or less tell when he gets there but the "there" is part and parcel of the story and its odd limitations, not to be abstracted or summed up. Malamud consistently throughout his career refused to speculate about the meaning of his stories: "I don't like questions of explication: What did I mean by this or that? I want the books to speak for themselves. You can read? All right, tell me what my books mean. Astonish me."[45]

From this critical perspective, Poe's story of the Raven—in spite of its vaunted psychological realism—is less real than Malamud's much more

---

[43] Poe, "The Philosophy of Composition," ibid. Poe's literary genres are all ones where the end-in-view is essential, the who-done-it, the other-worldly fantasy, the lurching gotcha. Literary qualities for these stories, if any, are just icing on the cake.

[44] In a letter to the artist Rosemary Beck, who became a close friend when they both were in residence at Yaddo in 1959, he explained, "Rewriting tends to be pleasurable, in particular the enjoyment of finding new opportunities in old sentences, twisting, tying, looping structure tighter, finding pegs to tie onto that were apparently not there before, deepening meanings, strengthening logicality in order to infiltrate the apparently illogical, the apparently absurd, the absurdly believable." Quoted in Phillip Davis, *Bernard Malamud: A Writer's Life* (Oxford: Oxford University Press, 2007) 155.

[45] Stern, "The Art of Fiction, Bernard Malamud No. 52," *The Paris Review*.

fabulous tale. Poe's raven is mere device croaking meaninglessly, "Nevermore." The narrative has nothing to do with the bird and everything to do with the young aesthete revealing his soul as he revels in his exquisite anguish, while increasingly over-interpreting the raven's croak—and plunging deeper into his narcissistic despair. Cohen's soul is also revealed in the bosom of his family, but as the result of his crude egoism. And Mr. Schwartz's fate—and the way in which he meets it—becomes the heart of the story. Poe's own parody of his poem exposes its phoniness—we can almost hear "The Raven" as written for a vaudevillian take-off with Groucho Marx as the Raven waving a big cigar and Zeppo as the histrionic lover. By contrast, Malamud's fable has a homely authenticity. Where Poe's raven, in the last verse "never flitting, still is sitting," will end up shitting on the pallid bust of Pallas (that's what birds do to statues), Mr. Schwartz has the moxie to fly across the street to the plane trees to "make dirty." It's magic realism gold versus ghost story brass. Most importantly, in spite of his success in achieving the effect he wanted, Poe's story goes nowhere. He simply wallows in his effect. Whereas Malamud uses comedy, fantasy, and bitter critique to leave us wondering what could be the alternative to this ending, how could we retell this story to save Mr. Schwartz or redeem Cohen or blame God? Unlike Poe's mathematizing poetry, this is moral geometry where a straight line is fortunately not the shortest distance between two points.

The mythic realms that Poe summons up to our fascination and horror are "wormy" archetypes buried deep in our psyches. Bloom describes them as expressing America's hysteric Promethean narcissism or, as I might venture, the guilt of self-serving parricides (rebels against paternal England) and fratricides (murdering, raping, and emasculating homebred brother/sister/slaves).[46] As Marilynn Robinson notes, "Poe's great tales turn on guilt concealed or denied, then abruptly and shockingly exposed.…Poe explores the thought that reality is of a kind to break through the enthralling dream of innocence or of effective concealment and confront us—horrify us—with

[46] Poe's wife Virginia Clemm, his first cousin whom he married when she was 13, blamed her own early death on Poe's very public flirtations as she declined from tuberculosis in the years leading up to "The Raven" and afterward. Poe died three years later.

truth."[47] Poe, like many enlightened Southerners of the time, had a deeply ambiguous relationship to the slavery surrounding him: racist, fearful, guilty, self-deceiving—whipsawed by myths of White female sanctity, Black bestiality, and divine retribution.

If Poe's American mythos is one of Whiteness/innocence and the Other ("black" beasts, "redskin" savages), Malamud's mythos *is* the Other. The Jew, the tribe of Judah, begins in myth as the Chosen People; perpetuates itself in myth as led out of bondage into the Promised Land and eventually into exile and as awaiting the Messiah and return to the Promised Land. As a sojourner the Jew becomes a ubiquitous mythic image in its enemies' eyes as demonic, excluded, and exterminated. And, finally, the Jew perdures as myth and uncomfortable reality—a stiff-necked people—against all likelihood to this latter day. As Walker Percy liked to ask, "If there are Jews here, why are there not Hittites here? Where are the Hittites? Show me one Hittite in New York City."[48] The establishment of modern Israel, an explicitly ethnically and increasingly religiously-based democracy, brings the myth full circle with enormous political and religious significance in Europe, the United States, and the Middle East. At the same time, as immigrants and refugees Jews have a distinctive world-wide presence, spawning tropes of Jewish humor, Jewish wealth, Jewish intellectual brilliance, Jewish domination of popular culture and media, and Jewish promotion of revolution and reaction, which function as unique ethnic myths. The shadow myths of anti-Semitism and Jewish racial/religious impurity were the backbone of the Nazi Third Reich and continue to this day as one of the convening "dog whistles" for neo-fascist populism. The Protocols of Zion, spurious as report but effective as propaganda, spin out a myth that is alive and well today across the world: "God has granted to us, His Chosen People, the gift of dispersion, and from this, which appears to all eyes to be our weakness, has come forth all our strength, which has now brought us to the threshold of sovereignty over all the world." (Protocol XI)[49]

---

[47] Marilynn Robinson, "On Edgar Allan Poe," *New York Review of Books* 62.2 (2015) www.nybooks.com/articles/2015/02/05/edgar-allan-poe/

[48] Walker Percy, *The Message in the Bottle* (New York: Farrar, Straus, and Giroux, 1975) 6.

[49] Following the Bolshevik Revolution and during the interim between the two World Wars with Germany, American icons like Henry Ford and Charles Lindberg promulgated the *Protocols* as legitimate. As the U.S. Holocaust Museum concludes, "The Internet has dramatically increased access to the *Protocols*. Even though many Web sites expose the *Protocols* as a fraud, the Internet has made it easy to use the

As the imaginary Other, the Jew is a Jew in-spite-of-himself. What is it to live out someone else's dream/nightmare of you—already a mésalliance? Does imagination/myth finally collapse and leave you standing there—where? At his most intuitive, Malamud explores this mythic Jew in order to resist and undermine the power of myth to express and shape the moral agents of his fictions. Unlike Poe, he is most interested in what cannot be expressed mythically, in the genuinely transcendent, in the sacred beyond Reality. The Jew beyond "the Jew." *All men are Jews but few men know it.*[50]

## "The Silver Crown"

"Gans, the father, lay dying in a hospital bed.... One doctor said cancer. 'Of the heart,' the old man said bitterly. 'It wouldn't be impossible.' The young Gans, Albert, a high school biology teacher, in the afternoons walked the streets in sorrow. What can anyone do about cancer?"[51] What can anyone do about dying? Of dying there is no cure—now or later. A scientist, Albert knows this. Yet, he is frantic, easily irritated by everything: "angered by the war, atom bomb, pollution, death." The narrator shares the character's voice, "To be able to do nothing for him made him frantic. He had done nothing for him all his life." Him, him, He, him, his. Who? Father? Son? Maybe it is not the character's voice at all, but solely the omniscient narrator's? What is the backstory? What is really going on? What is the relation between father and son? What does the father's death mean to the son? What does the son's sorrow and support mean to the father? Of all of this, we will receive scarcely a hint in the story. A colleague (a "visibly aging" girl with whom he'd once gone to bed, the fused narrator tells us) suggests a faith healer. ("If you've tried everything, what else can you try?" rationalizes the invested narrator. A

---

*Protocols* to spread hatred of Jews. Today, a typical Internet search yields several hundred thousand sites that disseminate, sell, or debate the *Protocols* or expose them as a fraud." United States Holocaust Memorial Museum, "Protocols of the Elders of Zion," *Holocaust Encyclopedia*, www.ushmm.org/wlc/en/article.php?ModuleId=10007058.

[50] Leslie A. Field and Joyce W. Field, "An Interview with Bernard Malamud," *Bernard Malamud: A Collection of Critical Essays*, eds. Field and Field (London: Prentice-Hall, 1975) 11. In this interview he put it this way: "All men are Jews except they don't know it." He often repeated this cryptic claim in other words; my wording here is from personal correspondence.

[51] "The Silver Crown," *The Complete Stories* 536–552. All references to "The Silver Crown" are to this edition.

thought that perhaps applies to Albert's romantic life as well?) By a cosmic accident, after another long lonely walk, an idiot girl—"stupefying" in her gurgling, unfocused bulk—thrusts a soiled card at him. Out of conflicting impulses (even the narrator seems unsure what is in his mind), he takes the card: "Heal The Sick. Save The Dying. Make A Silver Crown." The address on the card for a Rabbi Jonas Lifschitz is nearby: "The silver crown mystified him. He had no idea what it had to do with saving the dying but felt he ought to know." At first repelled by the thought, he quickly makes up his mind to visit the rabbi, "and felt, in a way, relieved." And an entirely—OK, maybe not *entirely*—other story is launched of rabbi and his daughter, of God's grace and our hardness of heart, of superficial convictions and bone-deep doubts.

But before we burrow deeper into the soul's nakedness before the ultimate, let us see what fragments we can glean from "The Silver Crown" of the original story of father and son. Five times over the course of several days, Rabbi Lifschitz asks him in different ways "Do you love your father?" Each time Albert brushes off the question:

> "You love your father?" the rabbi clucked, a glaze of sentiment veiling his eyes. "What I feel is obvious. My real concern right now mainly is how does the crown work?" "Doubts we all got. We doubt God and God doubts us....Of this kind doubts I am not afraid so long as you love your father."..."My father wasn't the easiest man in the world to get along with, and neither am I for that matter, but he has been generous to me and I'd like to repay him in some way."

The framework for the story is established. Albert has three concerns. He is curious about the phenomena proffered: "In the subway, Albert figured he would call it an investment in experience and see what came of it. Education costs money, but how else can you get it?" On the other hand, he does not want to be suckered. "I'm considering this recourse even though it goes against the grain of some of my strongest convictions." How much does it cost? "Tell me please what can a 986 crown do that a 401 can't?" Can he see one? "'Mr. Gans,' replied the rabbi, 'this is not a showcase business. You are not buying from me a Chevrolet automobile. Your father now lies dying in the hospital. Do you love him? Do you wish me to make a crown that will cure him?' The teacher's anger flared. 'Don't be stupid, rabbi, I've answered that. Please don't sidetrack the real issue.'" Finally and most crucially, Albert wants a clean conscience: "I don't want anything to go untried." "Not much will happen, I suppose, but whatever does, my conscience will be in the clear." But nothing is clear. Back and forth, back and forth goes Albert's heart: "He felt relieved, almost euphoric. But by the next morning, after a difficult night, Albert's mood had had about-faced." What does he really want; why does he want it; why can't he face his own desires?

The crown—the $986 one ("What a dope I was to order the $986 job instead of the $401. On that decision alone I lost $585.") will be done tomorrow night before Shabbos. But on the way home on the subway it comes crashing in on Albert that the hocus-pocus image of a crown ("constructed of bars, triangles, half-moons and crescents, spires, turrets, trees, points of spears") that he had seen by candle light in the rabbi's mirror was a mirage; he'd been hypnotized. "He was outraged by the knavery, hypocrisy, fat nerve of Rabbi Jonas Lifschitz," the narrator tells us. He rushes back to demand his money returned. No rabbi. He decides to wait until the Sabbath, then no crown in hand he'll go to the police. The Sabbath comes. He waits. And still no rabbi. Finally at 1:00 a.m. the rabbi and his daughter Rifkele trudge back home from shul down the dark street. He accosts the rabbi in his home: "I came to see my crown." It's finished; go home; soon your father will be better. "I insist on seeing the real thing, for which I paid close to one thousand smackers."

> "Listen, Mr. Gans," said the rabbi patiently, "there are some that we are allowed to see which He lets us see them. Sometimes I wish he didn't let us. There are other things we are not allowed to see—Moses knew this—and one is God's face, and another is the real crown that He makes and blesses it. A miracle is a miracle, this is God's business."

Accusing the rabbi of being a faker, Albert threatens to swear out a complaint to the Bronx D.A.: "A thief is a thief," Albert rants at him as Rifkele blubbers and squeals.

> "Be kind," begged the rabbi, tottering as he wandered amid empty chairs. "Be merciful to an old man. Think of my poor child. Think of your father who loves you." "He hates me, the son of a bitch, I hope he croaks."

There we have it. God has allowed Albert to see who he truly is. His knavery, hypocrisy, and fat nerve are exposed. "Murderer," cries the rabbi aghast—his finger pointing as witness to God in heaven.

> Moaning, father and daughter rushed into each other's arms, as Albert, wearing a massive, spike-laden headache, rushed down the booming stairs. An hour later the elder Gans shut his eyes and expired.

Albert thought his hocus-pocus of concern and effort would fool God—and himself. The rabbi and his daughter are Albert's foil. The rabbi believes without seeing, while Albert's "cast of mind is naturally empiric and objective." To the rabbi's eyes his idiot daughter is in her way perfect: "'She's not perfect, though God, who made her in his image, is Himself perfection. What this means I don't have to tell you.' His heavy eyelid went down in a blink, apparently involuntarily. 'What does it mean?' Albert asked. 'In her way she is also perfect.'" Father and daughter hold each other as Albert rushes down the stairs crowned with his own pain, a miracle of its own. The second miracle, his father's death, shortly awaiting.

What does it take to accept a miracle? Or even to accept that there could be a miracle? As Rabbi Lifschitz admits under pressure from Albert, "'Don't you see it?' 'Not with my eyes.' 'I don't believe a word of it, you faker, two-bit magician.' 'The crown is a real crown. If you think there is magic, it is on account those people that they insist to see it—we try to give them an idea. For those who believe, there is no magic.'" Albert's questions are meant to dispel the mystery: Don't you see it? Is it believable? Could I have a receipt? The rabbi's responses are nonsensical: "'What is the crown?' he asked, at first haughtily, then again, gently. 'It's a crown, nothing else.'" "'We got two kinds crowns,' said the rabbi. 'One is for 401 and the other is 986.'" "'How would that work?' 'Like two winds that they meet in the sky. A white and a blue. The blue says, "Not only I am blue but inside I am also purple and orange." So the white goes away.'" "'I would like to give you a receipt,' said Rabbi Lifschitz earnestly, 'but for the crowns there are no receipts. Some things are not a business.'" The minute the mystery is dispelled, the miracle is gone: "'Miracle,' Albert bellowed, 'it's a freaking fake magic, with an idiot girl for a come-on and hypnotic mirrors. I was mesmerized, suckered by you.'" On the one side of the equation there is the dying man, the conflicted son, the idiot daughter, and the biology and psychology that explain them, as well as the magic that suckers us for the moment into believing what we don't believe in—and the laws against fraud when the magic suckers us out of close to one thousand smackers in the Bronx. On the other side of the equation, is the rabbi, his daughter just as God made her, his father and grandfather before him (who also did not give receipts), and his notebook of hundreds of testimonials: "'Never before have I believed in miraculous occurrences, but from now on I will have less doubts. My thanks to you and God. Most sincerely, Daniel Schwartz.'" Mr. Schwartz being a lawyer whose father had recovered from cancer of the pancreas, with serious complications of the lungs—the $986 crown and God's grace working a miracle. And—of course—standing with the rabbi is God and his law in heaven. Reading to Albert in Hebrew from a thick "mystic" book, the rabbi translates, "The crown is the fruit of God's grace. His grace is love of creation."

Albert can conceive of God, he can conceive of a miracle, he can conceive of the silver crown, he can conceive of Rifkele's ideal perfection, he can conceive of his obligation to his father. He can conceive of love. But he can truly imagine none of it. None of it is real to him—just words and shifting thoughts. But his father's death will pursue him endlessly, the one miracle where he starts with belief not doubt, the one miracle that he would give anything to doubt, because he knows it to be real in his heart. His true bitter desire went straight from his heart to God's ears. The fact that the rabbi is a fraud (giving Albert a portentous—if possible involuntary—wink at key moments) doesn't change whether or not Albert was there to do everything he could to help his father recover his health. *That*, the rabbi could guarantee—whatever the outcome; a grateful son would have his chance to show his gratitude—$986 worth. If it doesn't "work," the rabbi—or even God—is to blame, not the son. Albert, unfortunately, is unable to transcend or even recognize his archetypical Oedipal rage against his father—until the bitter end. The imagination that failed him will now crown him with an inescapable pain, conflicted no longer. A miracle at the last minute and God's grace, after all? Who would say "No" without at least some hesitancy?

We have sampled just a few of Malamud's dozens of stories, but I hope we have tuned our ears to listen in them for the something more than can be said at the limit of storytelling, the insinuation of an ultimacy before which our imagination fails. The trope of mésalliance that underlies the best of Malamud's stories means that closure, reconciliation, or satisfaction will always be elusive. As Emmanuel Levinas insists, "my freedom does not have the last word; moral consciousness is essentially unsatisfied, or again, is always a desire."[52] Curiously, Malamud tests this hypothesis at the very beginning of his career with his first published novel, *The Natural*, a baseball novel.[53]

[52] Levinas, "Philosophy and the Idea of Infinity," 58.

[53] By and large, Malamud's novels are not as successful as his short stories in sustaining this vatic voicing. The radical openness of amphibolous beginnings and staccato endings requires compression to retain its elusive suggestiveness. Too often, Malamud in his novels falls back on moral allegory and sententious moralizing.

## *The Natural*

It was an attempt to start over. The long autobiographical novel he had worked on for five years (1943-1948), The Light Sleeper, was rejected by a dozen publishers. He burned his only manuscript of it in early 1952, after *The Natural* had been accepted for publication. *The Natural* is curious, indeed. It is his only novel without a Jew in it. It is drenched with allusions to chivalric and classical literature and replete with Freudian symbolism, which Malamud felt necessary to introduce because, as he wrote, "baseball in itself is a not very important phenomenon."[54] Malamud thought it was his ticket into the world of high literature and true-blue Americanism, far away from failing grocery stores and Jews writing about Jews for Jews. As he wrote his wife Ann a few days after the publication of *The Natural*, "Now I join the sacred company."[55] It puzzled critics then and now.[56] Sidney Richman, one of the earliest and best commentators on Malamud, pronounced it one of the most baffling novels of the 1950s: "weakest in those sections in which the metaphysical coupling of tongues prompts Malamud into parody."[57] Ihab Hassan, another early admirer of Malamud's work, had already judged *The Natural* to be "an allegorical tale...[that] fails ultimately to make itself comprehensible."[58] These and other critics identified what appeared to them to be two didactic weaknesses: the mythic parallels seem finally to lead nowhere, and the parody is too insistent. Let us see.

---

[54] Quoted from the Malamud Holding in the Library of Congress in Davis, *Bernard Malamud*, 104. Cynthia Ozick, the superb Jewish-American writer and critic, is a great admirer of Malamud. But, she has never read *The Natural* and says she never will, because it is about baseball! The profusion of literary allusions is, perhaps, motivated also by the fact that for years Malamud was precluded from teaching literature classes at Oregon State because he was without a Ph.D. (he taught composition only, although in recognition of his publishing success he was eventually allowed to teach some creative writing classes). Perhaps Malamud felt he had something to prove.

[55] Smith, *My Father Is A Book*, 119.

[56] Ironically, it is his best known novel thanks to the movie made of it starring Robert Redford, Glenn Close, Kim Basinger, and Robert Duvall, which changes the ending of the book and thus falsifies the whole story.

[57] Richman, *Bernard Malamud* 45.

[58] Ihab Hassan, *Radical Innocence: Studies in the Contemporary American Novel* (Princeton: Princeton University Press, 1961) 162.

Suppose a world where mésalliance was not the rule, a world where the extremely gifted and extremely lucky will naturally flourish, where some men/women are simply "naturals" at what they do, succeeding without even trying. As an untested young man, Roy Hobbs (a mythicized version of Eddie Waitkus and Babe Ruth and Shoeless Joe Jackson) sets out from Western forests for the Big Leagues. Along the way cross-country, he challenges the aging Walter (the Whammer) Wambold, three times Most Valuable Player, to an impromptu contest of skill—and strikes him out with three pitches (and unknowingly leaves him dying). He confesses that he wants to be the best there ever was. And, he was. The End. No, not quite. We know from our fairy tales and romances that the hero must be tested and overcome challenges before he can live happily ever after with the princess. There are dragons and giants to slay in order to prove the hero worthy of his natural gifts—and when the trial is internal to the hero, a fault that is not truly his fault, there are sometimes even stables to clean, the humiliation of a mad Heracles or of a seduced Roy Hobbs.

Natural lust and a naive pride lay Roy low before he even makes it into the game—a silver bullet in the gut from the gun in seductress Harriet Bird's hat box (Eddie Waitkus). An obscure period of trial ends fifteen years later when he finally returns to the game, a rookie hitter of thirty-four. His first hit for Pop Fisher's team, the New York Knights, literally knocks the cover off the ball—and a few drops of rain fall on the drought-stricken field. With Roy's astounding hitting, the team begins to win; the field turns green; and Pop Fisher's athlete's foot infection (on his hands) starts to heal. But, once again pride, lust, and a curious gluttony (Babe Ruth) disable him at the height of his powers—in spite of the loving ministrations of a highly fertile Lady of the Lake, Iris Lemon. His appetite for Iris spoiled by her status as a (thirty-three year old) grandmother, he is unable to embrace his Loathly Lady. Instead, he is seduced by the temptress Vivian, Memo Paris. Because she hates him for overthrowing her Knight's champion, Bump Bailey, she lures Roy into fixing the decisive game of the pennant race (Shoeless Joe Jackson and the "Black Sox" scandal). His change of heart at the last minute is fruitless. Wonderboy, his bat, shatters; he beans Iris, pregnant with his child, with an intentional foul ball; a rookie fresh off the farm, called up for the pennant drive, strikes him out; Pop Fisher will lose his job, his team, and his dream:

> "He coulda been a king," a woman remarked to a man.... A boy thrust a newspaper at him.... The headline screamed, "Suspicion of Hobbs's Sellout—Max Mercy...." Roy handed the paper back to the kid. "Say it ain't true, Roy." When Roy looked into the boy's eyes he wanted to

say it wasn't but couldn't, and he lifted his hands to his face and wept many bitter tears.[59] (237)

So, we say with the critics, where is this going? The key is in the parody, which is much more exact than has been appreciated. Adorned as it is with multitudes of allusions, at its heart *The Natural* is a parody of *Le Roman de Perceval ou le Conte du Graal* of Chrétien de Troyes (fl. c. 1160-1182), the oldest surviving literary work in the Arthurian tradition and regarded in its narrative structure as the primary precursor to the novel—sacred company, indeed. The novel's title, as it often is in Malamud, is the clue. Perceval is, of course, the "natural" of medieval romance. The youthful Perceval, living with his widowed mother far from scenes of chivalric glory, is a "natural" in several senses. His mother has purposively kept him uncultivated in the chivalric arts and virtues. This rustic simplicity is deepened by an ingenuousness verging on simple-mindedness; Perceval appears a Dümmling, or natural, in his comic literalness and indifference to convention. And, of course, he proves astonishingly adept at knightly crafts once introduced to them—a gifted natural. With an inversion or two, Roy Hobbs mimics these features of the young hero. For Chrétien, Perceval's extraordinary naiveté is illustrated in the questions he asks and, more fatefully, in the questions he neglects to ask. As a consequence of his naiveté, Perceval will disastrously misinterpret advice he is given—and fail at his heroic task, a task that only he can accomplish. Out of remarkable naiveté, the gifted "natural" fails to ask (Perceval) or fails to answer (Roy Hobbs) the saving questions when presented with the opportunity to accomplish a great good for the community. Perceval thinks too literally of obeying his knightly vows not to speak lightly. Roy thinks too prosaically of the game in terms of four bases, records, and bucks. For this ingenuousness, they suffer and those around them suffer. The moral meaning of this gratuitous suffering becomes the key question for those who reflect on this waste of possibility and its implications for our mortal hopes.

Both Perceval's female cousin and his hermit uncle explain that his spectacular failure was the result of a sin against his mother, who died of grief when he rode off with a troop of shining knights—to his untutored eyes more beautiful than God. But Perceval, the Dümmling, knows nothing of her death and doesn't even know what grief is. He is as naïve—and as innocent—as Adam and Eve when they first nibbled that apple. His uncle gives him a

---

[59] Bernard Malamud, *The Natural* (New York: Farrar, 1952); all references to *The Natural* will be to this edition and indicated parenthetically in the text.

formula to follow to regain his supposed lost virtues: go to church first thing every morning, drink spring water, eat cresses. But he takes this advice as literally as he did the advice his mother sent him off with or that his knightly sponsor Gorneman de Gorhaut gave him. Its moral meaning escapes him. Just so, Roy asks Iris Lemon,

> "What did I do to deserve it?" "Being stopped before you started?" He nodded. "Perhaps it was because you were a good person?" "How's that?" "Experience makes good people better." She was staring at the lake. "How does it do that?" "Through their suffering." "I had enough of that," he said in disgust. "We have two lives, Roy, the life we learn with and the life we live with after that. Suffering is what brings us toward happiness." "I had it up to here." He ran a finger across his windpipe. "Had what?" "What I suffered—and I don't want any more." "It teaches us to want the right things." "All it taught me is to stay away from it. I am sick of all I have suffered." (157–58)

Critics have taken the bait and assumed that this scene between Roy and his Lady of the Lake is the moral crux of the novel. As Jeffrey Helterman puts it, "Iris becomes Malamud's spokesman as she explains to Roy the theory that every person has two lives: one life teaches through experience how to live, and the other life is the life lived out of that knowledge."[60] Tellingly, Malamud came to this formulation at the very last minute in galley proof.

At the same time, however, the novel makes Iris a highly unreliable authority. She believes that happiness is the product of suffering ("Pregame") and of the learning that suffering brings good people ("Batter Up!"). But when the test of his learning comes, Roy flunks it even more badly and with less justification than he did the first time. Certainly, the implication that Harriet Bird had shot Roy fifteen years before because he was a good person and could benefit by the experience is sentimental twaddle. Harriet's previous two victims, both star athletes, had been killed by her silver bullets. Iris's approach to the moral life is also formulaic: "it's [the heroes'] function to be the best and for the rest of us to understand what they represent and guide ourselves accordingly." (154) This guidance is mocked within the novel by the penny-pinching Judge Banner (White Sox owner Charles Comiskey) with his slimy fondness for homilies: "Nihil nisi bonum," "All is not gold that glitters," and so on. And when Iris offers herself as living evidence of the efficacy

---

[60] Jeffrey Helterman, *Understanding Bernard Malamud* (Columbia: University of South Carolina Press, 1985) 30.

of her formula, she betrays her ironic blindness to her own situation. After Roy flees her grandmotherly embrace, she writes him a long letter telling him that her own life of suffering, loss, and denial as a guilt-ridden, unmarried, unsupported mother had gradually allowed her love for her daughter to blossom until finally "a change came—more a reward of standing it so long than any sudden magic." Her daughter grown, in love, married, a mother herself, "Suddenly everywhere I looked seemed to be tomorrow, and I was at last free to take up my life where I had left it off one summer night when I went for a walk in the park with a stranger." (210–11) But, of course, by the end of the story she is in precisely the same woebegone position as she was at the beginning of her life of suffering. Not only is "Batter Up!" a repetition for Roy, it is for Iris as well. She has had sexual intercourse twice in her life. Both times, looking for love from a stranger, she is surprised instead by need. Both times, she is left abandoned and pregnant—Roy's beanball adding injury to insult. Iris is no more a rescuing goddess than Roy is an exemplary hero—although the reader, with Roy, strains to see her as one.[61] Neither Iris nor Roy is likely actually to live out the mythoi they appear to embody. The readerly temptation to complete Malamud's tale in accord with mythic archetypes becomes the object of his playfully covert satire.

The point at which Malamud disavows the chivalric romance and its mythic reconciliations can now be located with precision. The end of *The Natural* is a matter of deep pessimism and total loss, and, as Malamud's parody makes us realize, this is true faute de mieux of Perceval as well. Chrétien never "finished" his heroic romance; there's some evidence he died while working on it. His 9,000 lines of poetry were succeeded by 54,000 lines of continuation from the hands of four different redactors over forty years, who finally added an ending where Perceval and Galahad complete the Grail Quest. By converting "interruption" to conclusion, by refusing the temptation to complete the story "as it should have gone," Malamud's text offers a strong reading or misprision of Chrétien's text and rescues Perceval from its

[61] Robert Ducharme detects "the implication that Roy will not make these same mistakes a third time." *Art and Idea in the Novels of Bernard Malamud: Toward The Fixer* (The Hague: Mouton, 1974) 81. Shelton Hershinow agrees: "We know that Roy will not repeat the same mistakes again." *Bernard Malamud*, (New York: Ungar, 1980) 23. Sandy Cohen goes a step further: "Though he 'weeps bitter tears' as the book closes, he has Iris and his child to look forward to. He has learned the lessons Iris and his suffering have taught him, and now he has a chance for a new, fertile, and meaningful life." *Bernard Malamud and the Trial by Love* (Amsterdam: Rodopi, 1974) 29.

epigones. Malamud's parody satirizes *Le Roman de Perceval*'s continuators and redactors by analogizing their spiritual glosses on Chrétien's truncated text to Iris's fatuous rationalizations of Roy's failures—and by assimilating both these "gnostic" interpretations to Roy's and Perceval's ingenuous misinterpretations. From this angle, critic and philistine, mythmaker and literalist, gnostic and simpleton are collapsed into the simple-minded didact. Malamud's moral is not one that can be taught, neither self-taught by the gifted innocent nor transmitted by the learned sophisticate. *The Natural* is a disarming work meant to disable mythoi and disrupt temporal concord—to baffle interpretation—in order to "represent" the primordially unrepresentable in our experience of life. Its ironic self-criticism bears the traces of an uninterpretable, because unthematizable, beyond: Mésalliance, original sin, the Sacred.

To give Levinas the last word, "It is experience in the sole radical sense of the term: a relationship with the exterior, with the other, without the exteriority being able to be integrated into the same."[62] Suffering is the burden of conscience—a different kind of story than the transformations of the hero. *The Natural* demythicizes the hero and humbles the reader in order to decontextualize human aspiration, to expose our true desire for a reality that opposes our freedom and for a goodness that is dispossession. Beyond either resistance or achievement, Roy Hobbs and Perceval are held inscrutably responsible for their freedom—the essence of a suffering that is not failure but approach to the Other. Roy Hobbs, with all his gifts, aspirations, appetites, disappointments, and betrayals, finally abandons his quest in the very moment when he discovers love:

> There were tears in her eyes. Her belly was slender....then the impact hit him. "Holy Jesus." Iris smiled with quivering lips. Bending over, he kissed her mouth and tasted blood. He kissed her breasts, they smelled of roses. He kissed her hard belly, wild with love for her and the child." (228)

Ironically, had he been able—mythically—to hit the homer and "win for us," his success within the circuit of his desire would have narcissistically accommodated what fundamentally challenges our self-regard: the radically other—and, thus, would have perversely confirmed him in his metaphysical solitude. Malamud's confounding moral is that love—love that is not disguised self-regard—necessarily is suffering. As Levinas insists,

---

[62] Levinas, "Philosophy and the Idea of Infinity" 54.

> Subjection to the order that ordains man—the ego—to answer for the other is, perhaps, the harsh name of love. Love here is no longer what this compromised word of our literature and our hypocrisies expresses, but the very fact of the approach of the unique one and, consequently, of the absolutely other, piercing what merely shows itself....It brings neither promise nor relief, but the absoluteness of an exigency."[63]

*The Natural* is situated within this conative incomprehensibility—primary suffering is our true desire. Love is precisely what always escapes our possession and enjoyment. Love is not a matter of contingency, a quest. Love is a matter of exigency, a subjection.[64] Malamud's parodic satire on the didactic impulse in life and literature allows us to glimpse a moral that ironically can only be represented in the collapse of intentionality and its formulary aspirations: love as an indictment of our very subjectivity.

## Imagined Jews

The human condition is one of mésalliance, of being shaped by intimate relations against type, interest, or desire. We live in time, knowing neither our beginning nor our end, our mortality a meaningless fragment of eternity. Yet as intentional beings, moral agents, our lives are deeply and uniquely shaped by desires and purposes, the meaning of our living. The Jew is a powerful figure for this cosmic mésalliance, inscrutably chosen by—and as willful creatures inevitably disappointing—an incomprehensible YHWH. The Hebraic moral imagination stretches to make sense of this imbroglio. This imaginative

---

[63] Levinas "Diachrony and Representation," *Time and the Other and Additional Essays*, trans. Richard A. Cohen (Pittsburgh: Duquense University Press, 1987) 116–17.

[64] Of all the critics, Marcus Klein comes closest to this insight. In a world of brute circumstance, the heroic quest is always bound to fail. He argues that in the face of this tragic fatality Malamud retreats into fancy and marvel: "the process of sensibility forced to extremities in order to withhold acknowledgement from the world." The higher possibilities glimpsed in the heroic are incomprehensible in a corrupt and corrupting world, except as suffering: "For the hero who can imagine something higher suffering is the one possibility of love. Therefore it is morality itself....It is expression of the way in which men are bound together, in their loss." Marcus Klein, *After Alienation: American Novels in Mid-Century* (Cleveland: World, 1965) 262–63. However, as Levinas argues and Malamud represents, suffering that is love is neither loss nor mutuality but something more metaphysically primordial: the desire for the radically Other.

engagement and its ultimate failure endlessly create the narratives of their lives, leaving them still listening for the Presence that transcends eternity and holds them accountable for their living. And in this sense—for Malamud—all men are Jews.

# 2

## O'Connor's Sacramental Freaks[1]

*The Catholic finds it easier to understand the atheist than the Protestant, but easier to love the Protestant than the atheist.*
—Flannery O'Connor

After straining to hear the whisper of God's voice in Malamud's stories, it's a bit of a relief to turn to Flannery O'Connor's equally brilliant but very different stories. They rely much less on compression, parody, and fantasy, although her instinct for extreme situations verges on the fantastic (she greatly admired Edgar Allan Poe's tales growing up).[2] Like Malamud she is a very gifted storyteller. Unlike him there is no layering of stories and no evanescent endings. Her stories barrel ahead concussively, with slam-bang endings. The mystery is in the meaning. Everything is as it is; even her most outrageous caricatures are spot-on. Her eye for sharply defining characteristics in those around her and her ear for their naive self-presentations are Dickensian. Her early career interests as a cartoonist point in this direction. Nevertheless, her characters and their world are rooted in a bedrock realism that has nothing to do with verisimilitude or naturalism, which are after all just authorial prerogatives like any other. Everything is as it is. As she wrote Betty Hester, who was to become one of her closest friends and confidantes, "I believe too that

[1] "Whenever I'm asked why Southern writers particularly have a penchant for writing about freaks, I say it is because we are still able to recognize one. To be able to recognize a freak, you have to have some conception of the whole man, and in the South the general conception of man is still, in the main, theological....In any case, it is when the freak can be sensed as a figure for our essential displacement that he attains some depth in literature." Flannery O'Connor, *Mystery and Manners: Occasional Prose*, eds. Sally and Robert Fitzgerald (New York: Farrar, Straus, & Giroux, 1969) 44–45.

[2] Her most recent biographer, Brad Gooch, nicely brings out her structural borrowings from other American writers within the tradition of the gothic romance, as well as the very homely origins of characters and settings for most of her stories. Brad Gooch, *Flannery: A Life of Flannery O'Connor* (New York: Little, Brown, 2009).

there is only one Reality and that that is the end of it."[3] Now, the question becomes: *from whose perspective?* Most of O'Connor's stories privilege a perspective from among many. The comedy comes from the divergence of these multiple perspectives, rich material for satire; the tragedy comes from the collapse of the privileged perspective, often in an act of violence; and the mystery comes from a dawning perspective that surpasses all of them, toward which narrator and author gesture without naming. It is a fabulous balancing act. As Joseph O'Neil discerns in his review of Brad Gooch's biography of O'Connor, "The narrating third person hovers in an almost miraculous fusion of proximity and comic distance. With O'Connor, there never seems to be space between the words and their creator's sensibility. You almost never catch a whiff of authorial self-consciousness."[4] Unfortunately, O'Neil—and many like him—read this as revealing an author simply taking delight in pinning her characters to a cross of misanthropy and, thus, as touched by evil herself. On the contrary, by making original sin her métier she can both acknowledge the truth in that charge and help us see it in her characters—and ourselves. If Malamud can claim that we are all Jews (but may not know it), O'Connor can confess we are all sinners (but may mistake our sins for virtues). *From whose perspective*?

Mary Flannery O'Connor was an exotic bird, indeed. Shy, introverted, over-protected, snarky, self-deprecating, and self-reliant, she later described her childish self as "a pidgeon-toed, only-child with a receding chin and a you-leave-me-alone-or-I'll-bite-you complex"—as this quotation intimates, she was a lifelong bad speller.[5] She was raised an Irish Catholic in the Protestant Bible Belt, where Catholics, Jews, and Negroes were still targeted by the Ku Klux Klan (she was personally well acquainted with local cross-burnings). Born in 1925, her preteen years were spent in Savannah, where the Irish had a strong presence and the O'Connors were well known and fairly well off if not as prominent as the Flannerys, kin by marriage.[6] She lived across Lafayette Square from the Cathedral of St. John the Baptist (rebuilt in 1900, after fire, under the leadership of Capt. John Flannery) and around the

---

[3] Flannery O'Connor, *Letters of Flannery O'Connor: The Habit of Being*, ed. Sally Fitzgerald (New York: Farrar, Straus, & Giroux, 1979) 92.

[4] Joseph O'Neil, "Touched by Evil," *The Atlantic* (June 2009) www.theatlantic.com/magazine/archive/2009/06/touched-by-evil/307422/.

[5] Gooch, *Flannery*, 30.

[6] Savannah's St. Patrick's Day Parade has a 190-year history and is now the third largest in the world. In Flannery's day, it was second in importance in Savannah only to the Confederate Memorial Day Parade.

corner from her parochial school St. Vincent's Grammar School for Girls run by the Sisters of Mercy (as was St. Joseph's Hospital, where O'Connor was born). During her father's illness (and business reversals in the Depression) they lived for a while in Atlanta, then following his early death, near her mother's family the Clines, in Milledgeville, Georgia. Milledgeville (the former capital of Confederate Georgia) sits in the middle of the historic Black Belt of upland cotton plantations stretching in a band from Augusta to Columbus (and on through South Carolina to the east and Alabama and Mississippi to the west).[7] She attended the local college, Georgia State College for Women, during the war and then studied at what was rapidly becoming the famed Iowa Writers' Workshop at the University of Iowa. She had rather dazzling early success as a writer, including forging lifelong friendships with the poet Robert Lowell and his wife, the critic and writer Elizabeth Hardwick, with the critics and writers Allen Tate and his wife Caroline Gordon, and with the classicist Robert Fitzgerald and his wife Sally Fitzgerald, who became one of O'Connor's greatest literary champions. She seemed launched on an unprecedented career (in a "compliment" she treasured—in part because it offended her mother Regina so much—Eveyln Waugh doubted that *Wise Blood* could possibly have been written by a young lady). At age twenty-five, she was diagnosed with lupus, the autoimmune genetic disease that had killed her father at age forty-five, nine years before. She moved back home from Connecticut (where she had been living with the Fitzgeralds) and spent the rest of her shortened life living with her mother on their 550-acre family dairy farm, Andalusia, just outside Milledgeville. Her mother, Regina Lucille Cline O'Connor, was a formidable woman in the genteel Southern mode, who lived to be ninety-nine.[8] Flannery O'Connor died at thirty-nine in 1964, disabled and disfigured by the disease and its severe steroid treatment. The evidence seems pretty clear that she was sexually inexperienced and died a virgin—like many of the nuns who taught her as a child, some of whom she despised. She had several intense literary/romantic friendships with both men and women. From the age of five on, she raised and doted on exotic chickens

[7] The "Black Belt" is conventionally defined as those Deep South counties with historically a majority African-American population.

[8] Mrs. O'Connor, who turned out to be quite an astute businesswoman, eventually converted the farm to a beef cattle operation—with resident bull—to reduce her dependence on unreliable farm workers.

and waterfowl, including her famous peafowl at Andalusia. Birds that walked backward, like the peacocks, were an iconic fascination.[9]

She published two short novels to mixed reviews and thirty-one short stories, many of which were highly praised. Like Malamud she was a rewriter, turning characters and situations around and around as she recycled them in stories and novels. In an early letter to her recently acquired literary agent, she described her method: "I don't have my novel outlined and I have to write to discover what I am doing. Like the old lady, I don't know so well what I think until I see what I say; then I have to say it over again."[10] As she wrote a bit later to Paul Engle, her mentor at the Writers' Workshop, after her publisher at the time complained about the slowness of her progress on *Wise Blood*, "No one can convince me I shouldn't rewrite as much as I do."[11] She was a prolific letter writer and, in spite of her illness, an astute critic in frequent lectures (the honoraria were an important supplement to the O'Connor household budget). She considered herself an adamant Catholic. At a late night, Manhattan dinner party hosted by Mary McCarthy, the notorious *Paris Review* critic and social activist (and lapsed Catholic), after McCarthy had explained that she now thought of the Communion wafer as a symbol (and a pretty good one), the twenty-four year old O'Connor shakily rebuked her: "Well, if it's a symbol to hell with it."[12] In spite of this, whether or not she is explicitly a Catholic or even a Christian writer is highly disputed.[13] This

---

[9] Her first brush with fame was a Pathé newsreel short of her at five with a pet chicken—with backward growing, "frizzled" feathers—that she had trained to walk backwards.

[10] Gooch, *Flannery* 155.

[11] O'Connor, *The Habit of Being* 14.

[12] Gooch, *Flannery*, 174. McCarthy's celebrated memoir, *Memories of a Catholic Girlhood*, was published in 1957.

[13] Marshall Bruce Gentry identifies four different schools of critical thought about O'Connor's religious intent: 1. There is none, 2. It is orthodoxly Catholic, 3. It is overly harsh, and 4. It is demonic. Marshall Bruce Gentry, *Flannery O'Connor's Religion of the Grotesque* (Jackson, MS: University Press of Mississippi, 1986) 3. Early on, O'Connor's friend the surrealist novelist John Hawkes had argued that she wrote with the devil's voice. As he wrote later, "the creative process transforms the writer's objective Catholic knowledge of the devil into an authorial attitude in itself in some measure diabolical." John Hawkes, "Flannery O'Connor's Devil," *Suwanee Review* 70.3 (1962): 401. O'Connor disagreed with him strongly, insisting her devil only punctured pretensions, rather than devouring souls, although she wrote Hawkes that she liked the piece "very very much." Gooch, *Flannery*, 345.

in itself tells us something about her amphibolous beginnings and endings—what story is being told?

## "Revelation"

Let us begin with the virtuous. "Revelation" was one of her last stories, published in 1964. Her longtime publisher Robert Giroux called it "as nearly perfect as stories can be."[14] The action of the story is set in two venues, a small doctor's office and a pig "parlor" or upscale pigsty.

> The doctor's waiting room, which was very small, was almost full when the Turpins entered and Mrs. Turpin, who was very large, made it look even smaller by her presence. She stood looming at the head of the magazine table set in the center of it, a living demonstration that the room was inadequate and ridiculous. Her little black eyes took in all the patients as she sized up the seating situation.[15]

The very small and very full waiting room is a Southern microcosm. Between the narrator and Mrs. Turpin, characters and roles are very precisely sized and summed up. Mrs. Turpin and her husband, Claud, are among the few dignified with names—and Mrs. Turpin is "Mrs. Turpin" to the narrator from beginning to end and "Ruby Turpin" to herself only once seeing herself through a crazy girl's eyes. With one notable exception, the others in the room are mere stereotypes, their rubrics indicate as much. To start at the top, with the only one Mrs. Turpin considers her equal, there is a pleasant and stylish lady wearing red and gray suede shoes matching her outfit. Their eyes meet in a shared judgment of the dirty, mannerless child who is sprawled on a sofa, oblivious to Mrs. Turpin's need to sit down and ignoring the well-dressed lady's suggestion that he could move over. As soon as another patient is called, Mrs. Turpin eases into her seat next to Claud (Claud is there because of an ugly ulcer on his calf, a cow kicked him)—and she and the lady initiate conversation: "'I wish I could reduce,' she said, and rolled her eyes and gave a comic sigh. 'Oh, *you* aren't fat,' the stylish lady said. 'Ooooo I am too,' Mrs. Turpin said." After a little more byplay, the stylish lady opines that it doesn't matter what size you are so long as you have a good disposition: "You just

---

[14] Flannery O'Connor, *The Complete Stories,* intro. Robert Giroux (New York: Farrar, Straus, & Giroux, 1972) xv. The story came to her very quickly over eight weeks—and after a drought of inspiration of over a year.

[15] "Revelation," *The Complete Stories*, 488–509. All references to "Revelation" are to this edition.

can't beat a good disposition." This elicits a scowl from the nice lady's daughter sitting next to her, an ugly, fat girl of eighteen or nineteen (which is the author making sure we know that the narrator, however controlling, does not know everything), her face "blue with acne" and reading a thick blue book entitled *Human Development*. The doctor's office is a veritable field manual for human development. Mrs. Turpin gives the poor girl a friendly smile but the girl only scowls harder: "Mrs. Turpin herself was fat but she had always had good skin, and, though she was forty-seven years old, there was not a wrinkle in her face except around her eyes from laughing too much." This blended assessment from narrator and character sets the stage. Mrs. Turpin is in the habit of comparing herself to others, and it usually is plain to her where she and Claud fit in.

Next to the sprawling child of five or six (again a limited narrator) is a "thin leathery old woman" in a feedsack print dress, who apparently went with the child: "She could tell from the way they sat—kind of vacant and white-trashy, as if they would sit there until Doomsday if nobody called and told them to get up." At right angles, next to the pleasant lady was the child's mother, lips stained with snuff, dirty yellow hair tied in a bit of red paper ribbon: "Worse than niggers any day, Mrs. Turpin thought." Their shoes place them (Mrs. Turpin always noticed people's feet "without appearing to"): Mrs. Turpin with "her good patent leather pumps," the ugly girl with Girl Scout shoes with thick socks, the old woman with tennis shoes, the white-trashy mother had on "what appeared to be bedroom slippers, black straw with gold braid threaded through them—exactly what you would have expected her to have on." Next to the child's mother was a red-headed youngish woman vigorously chewing gum. Mrs. Turpin couldn't see her shoes: "She was not white trash, just common." A "tall, very Black boy in discolored white pants and a green nylon shirt" arrives on a bike with a drugstore delivery. Waiting at the receptionist's window, he sways to some internal music while chewing gum slowly. Mrs. Turpin advises him that he can ring for the secretary. His back to her he allows, "'Is thas right?'…as if he had never seen the button before." He buzzs and twists to look at the White folks looking at him. "'She sometime out,' he says." The crew of this thoroughly beached ship of fools is complete; who's in charge?[16]

[16] Katherine Anne Porter, who became a friend of O'Connor's, was from the previous generation of Southern writers. Famously, she had spent thirty years writing her novel, *Ship of Fools*, finally published in 1962.

For a moment after the boy leaves no one speaks—then the white-trash woman: "They ought to send all them niggers back to Africa." The pleasant lady: "Oh, I couldn't do without my good colored friends." Mrs. Turpin: "There's a heap of things worse than a nigger....It's all kinds of them just like it's all kinds of us." The pleasant lady, in a musical voice: "Yes, and it takes all kinds to make the world go round." Then the ugly girl makes the ugliest face Mrs. Turpin had ever seen anyone make and "for a moment she was certain that the girl had made it at her." The exchange of low and high platitudes continues until Claud interrupts with a deadpan joke: "Claud's eyes twinkled. 'White-faced niggers,' he said with never a smile. Everybody in the office laughed except the white-trash and the ugly girl. The girl gripped the book in her lap with white fingers. The trashy woman looked around from face to face as if she thought they were all idiots."

So, we have a boatload of perspectives to contemplate. First, neither Claud (who tends to his own business without ever even thinking about it), nor the vacant old woman and listless child, nor a "lean stringy old fellow" sitting with his "rusty" hands on his knees and eyes closed pretending to be asleep have perspectives per se. They are simply not in the game. Judge not lest you be judged. The three women, stylish lady, white-trashy woman, and Mrs. Turpin, are constituted by their judgments. The stylish lady with the ugly acting daughter, who goes to Wellesley College "way up north," believes that pleasantries and homilies should carry the day but is burdened with an ungrateful daughter:

> "I know a girl," she said, "who has parents who would give her anything, a little brother who loves her dearly, who is getting a good education, who wears the best clothes, but who can never say a kind word to anyone, who never smiles, who just criticizes and complains all day long."

She's the mother you should have, unless you're just looking for trouble. The white-trashy woman is feisty and—in her own way—articulate: "'One thang I know....Two thangs I ain't going to do: love no niggers or scoot down no hog with no hose.' And she let out a bark of contempt." Mrs. Turpin replies to her (continuing to defend her pigs, noting that "They're cleaner than some children I've seen"): 'When you got something,' she said, 'you got to look after it.' And when you ain't got a thing but breath and britches, she added to herself, you can afford to come to town every morning and just sit on the Court House coping and spit."

There are two outliers to these defining perspectives, the Black boy and the ugly girl. Neither Mrs. Turpin *nor the narrator* can penetrate their facades. The author (in spite of O'Neil's snide comment about O'Connor's lack of authorial self-consciousness) gives us only the Black boy's cool reserve, which could be mere empty headedness or else the sly mockery of the distained.[17] The ugly girl continues her slow boil at her mother's platitudes and criticisms and at Mrs. Turpin's self-satisfied judgments. We are tempted to suppose this is just the intellectually and morally sophisticated response of the Wellesley girl, who "Just reads all the time, a real book worm." Perhaps she is a stand-in for literary O'Connor herself, surrounded by backwater provincials. Or so we may think, until provoked by Mrs. Turpin's "Oh thank you Jesus, Jesus, thank you!" she hurls her book at Mrs. Turpin, leaps howling across the magazine table, and clamps her fingers on Mrs. Turpin's neck. After she is subdued, tranquilized, and taken by ambulance to the hospital, the white-trash woman is given the last word on Mary Grace's perspective (for her mother, embarrassed by her rudeness earlier, supplied her name, Mary Grace): "'I thank Gawd,' the white-trash woman said fervently, 'I ain't a lunatic.'"[18]

However, our sense of this microcosm goes deeper than this, thanks to the narrator/author's focus on Mrs. Turpin's internal life and thoughts—which are not stereotypical. In spite of her overweening self-confidence, she struggles with the order of things in her world. Who, indeed, is in charge?

> Sometimes at night when she couldn't go to sleep, Mrs. Turpin would occupy herself with the question of who she would have chosen to be if she couldn't have been herself. If Jesus had said to her before he made her, "There's only two places available for you. You can either be a nigger or white-trash," what would she have said?

And if she couldn't have convinced Him to do otherwise, she would have settled for being a so-called "nigger"—but not trashy: "a neat clean

---

[17] In a student interview after one of her lectures, O'Connor confessed that she didn't understand her Black characters like she did her white characters: "I don't feel capable of entering the mind of a Negro. In my stories they're seen from the outside." Gooch, *Flannery*, 336 This is more than a little disingenuous; she uses this distance strategically.

[18] As O'Connor wrote of Milledgeville in the early fifties, "We have a girl's college here, but the lacy atmosphere is fortunately destroyed by a reformatory, an insane asylum, and a military school." Ibid., 52. Founded in 1842 as the Georgia Lunatic Asylum, Central State Hospital grew to be the largest insane asylum in the world, 200 buildings on 2,000 acres with up to 13,000 inmates/patients.

respectable Negro woman, herself but black." She also sometimes mused falling asleep about the classes of people. On the bottom were most Black people (not the neat, clean, respectable ones) and next to them—on the same level but apart—were the white-trash. Then the homeowners, and then the home-and-land owners (like Claud and herself), and then—above them—rich folks with bigger homes and more land. Here, however, the calculations became confusing. Some people with money were common and should be below her and Claud. Some with good blood had lost their money and had to rent. And, then, some colored people owned homes and land as well. Why, one Black dentist in town had two red Lincolns and a swimming pool and a farm with registered white-faced cattle.

> Usually by the time she had fallen asleep all the classes of people were moiling and roiling around in her head, and she would dream they were all crammed in together in a box car, being ridden off to be put in a gas oven.

This jarring image from post-war newsreels was used to greater effect in "The Displaced Person," one of her finest stories. It feels like an authorial intrusion here. We will return to that question in a moment.

The scene in the doctor's office reaches its climax when Mrs. Turpin responds to the nice lady's criticism of Mary Grace's ingratitude. Mrs. Turpin declaims her gratitude for being who she is and "what all I got, a little of everything." She feels like shouting "'Thank you, Jesus, for making everything the way it is!' It could have been different!" Then as she is flooded with gratitude for having gotten Claud, she does cry out "Oh thank you Jesus, Jesus, thank you!" And Mary Grace and her book come flying across the table at her. Mrs. Turpin's command flees, as if through the wrong end of the telescope. Everything is small and far away. She can't move—as if everything is in slow motion. Claud is doubled up in pain in a corner, kicked in his bad leg by Mary Grace during the melee—but she can't move to go to him. Who is in charge now? Mary Grace, before she succumbs to the sedative, commands the center of this new world of reversals. Mrs. Turpin finally leans forward to look directly into the girl's "fierce brilliant eyes": "'What you got to say to me?' she asked hoarsely." "'Go back to hell where you came from, you old warthog,' she whispered."

It is a shocking accusation. Mrs. Turpin has been using the occasion—as she obviously often does—to count her blessings. Her beatitudes may coincide with the nice lady's platitudes, but they nevertheless are real blessings, real virtues, real gratitude. Plain as the nose on your face. Maybe she is a bit too complacent about herself and too judgmental about others, but Jesus made her a good woman and nothing else matters so much to her she thinks, not money, not high society, not a svelte figure. "Whenever she counted her blessings she felt as buoyant as if she weighed one hundred and twenty-five pounds instead of one hundred and eighty." How utterly arbitrary those blessings are is highlighted in the story by the narrator when the nice lady turned the conversation to the listless little boy. He has an ulcer. The white-trash woman allows that "He ain't give me a minute's peace since he was born." But she'd rather have him sick. She has no trouble out of him anymore: "Took sick and turned good." Thank you, Jesus. So, perhaps, Mrs. Turpin is mistaken about her blessings, what they are, where they come from, what they mean? But what exactly would the narrator demand differently from Mrs. Turpin? That she be a New York intellectual, filled with irony? That she be a saint, filled with self-sacrificial love? (As she knows all too well, trying to help the helpless is hopeless: "Because if you gave them everything, in two weeks it would all be broken or filthy or they would have chopped it up for lightwood.") Her kind does indeed make the world go around. Do we suppose that God sees it any differently when He judges us? Who speaks for Jesus here? Mrs. Turpin or Mary Grace? At home, lying on the bed growing more and more wrathful, Mrs. Turpin jabs her fist at the ceiling, "as if she was defending her innocence to invisible guests who were like the comforters of Job, reasonable-seeming but wrong." Is this the same Lord who set Satan loose on Job, a righteous man, to see if the Accuser could take him down a notch or two? What kind of God would make war on moral superiority? We'll take these questions to a deeper level when we turn to "Everything That Rises Must Converge."

Mrs. Turpin marches out to the pig parlor and orders Claud to carry their field hands off home from picking their cotton—"and then get off that leg." Squirting the old sow and her shoats blindly with the stream of water, she demands in a low fierce voice "What do you send me a message like that for?…How am I a hog and me both? How am I saved and from hell too?" The sun is setting behind the distant woods "very red, looking over the paling of trees like a farmer inspecting his own hogs."

> "Why me?" she rumbled. "It's no trash around here, black or white, that I haven't given to. And break my back to the bone every day working. And do for the church."
>
> She appeared to be the right size woman to command the arena before her. "How am I a hog?" she demanded. "Exactly how am I like them?"

Then in a final spasm of fury she roars, "Who do you think you are?" Mrs. Turpin is no hypocrite or merely conventional Christian. She knows Jesus is in charge, which is why His accusation against her makes no sense. Thank you Jesus! Like Job, she is outraged that she—of all people in that Southern microcosm—should have been found inadequate. Thank you Jesus! She, like Job, knows that the narrator's take on her sinfulness is wrong, wrong, wrong. Thank you Jesus! How could her Jesus judge her so? For the first time, she is up against a transcendence that is truly transcendent—who is this Jesus and what does it truly mean to be loved by Him? This is O'Connor's—the author's—question. The question she wants her readers to ask, to really ask.

The microcosm of the doctor's office has been exploded. The setting now—the arena—is both cosmic and vanishingly small. She sees Claud's truck in the distance; "It looked like a child's toy. At any moment a bigger truck might smash into it and scatter Claud's and the niggers' brains all over the road." At the same time, all Mrs. Turpin commands now is a pig pen with eight squealing pigs. And she has been sized up by Mary Grace and Jesus as one of them, no better—her, not the white-trash, not the Blacks, her. The plenitude of the doctor's office, "what all I got, a little of everything, and a good disposition besides," has been replaced with the poverty of a square of concrete covered in hog wash, a transient speck under the "crimson sky, burn[ing] for a moment with a transparent intensity."

As the sun slips behind the tree line, she raises her gaze to the purple streak "cutting through a field of crimson and leading, like an extension of the highway, into the descending dusk." Lifting her hands, she has a vision of a bridge extending upward, on which "a vast horde of souls were rumbling toward heaven":

> There were whole companies of white trash, clean for the first time in their lives, and bands of black niggers in white robes, and battalions of freaks and lunatics shouting and clapping and leaping like frogs. And bringing up the end of the procession was a tribe of people whom she recognized at once as those who, like herself and Claud, had always a little of everything and the God-given wit to use it right.... They were marching behind the others with great dignity, accountable as they had always been for good order and common sense and respectable behavior. They alone were on key. Yet she could see by their shocked and altered faces that even their virtues were being burned away.

Turning finally down the darkening path to the house, the cricket choruses around her become "the voices of the souls climbing upward into the starry field and shouting hallelujah."

This stunning denouement is almost enough to convince us that Mrs. Turpin has had her Damascene moment of conversion and now speaks, indeed, for Jesus—a Jesus of the pigs, we might say. However, her last words prior to her fierce challenge, "Who do you think you are?" are "'Go on,' she yelled, 'call me a hog!...Put that bottom rail on top. There'll still be a top and bottom!'" Indeed, this vision changes nothing. White-trash will still be trashy and Blacks will still be "niggers" and lunatics will still be freaks. At the bottom of the path, Claud will still "[pay] no attention to her humors"—including this one. O'Connor's issue is not going to be met head on, although she herself may have wished otherwise. "I write the way I do because (not though) I am a Catholic. This is a fact, and nothing covers it like the bald statement," she wrote in her first letter to Betty Hester. Or, as she responded to a student correspondent at year later, "Let me make no bones about it: I write from the standpoint of Christian orthodoxy."[19] This issue is much more tangled in the author's mind than these assertions or this hopeful ending to our story suggests. This is, indeed, a spot where—contra O'Neil—the author's self-consciousness peeps through the narrator's silken satire. The struggle with the order of things goes very deep in O'Connor's Deep South, "thirteenth century" Catholic sensibility.[20] As she confesses early in her correspondence with Betty Hester, "You are right that I won't ever be able entirely to understand my own work or even my own motivations."[21] Years later, her very close friend and sparring partner Maryat Lee concluded that "The writing is one thing and the thinking and speeches are another. Jekyl [sic] and Hyde if you will. Perhaps." Or, as Gooch reports, some of her more secular friends began to feel that "she did not accept, and perhaps in some truly shuttered way did not even allow herself to understand, the implications of her writings."[22]

Ruby Turpin actually has *two* visions. Her "hieratic and profound" vision of Judgment Day is a vast swinging bridge across which altered souls—still ranked class by class—will rumble into heaven. But, we are also told she

---

[19] O'Connor, *Habit of Being*, 90, 147.

[20] In the fifties, she became a daily reader of Thomas Aquinas (the Modern Library *Introduction to Saint Thomas Aquinas*) and liked to explain that her Catholicism was medieval.

[21] Ibid., 92.

[22] Gooch, *Flannery*, 347.

sometimes falls asleep to a subliminal vision of a box car crammed with "all the classes of people…moiling and roiling around in her head," being trundled down railroad tracks to be burned alive. Orthodoxy suggests that the contrast meant is between a prophetic Christian transfiguration and the existential hell of a depraved, modern Christendom (Nazi Germany being the debased cultural inheritor of both the Holy Roman Empire founded by Charlemagne and Pope Leo III and the Reformation of the Church inspired by Martin Luther). Between these extremes of grace and the demonic, between salvation and perdition, lies the broad country of ordinary, Middle Georgia original sin, including a carefully-raised young woman writing with delicious malice about her friends, family, and neighbors. But Middle Georgia original sin was heating up. The legacy of African slavery and the continuing terror and oppression of the Jim Crow South were being challenged in the courts and on the streets. As one example among many, the Birmingham church bombing on a September Sunday morning in 1963 that murdered four young Black girls is as focused an evil as any—and was in O'Connor's backyard. O'Connor's attitude toward the civil rights struggle was, in the words of her biographer, "one of complex ambivalence."[23] With her bohemian and often outrageous friend Maryat, she shared racist jokes, "regaling Maryat with offensive punch lines," which leads Gooch to observe that her mask as a bigoted Southern redneck "[fit] disconcertingly well."[24] Turning down a potential visit from James Baldwin, she explained to Maryat, "In New York it would be nice to meet him; here it would not. I observe the traditions of the society I feed on—it's only fair. Might as well expect a mule to fly as me to see James Baldwin in Georgia."[25]

Let us dig a little deeper. The Holocaust with its boxcars and ovens is an image of great evil that can smash and mash together all the ordinary human distinctions of virtue and affiliation in favor of a grand abstraction of ideal purity: Aryan vs. Jew, Slav, Romani. From 1935 on, *Rassenschande* or race mixing was a crime in Germany, whether you were a banker, lawyer, scientist, artist, cobbler, or shopkeeper. In formulating the Nuremberg Laws, German jurists looked to the laws against miscegenation in the United States, which at the time had the most developed legal system of segregation in the

[23] Ibid., 332.
[24] Ibid., 335.
[25] O'Connor, *Habit of Being*, 329.

world.[26] In 1924, the Virginia General Assembly passed The Racial Integrity Act outlawing marriages between "whites" and "coloreds" and defining "colored" as having African or Indian (Native American) ancestry, the so-called "one drop rule." The Act was not overturned until 1967 when the U.S. Supreme Court declared it unconstitutional. Ironically, the Nazis considered this standard impractically rigorous and, after much debate about it, defined a "Jew" as anyone with three or more Jewish grandparents.[27] With this as an optic, the end-times march into heaven envisioned by Ruby Turpin looks a little different. It too is an ideal of purification that pictures an abstract resolution of human difference beyond virtue and vice, "even their virtues burned away." In these contexts, the absurdities leap to mind. Will Ruby Turpin embrace her white-trash, snuff-dipping cousins? Will James Baldwin be walking hand and hand with Mary Grace? Will the Nazis bring up the rear behind their murdered victims, still goose-stepping? What's left of personality and character and identity anyway? It's all literally unimaginable.

It turns out that an O'Connor slam-bang end to a story can fail to be conclusive just as much as a Malamud staccato end can terminate rather than conclude. One of the worst mistakes a reader can make reading O'Connor is to suppose she is trying to get her characters somewhere, to redemption, purgatorial reflection, repentance, whatever.[28] O'Connor is not trying to get her characters somewhere; she is trying to stop them dead in their tracks from getting wherever it is they think they are going or want to go—in order for an alternative to all alternatives to begin to emerge. A turn from desires, goals, or passions can be represented. A realization of failure, loss, or sin can be represented. But as Bruce Gentry nicely puts it, "if the ultimate state of a character's soul depends upon a momentary acceptance of grace, an action impossible to dramatize completely, then the climax of virtually every work by O'Connor occurs, as it were, offstage."[29] However, a presumptive or

---

[26] See *Hitler's American Model: The United States and the Making of Nazi Race Law* (2017) by the distinguished legal historian James Q. Whitman.

[27] Legally, someone with two Jewish grandparents was a *Mischling* ("mixed blood") of the first degree and with one Jewish grandparent a *Mischling* of the second degree. *Mischling* has the connotation of "mongrel."

[28] This proscription is less true of the two novels, with which O'Connor struggled mightily over many years. The stories were a relief for her to write and came into focus much more easily. A short story is a glimpse of something, a novel is a walkabout. All we—here—will ever get of Eternity is a glimpse, not a guided tour. I think there was a very good reason she was unsatisfied with the novels.

[29] Gentry, *Religion of the Grotesque*, 7.

tendentious misreading of these narrative climaxes is made easier, almost inevitable, because O'Connor seems herself to have supposed that that was indeed what she was doing, writing rough-hewn morality plays straight out the Catholic catechism—with complications introduced by Southern Protestant emphases on unmerited grace rather than baptism, confession, and good works and on the prophetic/Scriptural rather than the communal/traditional.

In one of her last interviews, O'Connor pled for the continuity of manners "to preserve each race from small intrusions upon the other....All this may not be ideal, but the Southerner has enough sense not to ask for the ideal but only for the possible, the workable."[30] Here we have her awareness of yet another threatening abstract ideal, this time an ideal of racial equality, which has exploded into contemporary identity politics with all sorts of marginalized groups claiming equal access and equal respect—if not moral superiority. From whose perspective? And who's in charge? O'Connor admired Russell Kirk's *The Conservative Mind* (1953), underlining the phrase "Abstract sentimentality ends in real brutality."[31] As she glossed her innate skepticism of glamorizing social difference,

> If other ages felt less, they saw more, even though they saw with the blind, prophetical, unsentimental eye of acceptance, which is to say, of faith. In the absence of this faith now, we govern by tenderness. It is a tenderness which, long since cut off from the person of Christ, is wrapped in theory. When tenderness is detached from the source of tenderness, its logical outcome is terror. It ends in forced-labor camps and in the fumes of the gas chamber.[32]

Or maybe just in being "canceled," #MeToo. The sentiments of purity and freedom and forgiveness in individual lives are worth striving for, failing at, paying the cost of. As ideologies, whether fascist or progressive or religious, they are suspect and—if history is a guide—as likely to destroy what is valued as to repair what is flawed. One of the most fundamental conservative impulses is "better the devil you know, than the devil you don't." It was a bedrock conviction of both Russell Kirk and the dear departed Judge McIntyre in "The Displaced Person." So, where does this leave us? These disturbing dissonances are made the centerpiece of "Everything That Rises Must Converge," to which we turn for one more go at the virtues as saving graces.

---

[30] O'Connor, *Mystery and Manners*, 234.

[31] Gooch, *Flannery*, 271.

[32] O'Connor, *Mystery and Manners*, 227

## "Everything That Rises Must Converge"

The story is slight but complex. Julian and his mother are mirror images, each an example of small-mindedness in service to grand spiritual pretension. Her pretension is being someone in the world, her father a Chestny, her mother a Godhigh, her grandfather a former governor of the state with a plantation and two hundred slaves. Julian's pretension is his high intelligence (as he realized, "too intelligent to be a success") and first-rate education ("In spite of going to only a third-rate college"), which have made him "free of prejudice and unafraid to face facts" and able to see his mother "with complete objectivity."[33] In his expansive view, "with a few exceptions there was no one worth knowing within a radius of three hundred miles." The mother can, against all evidence, maintain her pretension for herself (and her son) because the times—but not them—are out of joint: "'With the world in the mess it's in,' she said, 'it's a wonder we can enjoy anything. I tell you, the bottom rail is on the top.'" Although these class and racial reversals go back a generation (her father had to bail out his father-in-law to save the family mansion, since decayed and occupied by Negroes), her small-minded prejudices and presumptions survive girdled by her innocence: "her eyes, sky-blue, were as innocent and untouched by experience as they must have been when she was ten." The other bulwark of her pretension is her love for Julian, which does not so much blind her to his insignificance, as wash him in a glow of optimism and encouragement and hardheaded determination: (as the narrator shares Julian's own judgment) "she was a widow who had struggled fiercely to feed and clothe and put him through school and who was supporting him still, 'until he got on his feet.'" This initial description of Julian's mother is already enough for us to wonder how much the widowed, conventional, shrewd, caregiving Mrs. Regina Cline O'Connor is refracted through Julian's mother (the Ward-Beall-Cline Mansion in Milledgeville served as the Governor's Mansion in 1838 and 1839). And this *ex cathedra* question gives rise to its reflection: how much of Miss Mary Flannery O'Connor is refracted through the character of Julian?

Julian's small-mindedness is focused almost entirely on his mother *and her small-mindedness* while concealing his own timidity and resentment at his

---

[33] "Everything That Rises Must Converge," *The Complete Stories*, 405–420. All references to "Everything That Rises Must Converge" are to this edition.

situation.[34] His self-ascribed moral superiority to her is a mere façade. Somehow being right (which he is) because he *wants* to be right because he wants *her* to be wrong fails to make it really right. This moralistic self-deception is the mirror image of her innocence and naïve bigotry: "'And I remember the old darky who was my nurse, Caroline. There was no better person in the world. I've always had a great respect for my colored friends,' she said. 'I'd do anything in the world for them and they'd…'" By the end of the story her pretension has become literally her private reality, while his has utterly collapsed into a private world of love and guilt. Let us unpack it a bit more; O'Connor dissects Julian with the delicate touch of a neurosurgeon. His very unoriginal original sin is angry nostalgia for what was lost that was never his;[35] he saw the Godhigh mansion only once in person, many times in his dreams: "He preferred its threadbare elegance to anything he could name." He feels that he—not she—could have truly appreciated it. Moreover, he blames his mother for struggling "to act like a Chestny without the Chestny goods, and to give him everything she thought a Chestny ought to have." Worse even than her lack of foresight which had made it all harder than it need to have been, "He could not forgive her that she had enjoyed the struggle and that she thought *she* had won. What she meant when she said she had won was that she had brought him up successfully and sent him to college and that he had turned out so well." His illusions of superiority are mocked by her misplaced, express confidence in him and supported only by his disenchantment with the actual world he has inherited, "as disenchanted with it as a man of fifty." In compensation, the narrator reveals, "he spent most of his time…[in] a kind of mental bubble.…From it he could see out and judge but in it he was safe from any kind of penetration from without." Within this bubble he entertains fantasies of "teaching her a lesson." They are on a city bus, with recently integrated seating. When a large, well-dressed Negro man gets on, Julian makes a point of changing his seat from alongside his mother to sit on the facing bench seat with him. She looks at Julian with reproach: "At that moment he could with pleasure have slapped her as he would have slapped a particularly obnoxious child in his charge." This particular fantasy will become all too real in a few moments. He imagines increasingly outrageous

[34] This shoe fits Flannery O'Connor almost too well. It's not the whole story by any means, but one sort of self-conscious self-portrait perhaps. Like the garishly painted, famous self-portrait with devilish pheasant cock?

[35] Could this dynamic be part of what drives Cain's murderous rage against his brother "east of Eden?"

scenarios "to teach her a lesson," inviting a distinguished Negro friend to their home (he has no Negro friends), calling a Negro doctor to treat her in a desperate illness, participating in a sit-in demonstration, bringing home "a beautiful suspiciously Negroid woman."[36] However, his mother suffers from high blood pressure: "He could not push her to the extent of making her have a stroke."

Then, "a large, gaily dressed, sullen-looking colored woman got on with a little boy": "She was a giant of a woman. Her face was set not only to meet opposition but to seek it out." Julian hoped she would sit down next to his mother, but instead she squeezed in between Julian and the well-dressed Black man, and her little boy climbed up onto the facing seat next to his mother, who "lumped all children, black and white, into the common category, 'cute,' and she thought little Negroes were on the whole cuter than little white children." (Only Julian and this little Black boy, Carver, receive an individuating name in the story. The others, including his mother, are all types. Carver is an unknown quantity, at a social/moral cusp, the future, unformed, irrepressible. As we shall see, the author is intensely interested in this looming future. And in Julian's case, he has depths that he has yet fully to uncover.) Julian's annoyance at the woman's overbearing presence is swept away in the realization that the arrangement seemed to have gravely dismayed his mother. Oblivious in his superior insight, as always, he thinks it is because in a sense she and his mother have swapped sons: "Though his mother would not realize the symbolic significance of this, she would feel it." In reality, the two women are confronted by their shared taste in tasteless hats—and shared dislike of each other. Julian's mother had splurged on a hideous hat that she is wearing for the first time downtown to the Y for her (*free*) exercise class for her blood pressure. She bought it because the salesgirl assured her that, in that hat, she "wouldn't meet herself coming and going." So, we have another mirror image, a fun house mirror this time—the same and utterly different.

> The vision of the two hats, identical, broke upon him with the radiance of a brilliant sunrise. His face was suddenly lit with joy. He could not believe that fate had thrust upon his mother such a lesson. He gave a loud chuckle so she would look at him and see that he saw. She turned her eyes on him slowly. The blue in them seemed to have turned a bruised purple. For a moment he had an uncomfortable sense

---

[36] These mini-stories in his head—he wants to be a writer—are in lieu of actually taking a hand in the messy world. One is reminded of O'Connor's wry comment to a visitor to Andalusia that she farmed from a rocking chair on the front porch.

> of her innocence, but it lasted only a second before principle rescued him. Justice entitled him to laugh. His grin hardened until it said to her as plainly as if he were saying aloud: Your punishment exactly fits your pettiness. This should teach you a permanent lesson.

Just how much of this is narrator's interpretation and how much is character's balloon bubble thought is impossible to discern. We are on very slippery ground here, and the author intends for us to take a pratfall before we are done. We—the readers—may need our comeuppance as well.

The narrator has been busily sharing and interpreting the character's thoughts and feelings throughout the story. Julian's sensitivity to himself and his condemnation of his mother's insensitivity ("She called her insensitivity 'being adjustable.'") have been shown up by the narrator as an higher-order obliviousness to who he is and how he appears. Now the irony steps up a notch into the cosmic or Sophoclean range. Fate is indeed bringing a profound judgment and a permanent lesson to bear. The narrator, who of course knows the end of the story already, is preparing us for it—Julian is oblivious to it, his bubble is about to be burst. The narrator's careful irony also begins to prepare for the author's even more profound judgment and very difficult lesson for us, the readers. For starters, we can see and begin to feel how principles (and manners, mores, and spiritual pretensions) can justify—honestly/dishonestly—any trespass. This is textbook original sin: "So, when the woman saw that the tree was good for food, and that it was a delight to the eyes, and that the tree was desired to make one wise, she took of its fruit and ate."[37]

The Negress is bristling, "rumbling like a volcano about to become active." Julian's mother is beginning—with her trademark resilience—to see the humor in the hat faceoff: "an amused smile came over her face as if the woman was a monkey that had stolen her hat." With a sinking heart, Julian saw that this "was going to be no lesson at all." Carver begins to cut the fool with Julian's mother, giggling and smiling. "'I think he likes me,' Julian's mother said, and smiled at the woman. It was the smile she used when she was being particularly gracious to an inferior....The woman stood up and yanked the little boy off the seat as if she were snatching him from contagion. Julian could feel the rage in her at having no weapon like his mother's smile." Carver persists in playing peek-a-boo with Julian's mother from across the aisle: "The woman slapped his hand down. 'Quit yo' foolishness,' she said, 'before I knock the living Jesus out of you!'" Indeed, Jesus better look out.

[37] Genesis 3.6

Eager to escape the situation, Julian reaches for the cord for their stop. The woman reaches up and pulls it too: "Oh my God, he thought. He had the terrible intuition that when they got off the bus together, his mother would open her purse and give the boy a nickel. The gesture would be as natural to her as breathing." He tries to stop her; she insists, finding only a penny. She steps rapidly after the woman down the street, and under the lamppost holds out a bright new penny for Carver. Frozen for a moment "in frustrated rage," the huge woman explodes, swinging her "mammoth red pocketbook that bulged throughout as if stuffed with rocks": "[Julian] shut his eyes and cringed as he heard the woman shout, 'He don't take nobody's pennies!'"

Julian's mother is left sitting on the sidewalk, her face expressionless. Julian now has his chance for the perfect, angry lesson. Helped to her feet, she takes off in the wrong direction. She says one word: "Home." He follows along to explain the meaning of this lesson:

> "Don't think that was just an uppity Negro woman," he said. "That was the whole colored race which will no longer take your condescending pennies. That was your black double.... The old manners are obsolete and your graciousness is not worth a damn." He thought bitterly of the house that had been lost for him. "You aren't who you think you are," he said.

She drops her pocketbook. He says let's wait on the bus. She repeats thickly, "Home." Julian tells her she is acting like a child—and he childishly refuses to go any further.

> She continued to go on as if she had not heard him. He took a few steps and caught her arm and stopped her. He looked into her face and caught his breath. He was looking into a face he had never seen before. "Tell Grandpa to come get me," she said. He stared, stricken. 'Tell Caroline to come get me.'"

Staggering, she collapses to the pavement. Calling "Mother," "Darling, sweetheart," "Momma, Momma," he looks into her face: "One eye, large and staring, moved slightly to the left as if it had come unmoored. The other remained fixed on him, raked his face again, found nothing and closed." Wait here, wait here, he cries. Help, help, he shouts. The narrator describes his numb feet carrying him faster and faster nowhere, toward lights that drift away from him. But it is the author who concludes, "The tide of darkness seemed to sweep him back to her, postponing from moment to moment his entry into the world of guilt and sorrow." However briefly before she loses consciousness, Julian's mother recedes mentally back into her childhood of Home, Grandfather, and old nurse Caroline—her world restored to her in her loss, as it were. In bitter contrast, a whole new world opens up before him, his pretension of "objectivity" shattered, his love *and* his guilt exploding his bubble of feigned superiority and righteousness. Like Oedipus, his self-knowledge is heightened—by Fate—just in time to contemplate unending pain and sorrow.

With its authoritative last judgment and its highly intellectual title, taken from Teihard de Chardin's evolutionary theology,[38] O'Connor clearly stakes out the author's territory in this story. As she summed it up a couple of years later in a letter to Betty Hester, "The topical is poison. I got away with it in 'Everything That Rises' but only because I say a plague on everybody's house as far as the race business goes."[39] Well, that's our house, too, whatever it may be. There is much more to be unpacked in this devastating story. Original sin leaves no one off the hook, in spite of Teilhard de Chardin's apologia for the human race.

O'Connor places a significant authorial milepost at the beginning of the story: "She was almost ready to go, standing at the hall mirror, putting on her hat, while he, his hands behind him, appeared pinned to the door frame, waiting like Saint Sebastian for the arrows to begin piercing him." There's no question that Julian feels like a martyr every Wednesday night taking her downtown for her reducing class. But, to throw in St. Sebastian as a specific reference is punching way above the narrator's weight class, a narrator who almost never says anything about Julian or his mother that Julian couldn't more or less have thought himself. The narrator's ironies work by juxtaposition, with situations and self-revelations that give the lie to his apparently innocuous commentary. They are just Julian's thoughts and instincts as viewed, perhaps, from within the Devil's cynical, knowing, global perspective. So, why does O'Connor—the author—begin by introducing the plague

---

[38] Pierre Teilhard de Chardin, a Jesuit priest and paleontologist, was censored by the Church primarily for his views on original sin (concluding that evolution shows that human spirituality moves toward an omega point of divine awareness, called into being by Jesus' love, rather than departing from a deplorable fall remediable only by Jesus' death). O'Connor was deeply attracted to him in part because she suspected he was a rare Catholic thinker of the stature of a Tillich or Barth, but even more so because of his analysis of "passive diminishments" or unavoidable sufferings as opportunities for spiritual growth. As she had already opined, sickness is "more instructive than a long trip to Europe." Gooch, *Flannery*, 297.

[39] Ibid., 336.

saint? The famous images of St. Sebastian, shot full of arrows like a hedgehog, were and are a metaphor for multiple and disseminated pains and disabilities, as apt a metaphor for lupus as for the plague—and even perhaps for her mother's (and others') insensitive and critical barbs.[40] It is not a throwaway allusion, however. A few pages later, as his mother struggles with remorse for purchasing the atrocious hat ("I can pay the gas bill with the seven-fifty."), "Julian thought he could have stood his lot better if she had been selfish, if she had been an old hag who drank and screamed at him. He walked along, saturated in depression, as if in the midst of his martyrdom he had lost his faith [so concludes the narrator in Julian's voice]." But it is not he who is struck down, a martyr to a despised faith. St. Sebastian miraculously survived the barrage of arrows and was nursed back to health. Stubbornly, he pursued his martyrdom again, personally confronting Emperor Diocletian with his Christianity. This time he was clubbed to death and his body thrown into the common sewer. Our martyr is not Julian, but Julian's mother beat down in the street by the giant Negress. In spite of all the warning signs, in spite of all Julian's betrayals, she persists in her faith, refusing to believe that "The old manners are obsolete and...graciousness is not worth a damn."

O'Connor valorizes those faithful to the old ways, the traditions of the society she feeds on. Consequently, her portrayal of his mother's Black double, as Julian called her, has discomforting implications for the *bien pensant* reader who, like Julian, is too intelligent, too educated, too woke to have anything but disdain for the old traditions, as invidious and destructive. Where does that disdain take us? The massive Negress has her own spiritual pretension, girded by her own pettiness. She will take "nuthin'" from no White man or woman, not even a shiny penny. She has embraced a freedom that *demands* equality. She doesn't ask for it as a gift from condescending or presuming betters. Julian's little fantasies of racial solidarity as gifts of himself (and, of course, goads to his mother) are worse than shiny pennies, because they invite superior types of Negroes to join him in his superiority—and because they presume superiority is still the price of admission. Julian's little forays into solidarity have already shown him that not every well-dressed Negro is a lawyer or professor; they are as likely to be an undertaker or numbers runner. This sullen and truculent Black woman, yanking her kid around, crushing a well-meaning if foolish woman to the ground over a penny, is no

[40] When *Wise Blood* came out, Aunt Mary Cline drew herself up and declared, "I don't know where Mary Flannery met those people she wrote about, but it was certainly not in *my* house." Ibid., 208.

role model for equality. And this is exactly the point. The freedom she demands for herself is to be just as small-minded, just as sinful, as any privileged White person. She is free of imposed community standards, to hell with mores and morals.

Presciently, O'Connor has anticipated the backlash of enlightened, liberalizing White Southerners in the seventies and eighties. Surveying the outcome of desegregation and the demise of Jim Crow legislation, these civil rights activists—many of them Pauline Protestant Christians[41]—realized to their dismay that repression and resistance had held together Black families and Black businesses and Black churches. In the relative absence of these restraints, the Black community fragmented, with elites escaping into prosperity and the poor and uneducated being left behind in new ghettos and rural wastelands, often preying on each other. The liberal Southerner, aghast at this social collapse, blamed the successfully liberated for not taking responsibility for their Black "brothers and sisters." Look at what you've gained, look at what it *cost* you, look at what it cost *us*. You should be better than this, more responsible, committed to something bigger than your own advancement. This was wishful thinking and scapegoating. Finally, many of these enlightened, good men and women sheepishly and regretfully concluded: Better the devil you know than the devil you don't.

Principles, mores and manners, ideals? A plague on all their houses. Here, every privileged perspective that we might choose acting for the good *as we see it* founders. From what perspective are all virtuous perspectives suspect? What *is* original sin? Let us grab the Devil by the hindmost and see what He has to say about it. How does Mary Flannery, well-raised and precluded from most temptations by her illness, depict real evil, true sinners?

## "A Good Man Is Hard to Find"

Her breakthrough story, "A Good Man Is Hard to Find," was also her favorite story to read aloud to audiences—in a deadpan, steady Georgia drawl. The story is a contest between competing privileged perspectives. The narrator gets the first but not the last word. The character self-called "The Misfit" gets the last word but contradicts himself with it. And the anonymous grandmother has the only transformative word and moment—although its effect is opaque and ambiguous even for O'Connor as it turns out. As O'Connor

[41] "There is neither Jew nor Greek, there is neither slave nor free, there is neither male nor female; for you are all one in Christ Jesus." Galatians 3.28.

confessed to Cecil Dawkins, a younger writer and teacher whom she closely mentored, "Point of view runs me crazy when I think about it but I believe that when you are writing well, you don't think about it. I seldom think about it when I am writing a short story, but on the novel it gets to be a considerable worry."[42] Her genius depends on a perspicaciously tangled point of view, which she gets away with in the stories, nowhere more successfully than in "A Good Man Is Hard to Find." As dark and melodramatic as anything in Poe, nevertheless the story doesn't add up; its narrative logic fails at a crucial point, which means that in effect the author displaces us, the readers, and any judgments *we* would bring to bear. O'Connor was well aware of the role of negative capability in her stories (although she doesn't describe it as such). In her prefatory remarks to Hollins College students before reading "A Good Man Is Hard to Find," she beautifully summed it up:

> I often ask myself what makes a story work, and what makes it hold up as a story, and I have decided that it is probably some action, some gesture of a character that is unlike any other in the story, one which indicates where the real heart of the story lies. This would have to be an action or a gesture which was both totally right and totally unexpected; it would have to be one that was both in character and beyond character; it would have to suggest both the world and eternity....It would be a gesture that transcended any neat allegory that might have been intended or any pat moral categories a reader could make. It would be a gesture which somehow made contact with mystery.[43]

This is the essence of her sacramental view of the world, which she may or may not be correct in connecting to a moment of Divine grace. In an earlier letter, she makes this same point and then curiously adds, "for me, this is always an action which indicates that grace has been offered....This is not a piece of knowledge that I consciously put into my stories; it is a discovery I get out of them."[44] Having put herself on the same interpretive level as her readers, let's see if we too can discover mystery.

The tale begins in comedy. The narrator and the sophisticated readers for whom O'Connor was writing[45] have fun mocking the characters and their

---

[42] O'Connor, *Habit of Being*, 239.

[43] O'Connor, *Mystery and Manners*, 111.

[44] Ibid., 118.

[45] For a decade, O'Connor's first reader and primary literary tutor was Caroline Gordon, a fabled writer and teacher at Columbia University, who was thirty years

family dynamics: the grandmother self-concerned, provincial, enthusiastic, and calculatedly manipulative; her son, Bailey, long-suffering and withdrawn; the children John Wesley and June Star smart-mouthed, disrespectful, and instinctively manipulative (their respectively sanctified and pagan names signaling the nowhere character of post-War Atlanta); the children's "cabbage" faced, rabbity mother; a bland baby; and Pitty Sing, the grandmother's cat, which will be the agent of Fate in the story, a kind of Trojan horse. They are fixing to take a Florida vacation. The next morning they will be off with the grandmother sitting in the rear seat between the two kids, with her big black valise shaped like "the head of a hippopotamus" in one corner concealing a basket with Pitty Sing in it: "Her son, Bailey, didn't like to arrive at a motel with a cat."[46]

From the get-go the question of where they are headed is raised; "The grandmother didn't want to go to Florida. She wanted to visit some of her connections in east Tennessee and was seizing at every chance to change Bailey's mind." As he reads the sports pages, she shakes the paper at him and warns that it says that The Misfit "is aloose from the Federal pen and headed toward Florida." Getting no response she turns to the mother and urges that the children be taken somewhere else they haven't already seen, so they would "be broad," like east Tennessee. The only response she gets is from the children, who sass her and sum her up: "'She wouldn't stay at home to be queen for a day,' June Star said without raising her yellow head." When the grandmother responds with the threat of meeting up with The Misfit, John Wesley says "I'd smack his face."

She's the first one in the car the next morning, carefully dressed so that "anyone seeing her dead on the highway would know at once that she was a lady." The narrator shares the grandmother's continual commentary on the journey and the passing scenery, as she remarks the blue granite outcroppings, the brilliant red clay banks, the green lace-work of crops. Then out of the blue the narrator becomes a distinct sensibility and judge, not just a commentator: "The trees were full of silver-white sunlight and the meanest of them sparkled. The children were reading comic books and their mother had gone back to sleep." None of this is the grandmother's thought or language. "The meanest of them sparkled" is well beyond her perception or articulation. The

senior to O'Connor. The literary friends she had met at the Writer's Workshop or in New York and Connecticut made up her ideal audience.

[46] "A Good Man Is Hard to Find," *The Complete Stories*, 117–133. All references to "A Good Man Is Hard to Find" are to this edition.

sharp contrast with the sensibilities of the children and mother is intended. A judgment of these people is beginning to take shape. From this point on, we don't read merely for the comedy; we read for the insight we are led to expect from the narrator. The grandmother continues her commentary. Look at the cute little pickaninny. Look at the plantation graveyard. Look at the shapes of the clouds. Her mind is carried back to when she was a maiden lady, being courted by a Mr. Edgar Atkins Teagarden (E.A.T.). She tells the comic story of his courting her with Saturday afternoon watermelons with his initials carved in them. At the end of the story, she muses that she would have done well to have married Mr. Teagarden, who was "a gentleman and had bought Coca-Cola stock when it first came out." Instead, she is here now. Where that is exactly in her journey through life will be the question deeply explored by the narrative.

Well, they are at The Tower, stopping for barbeque sandwiches at a wood and stucco gas station/dance hall in a clearing outside of Timothy (which—because it doesn't exist—is even more nowhere than Atlanta).[47] This comic interlude outside of nowhere is a brilliant set piece, featuring the proprietor Red Sammy Butts, his wife, and pet monkey. It interrupts the plot, except to reintroduce The Misfit back into the conversation. It tells us nothing new about the grandmother or the family, who are all true to type. But, most oddly, it is Red Sammy ("THE FAT BOY WITH THE HAPPY LAUGH! A VETERAN! RED SAMMY'S YOUR MAN") who introduces the story's title "'A good man is hard to find,' Red Sammy said. Everything is getting terrible. I remember the day you could go off and leave your screen door unlatched. Not no more." Red Sammy agrees with the grandmother's opinion that "Europe was entirely to blame for the way things were now. She said the way Europe acted you would think we were made of money." They set off again on their journey, which will soon turn into a pilgrimage (at the

[47] Timothy was a sainted martyr who was Paul's most faithful companion on his journeys. His circumcision by Paul raised questions for the young church about the status of the Mosaic law for Christians, which hints forward at the antinomianism of The Misfit (see below). When O'Connor finished *The Violent Bear It Away*, she reported to Betty Hester that her mother had (slowly) read the manuscript and asked her "Does it have symbolisms in it? You know when I was coming along, they didn't have symbolisms." Flannery O'Connor, *O'Connor: Collected Work*, ed. Sally Fitzgerald (New York: Library of America, 1988) 1101–1102. The question is always how far to go in interpreting the symbolism. To this point, see Matthew Fike, "The Timothy Allusion in 'A Good Man Is Hard to Find,'" *Renascence: Essays on Value in Literature* 52.4 (Summer 2000).

grandmother's insistence) and then at their penultimate destination will inspire a second, outrageously sophisticated meditation on why men go bad (in The Misfit and the grandmother's dialogue) and at the end will finally conceal/reveal how men/women become good (in The Misfit's ironic/transcendental judgment).

But, at this moment, the author chooses to conceal more than reveal and introduces a red herring: *trust.* Red Sammy plops down at a table beside the family after they have ordered and begins the story's first ethical dialogue: "'You can't win,' he said. 'You can't win,' and he wiped his sweating red face off with a gray handkerchief. 'These days you don't know who to trust,' he said. 'Ain't that the truth?' 'People are certainly not nice like they used to be,' said the grandmother." Red Sammy's response is a lament for his trusting nature. A week ago he had trusted two fellers for some gas he pumped them on credit. "'Now why did I do that?' 'Because you're a good man!' the grandmother said at once. 'Yes'm, I suppose so,' Red Sam said as if he were struck with this answer." Red Sam's wife, "a tall burnt-brown woman with hair and eyes lighter than her skin," brought their order from behind the counter and brings the discussion down to earth, "'It isn't a soul in this green world of God's that you can trust,' she said. 'And I don't count nobody out of that, not nobody,' she repeated, looking at Red Sammy." Red Sammy is probably about as trustworthy as his pet monkey (little homunculus), which climbs to the top of the small chinaberry tree it's chained to in the yard as soon as the children get out of the car and run toward him. The monkey certainly knows not to trust the puerile children. And the grandmother with concealed cat is exactly as trustworthy as those Greeks with their gift horse before the walls of Troy, except she *really* doesn't know what she is doing when she deceives her son Bailey.[48] And so it goes—until we finally meet The Misfit. He is utterly trustworthy. He knows who he is, says what he thinks, and does what he says he will do, without second thoughts. He is as trustworthy as a rattlesnake.

---

[48] Of course, the Greeks—all unknowing—would also pay dearly on their way home for their success at deception. For most of the time that O'Connor knew Robert Fitzgerald (named by her as her literary executor) he was working on his famous poetic translation of *The Odyssey*, begun in the early fifties and finally published to major awards in 1961. It is not an accident that the black valise concealing Pitty Sing is shaped like the head of the Greek-named "river horse," one of those dreaded "symbolisms."

The games that the virtuous play with truth, honor, and filiation are not applicable when it comes to the truly evil who come only to destroy.[49]

Outside of Toomsboro, Georgia,[50] the grandmother remembers an old plantation she once visited in this neighborhood as a young lady, with twin arbors "where you sat down with your suitor after a stroll in the garden": "the more she talked about it [the narrator tells us], the more she wanted to see it once again." So, she tells a fond lie about a secret panel and concealed Civil War treasure. The children go into action, screaming, whining, kicking the back of the seat. The grandmother says it's not far from here, but it will turn out that it is farther and farther away as they set off on what is becoming a kind of pilgrimage: homage to lost youth, lost loves. It becomes a quest for hidden treasures and secret places, a place at which to arrive—not just more scenery. Traditionally, pilgrimage sites—like Lourdes visited by Flannery and her mother in 1958—are sacred places of spiritual renewal, physical healing, and abundant grace. We shall see. "The road looked as if no one had traveled on it for months. 'It's not much farther,' the grandmother said and just as she said it, a horrible thought came to her." In her acute embarrassment, she jumps in her seat, kicking over her valise in the corner. Pitty Sing springs out and leaps onto Bailey's neck. The car turns over into a gulch off the side of the road, landing right-side-up. The grandmother [the narrator tells us] had suddenly realized that "the house she had remembered so vividly was not in Georgia but in Tennessee." It's not the pilgrimage she had envisioned—or the destination Bailey had originally chosen—they, as it turns out, were headed nowhere. Only the children are excited by this turn in the road, "'We've had an ACCIDENT!' the children screamed in a frenzy of delight. 'But nobody's killed,' June Star said with disappointment." High comedy blends with an unsettling twist of fate. Hold on to your hats.

It is the last comedy in the story—the funny moments to come (and there are several) are so pitiful that only the Devil would laugh at them. The

---

[49] O'Connor's specialty, as she insisted to John Hawkes, was pretensions. When she deals with real evil, soul destroying evil, she is brilliant. But she rarely takes on this territory. Too rough on her? Too rough on her readers? At any rate, few of her stories force us to the edge of despair. Perhaps the most devastating of them is "The Lame Shall Enter First," whose situation consumed her thoughts over a number of years and versions: the pretensions of an educated, liberal do-gooder who devastatingly fails his dearest responsibility in the self-serving delusion that he—not Jesus—can save the proudly evil.

[50] Toomsboro is a railroad town thirty miles south of Milledgeville and maybe another one of those "symbolisms," homophonic "tomb-town."

narrator takes over. The scene becomes deeply menacing, and, as it does, this cartoon family becomes humanized by shock, terror, incomprehension, and instinctive dignity. The narrator pours it on: "woods, tall and dark and deep," "a big black battered hearse-like automobile," "He had on blue jeans that were too tight for him and was holding a black hat and a gun," "Behind them the line of woods gaped like a dark open mouth." When the grandmother finally recognizes The Misfit and blurts it out, "Bailey turned his head sharply and said something to his mother that shocked even the children. The old lady began to cry and The Misfit reddened." The grandmother, true to type, continues her self-inflation and manipulation: we turned over twice, oncet The Misfit corrects; she has a feeling that he is someone she knew, then declares she recognized him at once; you wouldn't shoot a lady, would you?; I know you're a good man; I know you must come from nice people. From this point on, the narrator backs off, simply supplying brief observational details that continue to humanize the grandmother and her family—as two (Bailey and John Wesley) by three (mother, baby, and June Star), they are led off into the woods by Hiram and Bobby Lee to be slaughtered. The verbal exchanges with and between family members are brilliantly written to be psychologically true and situationally surreal, while surfacing wrenching glimpses of love and dignity: "The children's mother had begun to make heaving noises as if she couldn't get her breath. 'Lady,' he asked, 'would you and that little girl like to step off yonder with Bobby Lee and Hiram and join your husband?' 'Yes, thank you,' the mother said faintly. Her left arm dangled helplessly and she was holding the baby, who had gone to sleep, in the other."

We now know where this family has been headed all this time: thrown in a backwoods ravine with flies buzzing in and out of their mouths. They are truly nowhere in this green world of God's (as Red Sammy's wife might put it). Of course, they were always headed that way, just as we all are. But, they—like we—usually think we have someplace else to get to, somewhere our desires, goals, and passions propel us. Even in death we expect our memory to live on in those we care about, maybe if we're lucky a tombstone. These pretensions to meaning stripped away by an unexpected encounter with the Devil in the wilderness (the penultimate nowhere), we realize that we are finally just food for worms, rotting meat (the ultimate nowhere). Nothing this inconsequential family does, says, feels, or suffers has any significance in the scheme of things. Even if the grandmother were queen for a day, even if she could make the sun stand still, they are nothing but dead meat. *Or*, a soul awaiting Judgment Day? So now, just the grandmother and The Misfit alone, they get down to the licklog on life and death. Their astonishingly detailed argument back and forth has the flavor of a medieval Thomistic disputation, with the grandmother as master raising the question "Should we pray?" and The Misfit as pupil offering reasons for the negative, to be resolved—we hope—by the master through both affirmative arguments and responses to the critical arguments.[51] Certainly, there is a density of thought and self-reflection here that gives The Misfit an other-worldly, perhaps even prophetic, character. As his father put it growing up, "a different breed of dog": "it's some that can live their whole life out without asking about it and it's others has to know why it is, and this boy is one of the latters. He's going to be into everything!"

The grandmother keeps insisting that he, like Red Sammy, is a good man, "not a bit common." She can tell by looking at him that he is good at heart. And, indeed, he is naturally polite, self-possessed, easily embarrassed by impropriety (like apologizing to the grandmother for Bailey's shocking profanity or for having no shirt on before ladies). There is something vulnerable about him. The narrator notes his silver-rimmed spectacles and the "scholarly" look they gave him, his sockless, red, thin ankles, and how thin his shoulder blades appeared to the grandmother looking down on him as he squats in the dirt drawing circles with the butt of his gun. The Misfit remarks twice that the children make him nervous. "'Do you ever pray?' she asked. He shook his head.…'Nome,' he said. There was a pistol shot from the woods, followed closely by another. Then silence. The old lady's head jerked around. She could hear the wind move through the tree tops like a long satisfied insuck of breath. 'Bailey Boy!' she called."

In spite of his daddy's singling him out, the man who would become "The Misfit" presents himself as everyman; he's done and seen it all, by land and by sea, at home and abroad. Pray, pray, the grandmother implores. Such a man as he was—insistent to understand the why of all he's seen and done—should seek God in prayer. He was not a bad boy, he insists, but somehow he did something wrong and got send to the penitentiary. This big word in

---

[51] One of the last classes O'Connor took at Georgia State College for Women was "Introduction to Modern Philosophy" taught by a new and cosmopolitan professor, George Beiswanger. She was unusually outspoken in class with her criticisms of philosophical modernism and defense of St. Thomas Aquinas. As Beiswanger later recalled, "She knew Aquinas in detail, was amazingly well read in early philosophy." His urging that she apply to graduate school at his alma mater, the University of Iowa, and his lobbying for a scholarship for her there (in the School of Journalism—she was still aiming to be a cartoonist) set her course forward. Gooch, *Flannery*, 114–115.

The Misfit's mouth means what it says, a place for penance, regret, contrition. That's when you should have started to pray says the grandmother. She, of course, is right. Pray for forgiveness, pray for a humble heart, pray for a turning from temptation. But immured, a wall to the left, a wall to the right, he could not remember what it was he had done that required forgiveness. As the Roman Catholic Church insists, original sin is not a personal fault but an inherited lack of originary grace, signifying the devil's dominion over man. The Misfit was punished for Adam's sin by the same logic that condemns unbaptized infants to hell if they die. It is a hard doctrine; the universal Church has struggled with it since the third century. The grandmother struggles too. Maybe it was a mistake? You must have done something to deserve it? According to The Misfit, a head-doctor at the penitentiary had diagnosed an updated version of St. Augustine's "concupiscence,"[52] a primal psychosexual acting out against his father.

> "If you would pray," the old lady said, "Jesus would help you." "That's right," The Misfit said. "Well then why don't you pray?" she asked trembling with delight suddenly. "I don't want no hep," he said. "I'm doing all right by myself."

This essentially Protestant self-assertion has, as Luther and Calvin soon found out, the seeds of antinomianism in it.[53] "I found out that the crime don't matter. You can do one thing or you can do another, kill a man or take a tire off his car, because sooner or later you're going to forget what it was you done and just be punished for it." If following the Mosaic laws will not save you

[52] "Although it is proper to each individual, original sin does not have the character of a personal fault in any of Adam's descendants. It is a deprivation of original holiness and justice, but human nature has not been totally corrupted: it is wounded in the natural powers proper to it, subject to ignorance, suffering and the dominion of death, and inclined to sin—an inclination to evil that is called 'concupiscence.'" *Catechism of the Catholic Church* (1992) Part 1, Section 2, Chapter 1, Article 1, Paragraph 7, Note 405.

[53] Calvin in particular railed against the so-called "Libertines" and Anabaptists and their "filthy" doctrines: "For their principles are to confound all differences between good & ill, & to mingle God so with the Devil that it should not be discerned between the one and the other, and so to make men not only without all feeling in their consciences before God: but also without shame before the world." The Libertine faction in Geneva was prominent enough to achieve Calvin's banishment from Geneva for a time. John Calvin, *Brief Instruction for Arming All the Good Faithful Against the Errors of the Common Sect of the Anabaptists*, 1549. www.truecovenanter.com/calvin/calvin_against_anabaptists.

and it is all up to unmerited grace, then sin bravely indeed. The case for prayer seems weaker and weaker.

Bobby Lee and Hiram come ambling back from the woods, dragging the yellow shirt with bright blue parrots on it that Bailey had been wearing. They toss it to The Misfit, who puts it on: "The grandmother couldn't name what the shirt reminded her of." They lead the mother and June Star off into the woods. The grandmother gaping and gasping for words begins cursing: "Jesus, Jesus." Or, at least, the narrator tells us it sounds like cursing but is meant as "Jesus will help you." The narrator tells us that The Misfit responds *as if* he agreed. "As if?" As if he agreed with what, the cursing, the pleading? The narrator clams up on us at this crucial moment. The Misfit speaks for himself from this point forward until after he has shot the grandmother to death. At the beginning of his remarkable soliloquy, The Misfit makes a bizarre claim. It's all Jesus' fault: "Jesus thrown everything off balance. It was the same case with Him as with me except He hadn't committed any crime and they could prove I had committed one because they had the papers on me." We won't know what he means by this until later. But, first, The Misfit explains why he is "The Misfit." Because, like Jesus, "I can't make what all I done wrong fit what all I gone through in punishment." What does the author intend for us here? Christ's "substitutionary atonement" is the heart of the Gospel. John 3.16 is the most famous verse in the New Testament: "For God so loved the world, that he gave his only begotten Son, that whoever believes in him should not perish, but have everlasting life." Salvation is found through an instrument of torture and death, the Cross. This too, like "original sin," is a hard doctrine with which the universal Church has wrestled since the days of Paul. The very fact that you need multiple conflicting theories to try to explain and justify the Crucifixion lends credence to The Misfit's charge that Jesus is the cause of a cosmic imbalance.

The Misfit's soliloquy is interrupted by the sound of pistol shots as the mother and her children are murdered and by the grandmother's last desperate attempt to bargain her way out of death: good blood, nice people, pray, Jesus, Jesus, I'll give you all the money I've got—and by her anguish: "the grandmother raised her head like a parched old turkey hen crying for water and called, 'Bailey Boy, Bailey Boy!' as if her heart would break." He continues, "Jesus was the only One [the author's faithful capitalization here is telling] that ever raised the dead....and He shouldn't have done it. He thrown everything off balance." The Misfit, natural theologian that he is, proceeds to a parody of Pascal's wager and thereby introduces Jansenism into the mix, together with a third hard doctrine of the universal Church "justification by grace (alone?)."[54] The workings of grace, O'Connor's leading fascination and dilemma, are put to the test in a looming moment that she confesses she doesn't understand any more than we do—yet it *is* the story, as she *did* understand.

The parody of Pascal is put starkly:

> "If He did what He said, then it's nothing for you to do but to throw away everything and follow Him, and if He didn't then it's nothing for you to do but enjoy the few minutes you got left the best way you can—by killing somebody or burning down his house or doing some other meanness to him. No pleasure but meanness," he said and his voice had become almost a snarl.

Please read this again, slowly. Pascal's wager has this same all or nothing, desperate quality. Pascal: Either God exists or He doesn't. Either we believe or we don't. If we believe and get it wrong, then we haven't lost much (maybe just our pleasure in meanness). If we don't believe and get it wrong, we lose eternal life in Heaven (and suffer eternally in Hell). Reason—according to Pascal—cannot figure out whether God exists or not, but reason can recognize good odds, infinite gain versus finite loss. Therefore, at least try to

---

[54] This hard doctrine, "*sola gratia*" in the Reformers' formulation, was the very crux of the Reformation split. Cornelius Jansen's *Augustinus*, published in 1640 two years after his death, looked to St. Augustine for a dark vision of the human will. Dead in sin no one can save himself, and God's grace neither requires nor allows any human assent. Jansenism was condemned as Catholic heresy because it seemed to verge on Calvinism's doctrine of predestination. Blaise Pascal was a Jansenist and perhaps the last great Catholic theologian (and a great mathematician, scientist, and inventor). Although she admired Pascal, O'Connor railed at what she saw as Jansenist tendencies in Catholicism (see O'Connor, *The Habit of Being*, 304) which George Niederauer (Archbishop of San Francisco) glosses as "a Jansenistic disdain for human weakness and struggle and distrust of questions, speculations and discussions of any depth." "Flannery O'Connor's Religious Vision," *America, The Jesuit Review* (2007) www.americamagazine.org/issue/639/article/flannery-oconnors-religious-vision. But Warren Coffey, writing after the publication of her posthumous collection of stories *Everything That Rises Must Converge*, argues persuasively that "[Irish] Jansenism, more than anything else, explains both her very considerable power at the short story and her limitations. The pride of intellect, the corruption of the heart, the horror of sex—all these appear again and again in her books, and against them, the desperate assertion of faith." "Flannery O'Connor," *Commentary* (November 1965) www.commentarymagazine.com/articles/flannery-oconnor/.

believe, seek God. It's explicitly an argument for mathematically inclined atheists—crystal clear.

Unfortunately, The Misfit is not an atheist; he is a Protestant. As the grandmother sinks down to the ground, dizzy, mumbling maybe he didn't raise the dead, "not knowing what she was saying," The Misfit goes into a Protestant rant: "'I wasn't there so I can't say He didn't.... It ain't right I wasn't there because if I had of been there I would have known. Listen lady,' he said in a high voice, 'if I had of been there I would have known and I wouldn't be like I am now.'" The poor, lonely, brilliant Misfit is wandering in a dark world of suffering seeking a God who is seeking him. But, when God doesn't present Himself—in Kierkegaard's marvelous image—like "the figure of a very rare and tremendously large green bird, with a red beak, sitting in a tree on a mound, and perhaps even whistling in an unheard of manner,"[55] he complains of God's lack of graciousness, not his own weakness of vision. Although even Moses could only get a glimpse of God's backside, the Protestant demands to receive God up close and personal, every revelation a personal revelation. What chutzpah! But as Mary Flannery would say, you gotta love him. He's just so mixed up! He wants it, but he wants it on his terms. Which is God and which is man? Say ten Our Fathers and fifty Hail Marys a day for a year and a day, then come back and the Holy Mother Church will teach you how to say the Rosary, with its twenty mysteries, concluding "we beseech thee, that while meditating on these mysteries of the most holy Rosary of the Blessed Virgin Mary, we may imitate what they contain and obtain what they promise, through the same Christ our Lord. Amen." We have gone as far as prayer as a disputatious concept will take us. If you were not raised in the Church, how do you turn to Her?[56]

We are at the crux of the story, its moment of negative capability. As she told her audience at Hollins College, "I find that students are often puzzled by what [the grandmother] says and does here, but I think myself that if I took out this gesture and what she says with it, I would have no story. What was left would not be worth your attention." Indeed, without the grandmother's response to The Misfit and his response to her gesture, this would be just another lurid True Detective story: maniac guns down family, including baby. The narrator steps back in. This is the moment the narrator's been

[55] Søren Kierkegaard, *Concluding Unscientific Postscript*, trans. David Swenson and Walter Lowrie (Princeton: Princeton University Press, 1941) 219.

[56] Some of O'Connor's most dramatic personal relationships were with Catholic converts: Robert Lowell, Caroline Gordon, Betty Hester.

waiting for—the rest is just incidental detail. The author keeps a tight rein on the scene, delicately balancing psychological realism, surreal effects, and deep compassion. The Misfit's voice "seemed" about to crack. The grandmother's head clears for an instant. His face is close to her face, twisted "as if he were going to cry." He's draped in Bailey's Florida holiday shirt, and she murmurs "You're one of my own children" and touches him on the shoulder. The narrator reports that "The Misfit sprang back as if a snake had bitten him and shot her three times through the chest." He puts down his gun and begins to clean his glasses. Hiram and Bobby Lee return, and he tells them "Take her off and throw her where you thrown the others." She was a talker, Bobby Lee says. "'She would have been a good woman,' The Misfit said, 'if it had been somebody there to shoot her every minute of her life.' 'Some fun!' Bobby Lee said. 'Shut up, Bobby Lee,' The Misfit said. 'It's no real pleasure in life.'"

Wow, what just happened here?

We have the three primary perspectives clearly arrayed for us. The grandmother—a good woman at the end? The Misfit pushing the limits of our humanity, giving the Devil his due—but somehow touched spiritually by the grandmother? The narrator with almost angelic dispassion and delicacy tenderly glossing the last moments on this earth of this doomed family—while reserving judgment on The Misfit? All three of these perspectives are blown up in the end.

It is the grandmother's story from beginning to end. She dressed for death at the start of the journey—death in a highway accident? by The Misfit's hand? because a mountain fell on her? It scarcely matters. In her shock and confusion—truly facing death—she reaches out and touches The Misfit with a mother's hand, momentarily transcending her pettiness, despair, and frantic hope. Was her whole world well lost to her in that gesture? But we surely cannot credit The Misfit's claim that she would have been a good woman if there had been someone to shoot her every minute of her life. This is O'Connor at a loss for an end to this tale, so she gives The Misfit an apparently profound and paradoxical last judgment on her soul. This is well in accord with her artistic credo discovered in 1948 as she read Jacques Maritain's *Art and Scholasticism*. The Catholic writer had above all to be a strong storyteller, not a moralist or a theologian. Follow the craft—Catholic or no, wrote Maritain. Much more interesting than The Misfit's pronouncement is the possibility that the grandmother—dying—becomes a Christ-like vehicle for God's grace, reaching out to a radically displaced Protestant—and thief. The Misfit like Saint Dismas, the thief crucified with and sanctified by

Jesus, is clear about one thing. He did what they say he did—they have the papers on him—but Jesus was innocent. As Luke 23.41 records the good thief saying, "And indeed, we have been condemned justly, for the sentence we received corresponds to our crimes, but this man has done nothing criminal."[57]

The narrator emphasizes The Misfit's vulnerability. He recoils from the grandmother's touch and tone—she has pressed on a tender spot in his psyche: "Without his glasses, The Misfit's eyes were red-rimmed and pale and defenseless-looking." In spite of his bravado—no pleasure but meanness—he's still stuck with Bobby Lee for companionship, fatuous and malignant at the same time. After all, murdering grandmothers in the backwoods scarcely registers on the scale of evil—he's not interested in torturing them. Even his nihilism is hollow. As the penitentiary psychologist divined, he's angry at the world and striking back at it. Finally, he confesses that "It's no real pleasure in life." He is a reflective man in despair. Will this moment open him to praying for forgiveness? O'Connor shared her druthers with the Hollins College audience:

> I don't want to equate the Misfit with the devil. I prefer to think that, however unlikely this may seem, the old lady's gesture, like the mustard-seed, will grow to be a great crow-filled tree in the Misfit's heart, and will be enough of a pain to him there to turn into the prophet he was meant to become. But that's another story."[58]

Damned unlikely. At best, he flips and becomes a peckerwood street preacher, ranting at the cars passing his corner of the courthouse square in some Appalachian mountain town. As she had just warned her audience, her fiction "takes its character from a reasonable use of the unreasonable, though the reasonableness of my use of it may not always be apparent. The assumptions that underlie this use of it, however, are those of the central Christian mysteries."[59] Or, as we've seen in particular, the mysteries of original sin, substitutionary atonement, and justification by grace. Yes, but does it all add up? It's both too pat (Christ-like grandmother and God-seeking Misfit) and too

---

[57] Saint Dismas is the patron saint of undertakers. As The Misfit rebukes the grandmother in her final appeal for his mercy, "Lady…there never was a body that give the undertaker a tip." According to some commentators, Dismas lived in the desert and robbed and killed travelers.

[58] O'Connor, *Mystery and Manners*, 112–113.

[59] Ibid., 109.

outrageous (the whole family—your family?—as collateral damage). Isn't it all over-ingenious?

Where is the narrator when we need him to tell us what it all means? At the crucial moment, with a sympathetic glance at The Misfit "defenseless-looking," the narrator discreetly withdraws. He has played no part in the prayer-full disputation between the grandmother and The Misfit—he has had no comment on The Misfit's fascinating soliloquy—he lets The Misfit have the last self-confounding word. At best, the narrator seems fascinated by this inconsequential, annoying family, trying to salvage some shreds of dignity for them in this moment of truth and terror. This, after having made easy fun of them for half the story.

In spite of her powers of narcissistic self-delusion, the grandmother's little world is crushed before her eyes. In spite of his powers of iconoclastic rebellion, The Misfit's transcendence of the world is mocked by his vulnerability and anger. In spite of his powers of omniscience, the narrator's understanding of the World that encompasses blue granite outcroppings, trees sparkling with silver-white sunlight, the grandmother, Bailey Boy, June Star, Red Sammy Butts and his monkey, The Misfit, and Bobby Lee hovers somewhere between amusement, affection, regret, and hope. What is really going on? The author, Mary Flannery O'Connor, would like to know—but doesn't. And that, dear reader, is the point. There is only one Reality and this is it—whatever *it* truly is. We can't know it—but we must live it. We are accountable. How, why, to whom—from whose perspective? We don't know, but, whether we are the grandmother, or The Misfit, or the narrator standing in for the author, in that cosmic perspective we are accountable for who we are and what we do and why we do it—no matter how hard it is to be that good man. And while faith can provide a metaphysical regime (or two or three) to rationalize our accountability, O'Connor had the good sense and good taste not to intrude didactically on her fiction. Instead, the story is pregnant with the possibility of heart-changing, heart-stopping response to a beyond—to the sacred—and that is enough. As Levinas describes it, "The true desire is that which the desired does not satisfy, but hollows out. It is goodness. It does not refer to a lost fatherland or plenitude; it is not homesickness, it is not nostalgia. It is the lack in a being which *is* completely, and lacks nothing."[60] We are full of ourselves; the grandmother, The Misfit, Red Sammy Butts, all full of themselves. We want what we want, but getting what we want reveals deeper need, not satisfaction: "It's no real pleasure in life." This paradoxical

[60] Levinas, "Philosophy and the Idea of Infinity," 57.

turning away from—before we know there is anything to turn towards—seems to be part of what is captured in the theological vision of "prevenient grace," i.e., enough grace to open us to grace (whether we accept it or not). Prevenient grace means that the Thomistic disputation between the grandmother and The Misfit ends with prayer inexplicably and triumphantly rampant: "Every time we begin to pray to Jesus it is the Holy Spirit who draws us on the way of prayer by his prevenient grace."[61]

## Sacramental Freaks

The comedy and tragedy of human life is that we live in one common Reality but form a multitude of different takes on what that is. From the ground of our own personal perspective, all other perspectives are either congruent with our own or diverge more or less profoundly. The outliers are freaks and fools from our viewpoint, to be reviled or feared or mocked or manipulated. This native pretension to the superiority of one's own perspective is endlessly explored in the stories we tell about our lives and world, whether addressing the author's, a narrator's, or a character's perspective. When such a privileged perspective is seen to collapse (as all of them must eventually, at death if no time else), a momentary radical openness to the overarching Reality dawns. For O'Connor, this moment is incipiently sacramental. Adapting Augustine's formulation, it is outwardly and visibly a moment of existential crisis that is spiritually a moment of transcending Presence, of a lacerating grace. To the extent that the privileged perspective in question is a virtuous or faithful stance in the world, an abyss opens for us: grace reveals us as sinners, whoever we are and whatever we do. This awareness of the inescapability of original sin becomes, paradoxically, our contact with the sacred.

---

[61] *Catechism of the Catholic Church* (1992) part 4, section 1, chapter 2, article 2, note 2670. "Prevenient grace" is both a Catholic and a Holiness/Wesleyan concept and stands in contrast to Calvinism, which insists it is all God all the way, i.e., no free will, no power of turning, no resistance to grace. With Calvinism, there is simply no story to be told between original sin and salvation—God's got it all worked out without our help.

# 3

## Updike's Secular Puritans

*"All things end under heaven, and if temporality is held to be invalidating, then nothing real succeeds."—John Updike*

Bernard Malamud and Flannery O'Connor knew very early that they—coming from modest backgrounds—wanted to be writers, real writers on a national stage. They both worked hard and with extraordinary discipline to refine their gifts and achieve the prominence they sought. John Updike, with a much more prestigious launching pad (Harvard *summa cum laude*, a postgraduate year at Oxford in the Ruskin School of Drawing and Fine Art, and staff writer at twenty-three for *The New Yorker*), was torn between cartooning[1] and writing, which came very easily, even gracefully to him. He very rarely revised what he wrote as he wrote it. As a prolific book reviewer, he complained that he could write faster than he could read. But, he too worked hard for fame. In his career, he published twenty-three novels, fifteen short story collections, seven volumes of poetry, thirteen collections of essays and reviews (over 375 book reviews in *The New Yorker* alone), a memoir, a play, and five children's books. For this writing, he won two Pulitzer Prizes, two National Book Awards, and four National Book Critics Circle Awards. He was inducted into the National Institute of Arts and Letters at thirty-two. He had hoped ultimately for a Nobel Prize.

In spite of this extraordinary success, there were strong critical disagreements about the artistry and value of his work. Bob Batchelor, in his rather uncritical *Critical Biography* of Updike, anointed him "the über American of the American century": "What I find so unparalleled about his work is that he shined this light, in his words, on 'the inner lives of hidden men,' with the

[1] While growing up, he dreamed of being the next Walt Disney. At age twelve, he fell in love with *The New Yorker* and its cartoonists and, as student editor, contributed over a hundred cartoons to the Harvard *Lampoon*. Begley, *Updike* 27–28, 68–71. He eventually published two volumes of well-received art criticism (originally published mainly in the *New York Review of Books*). His eye for visual detail obviously served his highly precise writing well.

deft skills of a social historian and the lyrical grace of a fabled poet."[2] In his tribute to Updike at his death, Julian Barnes, the novelist and critic (and Man Booker Prize winner), confirmed his early judgment that "the [*Rabbit*] quartet was the best American novel of the postwar period."[3] David Baddiel, British novelist, comedian, and script writer—with a double first from Cambridge—goes him one better by declaring: "Let's begin by making one thing clear. John Updike was the greatest writer in English of the last century."[4] By contrast, the first generation of *negative* critics doubted his seriousness. As Batchelor puts it, they accused him of valuing "style over substance" or, as Harold Bloom quipped, "a minor novelist with a major style."[5] And then there was all that slippery, slidey sex. If O'Connor had a maidenly horror of sex and Malamud a fascination with sexual shame, Updike—as man and as author—reveled in the erotic as the passion that drives life forward.[6] The second generation of negative critics, coming of age in the seventies and eighties, despised him: "Just a penis with a thesaurus," as the novelist and essayist David Foster Wallace reported.[7] If we take these criticisms as complaining that Updike—for all his gifts—didn't write in the right way about the right things, then we have presumptive evidence already of his exceptional negative

---

[2] Bob Batchelor, *John Updike: A Critical Biography* (Santa Barbara, CA: Praeger, 2013) ix.

[3] Julian Barnes, "Running Away," *The Guardian* (16 October 2009) www.theguardian.com/books/2009/oct/17/julian-barnes-john-updike-rabbit.

[4] Adam Baddiel, "Suburban Legend," *NewStatesman* (2 May 2014) www.newstatesman.com/2014/04/judging-john-updike.

[5] Batchelor, *John Updike* 9. Harold Bloom, *John Updike* (New York: Chelsea House, 1987) 7. A vicious early review pained Updike to the end of his life—and was echoed by other critics: "He does not challenge the imagination or stimulate, shock, or educate it....Mr. Updike has nothing to say." John Aldridge reviewing *Of the Farm* in the *New York Herald Tribune* in 1965, quoted in Begley, *Updike*, 272.

[6] His breakthrough bestseller, *Couples* (1968) barely skirted libel in its clinical portrayal of riotous suburban sex in Tarbox (Ipswich). The book and the movie rights made him a million dollars—and got him excluded from the tonier environs of Ipswich. Earlier, sexually explicit passages in *Rabbit, Run* (1960) had been deleted at the publisher's gentle insistence. In 1962, with a changing climate toward censorship, Updike restored the cuts, which were included in subsequent printings.

[7] David Foster Wallace, "John Updike, Champion Literary Phallocrat, Drops One; Is This Finally the End for Magnificent Narcissists?" *The New York Observer* (13 October 1997) observer.com/1997/10/john-updike-champion-literary-phallocrat-drops-one-is-this-finally-the-end-for-magnificent-narcissists/

capability—Keats' chameleon Poet with gusto for the mean as well as the elevated, the foul as well as the fair.

However, these critiques (misogyny, objectification of women, unbuckled fascination with sex, narcissistic amorality) would seem to confuse author and character. To accuse Updike of misogyny because his characters are misogynous seems to be a version of what C. S. Lewis called "the personal heresy," the neo-Romantic idea that our interest in the poem is as a revelation of the personality of the poet and that great poetry must have an admirable man or woman as its author.[8] If we knew nothing more about Updike's work than the works themselves, would we find *him* misogynous—if on the basis of his life history we find him misogynous would that explain the function of misogyny *in his works*? We still guess at Shakespeare's identity from the scanty historical record and the sense that a mere player could not have written such sophisticated, large-hearted plays. But the play's the thing—not to be significantly changed if Sir Francis Bacon turns out to have written them! Is Stephen King a monster because he can think his way into monsters' minds, even if it is true that his father abandoned him as a child and he became an alcoholic? W.K. Wimsatt and Monroe Beardsley take this line of reasoning a step further, decrying the "Intentional Fallacy" as supposing the author's intention tells us what is in the work itself.[9] When once gone from the author's hand the play/poem/novel must speak for itself, whatever the author thought he or she was up to in writing it—or whatever deep motives lie behind what he or she wrote. Clues from the author's life and, certainly from her milieu, may help us read more deeply—just as the public meanings of the words used are, of course, essential to grasping and unpacking the story told. But read we must, whatever little or much we think we know of the author.

This is not our last word on misogyny in Updike, however, just a caution to pay close attention to the text itself. We will need much more context before we attempt a decisive word on the relationship between Updike's men and women and their social setting.

Something, indeed, is going on that some elite critics get and some miss. As Lee Siegel observes, "No American novelist with Updike's accomplish-

---

[8] E. M. W Tillyard and C. S. Lewis, *The Personal Heresy: A Controversy* (Oxford: Oxford University Press, 1939).

[9] W.K. Wimsatt, Jr. and Monroe Beardsley, "The Intentional Fallacy," *Sewanee Review* 54 (1946) 468–488.

ments has ever been as dumped on."[10] The British critic, James Wood, led the charge. Wood is one of the most feared—and respected—critics in the world. In an irony that Updike's biographer supposed was "a bitter pill for Updike to swallow,"[11] Wood joined *The New Yorker* staff in 2007 as book reviewer.[12] In a letter written in 2008, Updike admitted that "Woods [*sic*] is a great annoyance, in part because he is so intelligent in a needling, fussy kind of way."[13] Wood's analysis and criticism points to something real and important about Updike's fictions, even if we—I—fundamentally disagree with his judgment. Before plunging into a close reading of Updike, let us see what guideposts we can identify from Wood's complaints.

Wood attacks where it hurts, charging that in various ways Updike is not an accomplished writer (so much for style over substance!): "The sentences have an essayist saunter; the language lifts itself up on pretty hydraulics, and hovers slightly above its subjects, generally a little too accomplished and a little too abstract."[14] Too "dainty," too "delicate," too "gauzy," too "upholstered," too "fine," too "perfect" for the "hard, coarse, primitive, misogynist worldview of these stories" (in *Licks of Love*). Or in *Roger's Version*, when Updike notes in passing a "poignantly breastless" young woman: "'Poignant' is both too poignant a word and not poignant enough....In striving to find good 'literary' words, like 'tender' and 'poignant', he both inflates and deflates language, almost as if he were condescending to himself."[15] Wood's argument is that, when you write about clumsy, broken, vulgar, unreflective people, your language should have analogous defects. Otherwise your prose runs the risk of becoming "high lyric kitsch," disguising a fallen, banal world in "beautiful...equalizing prose": "He is a writer for whom different subjects have the same sensuous textures, whether a vagina, an air-conditioner, or a petal." Curiously, Wood concludes that "Supremely, better than almost any other contemporary writer, he can always describe these feelings and states; but they

---

[10] Lee Siegel, "Writing Off Updike," *The Daily Beast* (1 February 2009) www.thedailybeast.com.

[11] Begley, *Updike*, 460.

[12] Updike published 146 stories in *The New Yorker*. Siegel, "Writing Off Updike."

[13] Begley, *Updike*, 460.

[14] James Wood, "Gossip in Gilt," *London Review of Books* 23 (19 April 2001) 30–31. Subsequent quotations from Wood are all from this review of *Licks of Love*.

[15] Speaking of condescending, one of Wood's central criticisms is that the later Updike is stuck in a rut and out of touch—pitiably retro—in believing that sex matters anymore, much less that it might have some spiritual significance.

are not inscribed in the language itself." This is not just the aesthetic need, in Wood's opinion, to add a "barbaric yawp" or two to his prose, it is a theological position that Wood finds "unmodern" in its "unwillingness, verbally, to acknowledge [God's] silence, failure, interruption, loss of faith, despair, and so on." So on, indeed. As we shall see below, yawping (apologies to Walt Whitman) about the need for transcendence is not the same as trying to find transcendence in sacred words for the mundane. Interestingly, Wood proposes that Updike is "really a kind of pagan writer, for in fact, traditionally, God does not always enable language and its easy flow, but beggars it, forcing the writer into approximations and helpless ineffabilities." Updike has already made that point himself, giving it a much sharper edge. In his memoir, "On Being a Self Forever," written as his mother was dying, he reflects, "Even the barest early facts are unbearably heavy, weighted as they are with our personal death. Writing, in making the world light—in codifying, distorting, prettifying, verbalizing it—approaches blasphemy."[16]

The thing that Wood has ahold of here, but doesn't know what to make of it, is *point of view*. Point of view is key, as we've already seen, to listening for God, listening for a story that is a fragment of something larger, deeper, higher (as I have said). As Wood very rightly warns, "One of the dangers for the stylist such as Updike—and one of the ways in which prose is unlike poetry—is that prose always forces the question: who is thinking in these particular words, and why? Point of view, a boring topic to most readers, is the densest riddle for the novelist, since words are either directly ascribed to characters (first-person narration) or indirectly ascribed to them (third-person narration)." Too often, Wood claims, Updike puts *his* words in his characters' mouths, as in "yet we did divorce, in painful piecemeal, as did Maureen and Rodney," "the pleasantly alliterative phrase 'in painful piecemeal'...slid[es] a filter between the reader and the supposedly pained narrator." But, as we've already explored with Malamud and O'Connor, this blending of voicing/point-of-view may be essential to an author's larger purpose. The accomplished stylist and highly successful British novelist (Man Booker Prize winner), Ian McEwan, sets this straight and is worth quoting at length:

> Like Bellow, his only equal in this, Updike is a master of effortless motion—between third and first person, from the metaphorical density of literary prose to the demotic, from specific detail to wide

[16] John Updike, *Self-Consciousness: Memoirs* (New York: Random House, 1989) 226.

> generalization, from the actual to the numinous, from the scary to the comic. For his own particular purposes, Updike devised for himself a style of narration, an intense, present tense, free indirect style, that can leap up, whenever it wants, to a God's eye view of Harry [Angstrom], or the view of his put-upon wife, Janice, or his victimized son, Nelson.... Updike once said of the Rabbit books that they were an exercise in point of view. This was typically self-deprecating, but contains an important grain of truth. Harry's education extends no further than high school, his view is further limited by a range of prejudices and a stubborn, combative spirit, and yet he is the vehicle for a half-million-word meditation on postwar American anxiety, failure, and prosperity. A mode had to be devised to make this possible, and that involved pushing beyond the bounds of realism. In a novel like this, Updike insisted, you have to be generous and allow your characters eloquence, "and not chop them down to what you think is the right size."[17]

So, we will take two main questions away from Wood's querulous quibbles. What is Updike using his finely crafted words to do that other more plebian and clumsy words cannot do?[18] And how do his characters see things and see themselves seeing things?—how does the narrator see the characters?—how does the author see the story, the narrator, the characters?—how does God see us all?—and how do we see *ourselves as readers* through these many shifting, merging vantage points?

Within Updike's huge corpus of work, the Rabbit Angstrom tetralogy stands out: *Rabbit, Run*; *Rabbit Redux*; *Rabbit Is Rich*; *Rabbit at Rest.* This extraordinary project is a historical novel in reverse. Instead of simply reconstructing a period of time through the lives of his characters, he projects his characters forward into a yet unlived future.[19] His creative task is to take the

---

[17] Ian McEwan, "On John Updike," *New York Review of Books* (12 March 2009).

[18] This is not to suppose that he always succeeds. His style walks a slack rope, so to speak, because it is so flexible. Often enough, he will fall off.

[19] The project evolved unintentionally. *Rabbit, Run* ended on the note of a future utterly unresolved. A decade later, uncharacteristically stymied on a major writing project begun while living in England, feeling he owed his publisher another novel, and unnerved by the Sixties attacks on American pieties, he cranked out in very short order *Rabbit Redux* "as a receptacle for my disquiet and resentments," he tells us. John Updike, "Introduction," *Rabbit Angstrom: A Tetralogy* (New York: Knopf, 1995) xiii. Now, he had a saga going, "a boxed life," with careful symmetries between the first two Rabbit novels. Ibid., xviii. As he said at the time, "Anybody

measure of the social moment decade by decade, at the end of the Fifties, Sixties, Seventies, and Eighties, and, at the same time, of the seasons of a man's life, Rabbit born in 1933—like Updike (1932)—and dead in 1989—unlike Updike (2009). And the creative task is to do this not knowing in advance how to take the man we come to know (and his friends and family) into a future we do not. This precisely mirrors the amphiboly of our lives—endings and beginnings inextricably intertwined in the moment, but only seen as such retrospectively. And we must double-down on the fluidity of story told and story telling because, of course, the writer has no way of foretelling at the moment who he will be (or be seen to be) as writer, citizen, husband, father, man a decade later, i.e., no way of foretelling what or how he will write then. All this means that we must take care to read the novels in order and to read each novel as if we had no clue what was coming in the next one. Indeed, the speculation that *Rabbit at Rest* was not the last of Rabbit was kept alive by the final words of that novel: "… enough. Maybe. Enough."[20] (*Rest* 1516). But at the end of the Nineties, Updike instead published "Rabbit Remembered," a 189-page novella, which has Rabbit dead but not ended—yet.[21] And ten years later, John Updike was himself dead but not ended—yet.

In the beginning, Harold C. Angstrom (Harry/"Rabbit" to his teammates/"Hassy" to his mother) and John Hoyer Updike shared the same social and cultural space, growing up in the "same" place at the "same" time. Most of Updike's best work was patently autobiographical in its origin (and many of its details).[22] However, like Malamud and O'Connor, he was deeply ambivalent about his origins, honoring them and drawing on them while fleeing them. In Updike's case, this was doubly complex because he was deeply

who cared could get some really interesting formal things out of the two books together." Quoted in Begley, *Updike*, 341.

[20] References to the novels will all be from the Knopf edition of the Tetralogy cited above and hereafter indicated in the text parenthetically with an abbreviated title and page number, i.e., *Run, Redux, Rich, Rest.*

[21] *Rabbit Remembered* was published as a sequel together with twelve short stories in John Updike, *Licks of Love* (New York: Random House , 2000). References to *Rabbit Remembered* will be from this edition and included parenthetically in the text with abbreviated title as *Remembered.*

[22] In his memoirs, he describes the streets of Shillington, Pennsylvania, where he lived until he was thirteen, whose "deceptive simplicity composed their precious, mystical secret, the conviction of whose existence I had parlayed into a career, a message to sustain a writer book after book." Updike, *Self-Consciousness*, 24.

adored by his mother (an aspiring, modestly successful writer herself), who nevertheless was the one who insisted he must leave the small-minded, small town he grew up in (and not marry the girlfriend who would have kept him there). Interestingly, virtually the only lasting social friendships he made were with old high school friends. Again like Malamud and O'Connor, he also often strove to sympathetically represent characters from familiar but fundamentally alien milieus (e.g., wonder-working rabbis and murderous misfits, respectively). His most provocative creation in this vein is Henry Bech, twenty stories collected in three books about a comically "successful" Jewish-American writer with writer's block—a version of Norman Mailer with touches of Malamud: "I made Bech as unlike myself as I could."[23] Rabbit, on the other hand, is both autobiographical *and* alien. "Rabbit" Angstrom is made of the same stuff as John Updike but lives a mundane version of his life, the life Updike's mother feared would be his if he stayed in Shillington: "the muddy routine that seems to be the usual lot of God's creatures."[24] This imagined parallel universe, the one most similar to where most of "us" (White, lower to middle class, American) live out our lives, presents us with two critical, existential challenges.

*First*, how does Updike's life measure up from the perspective of Rabbit's?[25] Where is the glittering transcendence to be found that transfigures Updike's all too mundane adulteries, neglect of his children, narcissism,[26]

---

[23] John Updike, "One Big Interview," *Picked-Up Pieces* (New York: Random House, 1975) 486.

[24] In a letter to Updike from his mother, Linda Grace Hoyer Updike, written in 1951 and quoted in Begley, *Updike*, 75–76.

[25] This line of inquiry not only flouts Wimsatt and Beardsley's injunction against the Intentional Fallacy, it stomps all over it. But this whole extended essay, part and parcel, is asking how Malamud, O'Connor, Updike, and Morrison use their stories to help us "listen for God." This is not a question of how their characters "listen for God." It is a question of how we use these stories to—as I have said—tune our ears to the voice of the sacred in human life. Updike and his alter-ego, Rabbit Angstrom, offer us an extraordinary gamble on what matters most, not Rabbit's life, not Updike's life, but the words that convey them both, *about* Rabbit (whose life is given in full) *by* Updike (whose life is fully given to them). This will become a little clearer below.

[26] In a 1982 public television documentary, Updike's son David reproached his father, who "decided at an early age that his writing had to take precedence over his relations with real people." Updike acknowledged the charge: "my duty as a writer...takes precedence for me over all these other considerations." Begley, *Updike*, 9.

continuing emotional dependence on his mother's love and his father's respect, public struggle with a stutter and shaming psoriasis, literary focus on the banal, avid desire for fame and honors, and gleefully enjoyed social and financial success? Is it possible, instead, that Rabbit—*in his ordinariness*—is more memorable than his author? As Updike himself judged, "What I saw through Rabbit's eyes was more worth telling than what I saw through my own."[27] If so, does this paradoxically count as a kind of transcendence, the secular as sacral? As Updike himself put it in the poem "Earthworm," "Immersed in the facts, one must worship there."[28] Can mere description transfigure the world; can the word make God present to us in a way that mere living does not? Behind this question skulks one of the great Protestant theological dilemmas. When you insist on God's absolute Otherness and banish knowledge of Him from the workings of the world, from the authority of Church dogma, and from the categories of the human mind, you are left only with Scripture, *sola scriptura*, as guide and revelation. With its tattered history and tangled logic, the Bible is not only a deplorably weak and varying reed, but, as Karl Barth insisted, evangelical fundamentalism verges on idolatry—only Jesus is the Word of God made flesh. *Are there any mortal words that can reveal the sacred to us?*

*Second*, we can flip the first question and ask: how does Rabbit's life measure up from the perspective of Updike's authority? As he famously explained, "my only duty was to describe reality as it had come to me — and to give the mundane its beautiful due."[29] Comparing himself to Vladimir Nabokov,[30] he described "a writer's covetousness…akin to the fear of death," whose symptom was a "constant state of anxiety compelling one to fix indelibly this or that evanescent trifle."[31] When we take Rabbit straight, no symbolic sleight-of-hand, what do we have—and how does "the beautiful

---

[27] Updike, "Introduction," *Rabbit Angstrom*, vii.

[28] *John Updike and Religion: The Sense of the Sacred and the Motions of Grace*, ed. James Yerkes (Grand Rapids, Michigan: William B. Eerdmans, 1999) 2.

[29] John Updike, "Foreword," *The Early Stories, 1953–1975* (New York: Knopf, 2003) xvii.

[30] Nabokov's *Speak, Memory* (1966) is an astonishing feat of memory, preserving and transforming an utterly lost past in hallucinatory, precise sentences and phrases. In Updike's words, "inspired by an atheist's faith in the magic of simile and the sacredness of lost time, Nabokov makes of his past a brilliant icon—bejewelled, perspectiveless, untouchable." Updike, *Picked-Up Pieces*, 180.

[31] John Updike, "The Translucing of Hugh Person," *Picked Up Pieces*, 199, quoted in Begley, *Updike*, 363.

mundane" measure up to eternity? Is there anything in this life that gives us a purchase on a meaning that survives death? Behind *this* question lurks an immense Protestant *moral* dilemma. When you insist on God's absolute freedom and isolate Him from any consequences for His actions, salvation becomes a blind game, totally dependent on God's inscrutable, irresistible, irrevocable, antecedent grace, *sola gratia.* As we have already seen in the character of O'Connor's The Misfit, "filthy" antinomianism is a persistent temptation for the Reformed. If you are already saved, it doesn't matter what you do—it won't do you any ultimate harm. If you aren't already saved, it doesn't matter what you do—it won't do you any ultimate good. Sometimes, it may seem that both John Updike and Rabbit Angstrom are living out this moral ambiguity. *Is there anything we can do, think, or feel in this mortal world that will give us hope for redemption from sin and death?*

With these huge and ramifying questions in mind, we can dismiss the idea that Updike is an intellectual lightweight, all style and no substance. He does not mean to discuss big ideas; he means to enact them. Let us see how he does it.

## *Rabbit, Run.*[32]

The novel begins by looking backward to a founding moment in Rabbit's life that is already an irrelevancy, except in memory—his high school years as a basketball star in the little town of Mt. Judge, setting county scoring records as a junior and again as a senior. Twenty-six years old, heading home on a Friday evening from his job hawking MagiPeel Peelers in dime stores, he walks into a teenage pick-up game in a back alley. Incongruously, he carefully folds his suit coat and asks to play. His first shot swishes; his second is an air ball. But, it comes back to him: "That his touch still lives in his hands elates him. He feels liberated from long gloom. But his body is weighty and his breath grows short." (*Run,* 7) He jogs the rest of the way home, throwing his pack of cigarettes in a trash can as he passes. He climbs the stairs to the third-floor walk-up he shares with his pregnant wife, Janice, and their two-year-old son, Nelson. The door is locked; he scratches at the lock with his key and finds her in an armchair watching the Mickey Mouse Club show on TV, a

[32] Updike began writing *Rabbit, Run* early in 1959 and the first draft was completed September 11, 1959. According to the author, the fictional action of the novel takes place from March 20, 1959, to June 24, 1959.

glass with the dregs of an Old Fashioned beside her (he doesn't drink, still keeping his body pure):

> "You're *here*," he says. "What's the door locked for?" She looks to one side of him with vague dark eyes reddened by the friction of watching. "It just locked itself." "Just locked itself," he repeats, but bends down to kiss her glossy forehead nevertheless. (*Run* 8)

Immediately, there is an allusion to another founding moment, also rapidly becoming an irrelevancy. Janice is barely twenty-three, but Harry sees the new wrinkles shaping a "greedy" mouth, the thinning hair, and remembers the first days of sex with her, before marriage, in her girlfriend's bed after work: "She could be sudden then.... Nerves like new thread. Skin smelled like fresh cotton.... She made him keep his eyes shut. And then with a shiver come as soon as he was in her, her inside softly grainy, like a silk slipper" (*Run* 13–14). Now, it is always a struggle. He calculates that he has screwed her maybe 300 times in their three years of marriage. He's "an order-loving man," (*Run* 8) and the clutter and slop, as he looks around the room before going to retrieve their son from his mother's house, "clings to his back like a tightening net." (*Run* 14).

The narrator here and elsewhere provides commentary that glides from rendering Rabbit's musings and memories to painting a picture of Janice and Rabbit and their circumstances. The narrator's eloquence elevates Rabbit's internal monologue both directly and by association. Now, as he leaves, "Rabbit freezes, standing looking at his faint yellow shadow on the white door that leads to the hall, and senses he is in a trap. It seems certain. He goes out" (*Run* 15). How much of this is Rabbit and how much is narrator is uncertain—particularly Rabbit's "certainty." But we can be certain that the narrator is not going to miss anything of relevance. We will have a dispassionate, God's-eye view of what is in Rabbit's mind and feelings and in his circumstances. We are not allowed inside Janice's perspective, however. Her actions and words are glossed: "She opens her brown eyes and tears fill them and break over the lower lids and drop down her cheeks, pink with injury, while she looks at him and says, 'You bastard' very thoughtfully" (*Run* 12). What does Janice think or feel? We don't really know—anymore than Rabbit does: In what seems to be mostly Harry: "'Jesus. You're a mess.'... When confused,

Janice is a frightening person. Her eyes dwindle in their frowning sockets and her little mouth hangs open in a dumb slot" (*Run* 11).[33]

If the narrator is God-like, watching and helping Rabbit make his case, the author is much more directly involved in setting up the scene and its deep plot. In fact, in these first few pages, Updike literally as well as figuratively draws us a roadmap for the novel. The metaphor is too blatant and too extended not to be noticed—and it takes us far, far beyond Rabbit's timid angst. What is the story being spun here? Obviously, the basic plot is time itself. Twenty-six years old and your best days are already past, the days of bodily grace and quicksilver erotic energy. He runs up the alley, "Past the deserted ice plant with its rotting wooden skids on the fallen loading porch" (*Run* 7). "Just yesterday, it seems to him, she stopped being pretty" (*Run* 8). "She used to make it easier before they got married....After work, working both at Kroll's then, she selling candy and cashews in a white smock with 'Jan' stitched on her pocket and he lugging easy chairs and maple end tables around on the floor above" (*Run* 13). "He used to love to climb the poles. To shinny up from a friend's shoulders until the ladder of spikes came to your hands, to get up where you could hear the wires sing" (*Run* 15). "This farmhouse, which once commanded half of the acreage the town is now built on, still retains, behind a shattered and vandalized fence, its yard, a junkheap of brown stalks and eroded timber" (*Run* 16). "And then [at the summit of Mt. Judge], coming upon...a softened stone-filled cellar pit dug by some brave and monstrous settler centuries ago, you become vividly frightened" (*Run* 17). Now, "[sneaking] down the strip of grass between the two cement walks that go with the two brick walls" of the side-by-side duplexes where his parents live, he remembers his childish impressions of Mrs. Zim in the building next door screaming at her beautiful little daughter and at her husband when he defended her, of his mother's fury at the old, strict Methodist who succeeded the Zims and refused to mow more than his nine-inch half of the eighteen-inch-wide strip of grass, and of his parent's quarrels "cutting off air; his strength drained away and he had to go to a far corner of the house" (*Run* 19–20). Looking into his parent's kitchen, he has a momentary vision of his son Nelson as himself in a highchair, his father now looking old, tired, and grizzled. Sneaking past the Springer's, Janice's parents, to retrieve their car, he recalls how old man Springer pressured him to buy the newer car before

[33] When the narrator does condescend to give us Janice from the inside, it is to display her anxious slide into drunken incoherence from dawn to noon as she "prepares" to drown little Rebecca June in Rabbit's renewed absence (*Run* 217–27).

their wedding—ashamed because used cars were Springer's business. Driving away he distracts himself from what he is doing by recalling his little sister Mim on the handlebars of his bike or being pulled uphill on his sled (*Run* 18–23). Rabbit is surrounded by fragments of a decaying past with nothing of his own but memories of what is lost—the future is just a net, a trap, to catch a Rabbit.[34]

So, he runs. But here the plot thickens because you can run in space but not in time. Space must be traversed; time must ultimately be renewed or fulfilled or annihilated—or simply marked and wasted. It is clear what Rabbit is running from—domesticity. "Sheltered by his chest and arms she blurts with an earnestness he didn't know she still could hold, 'Don't run from me, Harry. I love you'" (*Run* 12). What is unclear is what he is running to. However, this particular Friday evening, as he slithers away from the Springer's in his '55 Ford, marks the day before the vernal equinox *and* the last two days of Lent. After trying all night to drive toward "the South": "orange groves and smoking rivers and barefoot women" (*Run* 23), he ends up back in Mt. Judge and on Palm Sunday he will awaken in the city of Brewer—on the other side of the mountain—in a whore's bed. He has taken the long away around to get not too far in space—but maybe he makes it to a new beginning in time: the new season of spring and Passion Week with its annual/eternal resurrection ahead of him.

The whole motif of roads and running is almost incidental. According to Updike, he intended *Rabbit, Run* as a parodic response to Jack Kerouac's recently published, much fabled *On the Road.* In the February 25, 1959, issue

---

[34] Updike claimed that he was thinking of Beatrix Potter's Peter Rabbit when he gave his character his nickname. And, indeed, the themes of *Rabbit, Run* play out true to her breakthrough, turn-of-the-century, children's book, the rabbits—like sex—both naturalistic and symbolic. To jump the gun a bit on our story, Peter, unlike his sisters, is naughty, poaching in a garden of forbidden delights. Caught in the act, he dodges and runs as Death (Mr. McGregor, who has already killed and cooked his father in a pie) pursues him, Rabbit hiding (like Peter) amidst "the flowerpot red" city of Brewer. Leaving his clothes behind him, he squeezes through the gate at the last minute and makes it home to Mommy (cooking dinner like Ruth, the whore) and, finally, he gets a dose of medicine (a dead baby—maybe two) for being a bad and reckless boy. There's no evidence he has learned his lesson—or wants to. Calling this a mythic mode, Updike admits it may be semi-conscious: "For example, only lately do I see that Brewer, painted the color of flowerpots, is the flowerpot that Mr. McGregor slips over Peter Rabbit." "John Updike, The Art of Fiction No.43," interviewed by Charles Thomas Samuels, *Paris Review* (Winter 1968).

of *The New Yorker* he published a satiric sendup of Kerouac's 1957 novel as "On The Sidewalk (After Reading, at Long Last, "*On the Road*," by Jack Kerouac)." The contrasts and consonance with Kerouac are notable. We can contrast Kerouac's manic, stream-of-consciousness style with Updike's refined, precise descriptions. We can contrast Kerouac and friends' ceaseless movement across the continent, across girlfriends, wives, and children, with Updike's endless mining of Berks County, Pennsylvania, and familiar suburban domestic arrangements. However, crucially, Kerouac and Neal Cassidy's flight from death and their search for IT ("two Catholic buddies roaming the country in search of God," as Kerouac later described it) seem to match Updike and Rabbit's quests. As Updike later explained, what he wanted to do in *Rabbit, Run* "was to write a book in which going on the road had consequences, to explore what might have happened had Kerouac's Sal Paradise left a wife and child behind."[35]

Let us follow the mile markers Updike has set out for us on this faux road to nowhere. It is, indeed, literally a roadmap of missed turns, misreadings, and bad instincts: "He drives through a thickening night. The road unravels with infuriating slowness, its black wall wearilessly rising in front of his headlights no matter how they twist" (*Run* 31). Route 422, Route 100, 23, 10, 222, 1, 137, 482, 26, 340. Pottstown, Coventryville, Elverson, Morgantown, Lancaster, Churchtown, Bird in Hand, Paradise, Intercourse, Mt. Airy, Mascot, and another dozen towns: "The names melt away and he sees the map whole, a net, all those red lines and blue lines and stars, a net he is somewhere caught in" (*Run* 33). Outside of Churchtown, he passes an Amish buggy in the dark, a bearded man and a woman in black "glaring like devils....Tall coffin lined with hair clopping along to the tune of a dying horse....Fanatics. Worship manure." who are stubbornly holding onto old, old ways in a fraudulent MagiPeel Vitaconomy (*Run* 27).

But the real map, the real net, is Mt. Judge, its familiar streets and alleys—and its topography, up to the mysterious, frightening, abandoned pine plantation at its scenic view top and down the other side into the city of Brewer (fifth largest in Pennsylvania). Wilbur Street, Potter Avenue, Kegerise, Jackson, Joseph, Central. At the beginning of the novel, his progress is down, from one scene of supposed domesticity to another: from his and Janice's third story walkup, down to his parents' duplex where his son is being fed supper, further down to the big, leafy Springer house where Janice left

[35] David Ulin, "For better or worse, John Updike produced a nearly endless stream of work," *LA Times* (27 January 2009).

their car parked going shopping with her mother. As he finally drives back around the mountain along the Shining Horse River from Brewer to Mt. Judge in the early dawn of the first day of spring, his flight aborted, he passes by his parents' house and parks in front of the Sunshine Athletic Association, an old man's back alley bar with card tables on the second floor, and—up in a corner of the attic—an Army cot and a bureau made of six beer crates, his old coach's flophouse digs since scandal had ousted him from his position at the high school and from his home ("My wife calls me a person to be abhorred") (*Run* 48). It is a surrogate parent's pitifully degraded domesticity. In the morning light, when Rabbit runs after him, Marty Tothero, "look[ing] like a big tired dwarf," says the "perfect" thing. "'Harry,' he says, 'wonderful Harry Angstrom.'" (*Run* 37–38). Harry sleeps fitfully in Tothero's cot all day, awakened by Tothero after six. He's set up a Brewer dinner date for himself and Harry, with his "tenuous" girlfriend, Margaret Kosko, and a friend of hers, Ruth Leonard. Tothero assures Harry he'll like Margaret, "'She is a remarkable girl, Harry, with seven strikes against her from birth, but she's done a remarkable thing.' 'What?' 'She's come to grips. Isn't that the whole secret, Harry; to come to grips?'" (*Run* 47).

Harry is looking for the secret, the secret of being an adult, having a family, making a living, making time count, making life happen—never so alive as he is in bed with a woman. Tothero is just one of several he looks to for the secret. With Janice he watches the end of the Walt Disney show. Jimmie, the big Mouseketeer, sings: "'Proverbs, proverbs, they're so true,' Jimmie sings, strumming his Mouseguitar, 'proverbs tell us what to do; proverbs help us all to *bee*—better—Mouse-ke-teers.'" Rabbit attends closely, expects to learn something helpful to him selling MagiPeelers: "[Jimmie] pinches his mouth together and winks. That was good. Rabbit tries it, pinching the mouth together and then the wink, getting the audience out front with you against some enemy behind" (*Run* 10). Know thyself, advises Mouseketeer Jimmie. Come to grips, advises Coach Tothero. The farmer who fills his tank from old-fashioned bubble-headed pumps on his run to West Virginia and back, asks him "'Son, where do you want to go?' 'Huh? I don't know exactly.' 'Where are you headed?' The man is patient. His face seems fatherly and crafty and stupid" (*Run* 25). The only map the farmer has is for New York State. As Rabbit slams the door, the farmer—the scent of whiskey on his breath—leans into the open window: "The only way to get somewhere, you know, is to figure out where you're going before you go there" (*Run* 26).

Two days later, Rabbit is moving in with Ruth in her Brewer apartment, a try at *illicit* domesticity: "She shakes her head heavily and says, 'You're bad news'" (*Run* 84). The *second* thing Ruth does for him is cook (Janice is no cook, just a dumb mutt, he says over and over). What does he want? His next mentor manqué, the Reverend Jack Eccles, arrives in a '58 Buick four-door Special, nosing up to him as he carries a ball of his clothes away from their abandoned apartment. He's about Rabbit's age, a little older, the Springer's Episcopalian minister:

> "Uh, what, exactly, is your plan?" "I don't really have a plan. I'm sort of playing it by ear." Eccles' laughter surprises him; it occurs to Rabbit that the minister is an expert on affairs like this – broken homes, fleeing husbands – and that 'playing it by ear' has struck a fresh note. He feels flattered. Eccles has this knack." (*Run* 90)

Unexpectedly, they make a date to play golf on Tuesday, Rabbit never having played. "Ah. Here's the hook" (*Run* 93).

We have most of the milestones in place. Within the first hundred pages of the novel, six versions of domesticity or *Kinder, Küche, Kirche* are set before us: dumb mutt, bad cook, sloppy drunk Janice (a nominal Christian who will undergo her own crucifixion: "the worst thing that has ever happened to any woman in the world has happened to her") (*Run* 226), tough working-class Mother Angstrom (Lutheran), judgmental middle-class mother-in-law Springer (social-climbing Episcopalian), Tothero the abhorrent and humiliated dwarf (an unrepentant pagan who sees women as repellant cunts, "They are monkeys, Harry. Women are monkeys.") (*Run* 47), Ruth the fat whore with a soft heart (who finds it impossible not to *not believe* in God), and Eccles' wife, a thoughtful non-believer, in her fashionable imitation Greek-temple Rectory, "A crisp little number with speckled green eyes" (*Run* 100). Four types of male mentors/models are consulted: Jimmie the Mouseketeer with his phony popular culture, the old farmer immemorial as dirt, Tothero the failed coach shaping the head, the body, and the heart of boys to play an elegant game, and Eccles the doubting priest burdened with his wife's, parishioners', and dead father's/God's expectations. Domesticity is women's business. Mentoring is men's. But only the women have any real force to them, even dumb mutt Janice who is finally selected for incomprehensible suffering. The men are supernumeraries. (Fritz Kruppenbach, the Angstrom's Lutheran minister is an exception to this, but he believes that in God's eyes we are all supernumeraries. The last thing he wants is to mentor anyone, especially not a *Schussel*—butterfingers—like Rabbit.) Now, Updike lets Rabbit speak his own piece—self-mentoring, as it were, a supernumerary too often to his own life. Then, the benchmarks for navigating the net will have been put in place. It will do no good. The elaborate roadmap is useless, its elaboration underlining its uselessness. The only destination is up Mt. Judge to a cemetery and a baby's grave—time annihilated before it even begins.

In his first encounter with Eccles, Eccles asks him what Janice did to make him leave: "I don't know, it seemed like the whole business was fetching and hauling, all the time trying to hold this mess together she was making all the time. I don't know, it seemed like I was glued in with a whole lot of busted toys and empty glasses and the television going and meals late or never and no way of getting out" (*Run* 91). Eccles challenges him: "You speak of the feeling of muddle. What do you think it's like for the other young couples? In what way do you think you're exceptional?" (*Run* 92). Rabbit has an implausibly articulate answer ready—it is so out of rhetorical character that Updike must have really wanted to draw our attention to it: the first rate, the exalted, the transcending. It is a homely first cousin to Kerouac's IT:

> "You don't think there is any answer to that but there is. I once did something right. I played first-rate basketball. I really did. And after you're first-rate at something, no matter what, it kind of takes the kick out of being second-rate. And that little thing Janice and I had going, boy, it was really second-rate." (*Run* 92)

Eccles brings God into it; what does God want for Janice in the situation? Rabbit has a response to that too, one of Mouseketeer Jimmie's proverbs: Be Yourself—"God doesn't want a tree to be a waterfall…God gives to each of us a special talent," says Jimmie/Harry (*Run* 10). Eccles tells him God wants him to grow up and protect his wife. Rabbit explodes: "Well, I'm not going back to that little soppy dope no matter how sorry you feel for her. I don't know what she feels. I haven't known for years. All I know is what's inside *me*. That's all I have" (*Run* 93).

And that is all we will have from beginning to end of *Rabbit, Run*. What is inside Rabbit. What is special about Rabbit. What Rabbit is holding on to against domesticity, against "maturity," against all the advice. He is even holding out against his own nature. As Eccles identifies for Mrs. Springer, "The strange thing about Angstrom, he's by nature a domestic creature" (*Run* 134). Ruth's judgment bookends our judgment of Rabbit. She likes him enough to put up with him moving in: "'Cause you haven't given up. In your stupid way you're still fighting.' He loves hearing this; pleasure spins along his nerves, making him feel immense" (*Run* 80). But, finally, confronting him with her own pregnancy and his abandonment—after Janice has accidentally drowned their new born daughter—she says what all of us have been thinking almost from the beginning: "Why don't you look outside your pretty skin once in a while?" (*Run* 259). Rabbit is likeable. His wife, his mother, his sister, Ruth, Marty Tothero, Jack Eccles, old Mrs. Smith for whom he gardens (paying off Peter Rabbit's debt to Mr. McGregor), all like him, like being around him. But he is despicable, selfish, disloyal, self-satisfied. Jazzed from attending church and flirting with the minister's wife afterwards, he insists that Janice satisfy him sexually while she still has stiches from child birth—and her refusal sends him off again, which puts in train the drunken drowning of his diarrhea-splattered baby: "'Why can't you try to imagine how I *feel*? I've just had a baby.' 'I can. I can but I don't want to, it's not the thing, the thing is how *I* feel. And I feel like getting out. 'Don't. Harry. Don't.' 'You can just lie there with your precious ass. Kiss it for me'" (*Run* 213).

Updike the author suffuses this climactic train of events with Harry's deepest sense of the world. The narrator tells us that the presence of the new baby Rebecca June "fills the apartment as a little casket of incense fills a chapel" (*Run* 200). "Thick sweet love" for Janice nursing the baby "burdens his chest" (*Run* 201). A week later at Eccles' invitation he attends church. "He hates all the people on the street in dirty everyday clothes, advertising their belief that the world arches over a pit, that death is final, that the wandering thread of his feelings leads nowhere. Correspondingly he loves the ones dressed for church,...[giving] substance and respectability to his furtive sensations of the invisible" (*Run* 201–02). As he kneels in the pew, "his head buzzes with joy, his blood leaps in his skull, and the few words he frames, *God, Rebecca, thank you* bob inconsecutively among senseless eddies of gladness" (*Run* 202). Lucy Eccles happens to be seated in front of him, half hidden behind a wide straw hat: "There is something sexed in her stillness in the church, in her obedience to its man-centered, rigid procedure" (*Run* 204). Walking her home after the service, Harry flirts with her, imagines she is flirting with him, presumes on her invitation to a cup of coffee, and has the door slammed in his face: "Whether spurned or misunderstood, Eccles' wife had jazzed him up, and he reaches his apartment clever and cold with lust" (*Run* 208). And baby Rebecca June dies, slipping out of her drunken mother's hands in the bathtub—a "baptism" that Eccles, Rabbit's weakly compliant alter ego, will strain later to see as a sacramental sacrifice.

Surrounded by a dense world of people and places, a world no worse or no better than it should be, Harry preserves a simple-minded purity or intention, perhaps a saintly purity:[36]

> Goodness lies inside, there is nothing outside, those things he was trying to balance have no weight. He feels his inside as very real suddenly, a pure blank space in the middle of a dense net. *I don't know*, he kept telling Ruth; he doesn't know, what to do, where to go, what will happen, the thought that he doesn't know seems to make him infinitely small and impossible to capture. Its smallness fills him like a vastness. (*Run* 264)

This reflection of German Lutheran Pietism's "inner light," with its distain for liturgy, sacrament, theology, the Law, the communion of saints, and God's saving word in Jesus the Christ, matches Jack Eccles' extra-ecclesiastical/golf course engagement with Rabbit. It harkens back even to the Desert Fathers, seeking God in themselves in their huts—with sexual repression *and* fornication the only real challenges to their detachment from the world. (As Eccles cattily remarks, "It's the strange thing about you mystics, how often your little ecstasies wear a skirt.") (*Run* 111) For a *Schussel* to have aspirations to be a saint is the *ne plus ultra* in narcissism.

More profoundly, Updike is evoking the whole Puritan tradition embedded in the literary form of the realistic novel itself. As Ian Watt first brilliantly identified, a secularized Puritanism was one of the two most important formative influences on the eighteenth-century evolution of the modern novel from its beginnings in the romance, *videlicet*, (1) the rise of bourgeois economic individualism and (2) the confusion of religious and material values in an ebbing Puritanism. The first replaced myth and allegory as plot with the individual actions of ordinary people in the various circumstances of life and discarded classical style and aristocratic virtue in favor of plain speaking and commercial values. The second, as Watt identifies it, "inherited of Puritanism everything except its religious faith":

[36] The boy who didn't drink, who never fouled on the basketball court. At the swimming pool, full of contentment, loving his Ruth, she asks him "'What's so special about *you*?' 'I'm a saint,' he says. 'I give people faith.' Eccles had told him this. Once, with a laugh, probably meaning it sarcastically....Rabbit took this to heart. He never would have thought of it himself. He doesn't think much about what he gives other people" (*Run* 124).

> [Novelists in this tradition of formal realism] all have an intensely active conception of life as a continuous moral and social struggle; they all see every event in ordinary life as proposing an intrinsically moral issue on which reason and conscience must be exerted to the full before right action is possible; they all seek by introspection and observation to build their own personal scheme of moral certainty; and in different ways they all manifest the self-righteous and somewhat angular individualism of the earlier Puritan character.[37]

In this tradition, egocentricity and isolation and a resistance to confining values of affection, family, community, and church are perennial problems for the novels' heroes. Even sex is a temptation threatening to draw the hero away from his or her pursuit of merit and distinction. And, for the novelist, the problem of formal realism becomes, as Watt describes it, "how to impose a coherent moral structure on narrative without detracting from its air of literal authenticity."[38] The novelist's moral sensibility had to gain purchase, not through direct comment or tendentious imagery or irony, but indirectly through point of view, the from-whence of literal description. Updike's hero—or as Robert Detweiler denominates him "nonhero"[39]—appears to us from the far shores of this intensely individualized spirituality, where even "Sunday" church is too much of a civic demand: a thoroughly secularized Puritanism. With this as deep background, let us look first more closely at Rabbit the character—and then more closely at Updike the author.

What is Rabbit's problem? He is looking within for a vaguely remembered God. Pure and simple: "Well, I don't know all this about theology, but I'll tell you, I *do* feel, I guess, that somewhere behind all this...there's something that wants me to find it" (*Run* 110). The narrator confirms this unequivocally as Rabbit prepares to attend Eccles's church: "His feeling there is an unseen world is instinctive, and more of his actions than anyone suspects constitute transactions with it" (*Run* 201). This quest—whose metaphor is a sweet set shot or a long, straight drive off the tee or his hands heating a woman's body to his touch—naturally elevates his diction.[40] He is straining

---

[37] Ian Watt, *The Rise of the Novel* (Berkeley: University of California Press, 1957) 85.

[38] Ibid., 117.

[39] Robert Detweiler, *John Updike* (Boston: Twayne, 1984) 38.

[40] These metaphors have in common a "hole" which you must penetrate, the basketball hoop, the golf cup, the vagina. The first two depend on a launch and a freely falling trajectory, once launched there is no longer any control, i.e., God may

towards something and away from something—looking for a touchstone for the unfathomable, something that marks the difference between just living and being alive, between prose and poetry, between oblivion and purpose. Eccles clearly distinguishes it from his own babbling, counterfeit belief. Yet, to his father, Earl Angstrom, he has become "the worst kind of Brewer bum." As a boy he didn't make such messes: "He was a tidy worker" (*Run* 140). What is he, this double-backed monster? The other characters in the novel emerge as complex and interesting personalities, with characteristic styles and perspectives on life, on Harry, on Janice. The narrator grooms them as if they are on a stage. They are almost all of them more fully realized and more humanly interesting than Harry. But none of them have his inwardness. They are sites of transactions with the world and with each other. None of them propose to transcend this world or even transcend their mundane acceptance and complaint about this world. They are thoroughly—brilliantly—who they are. Only Harry does not know. At the cemetery burying little baby Becky, he does the unpardonable. Feeling the rightness of the ceremonial words and attentive mourners, he senses a descending strength and emerging light: "All gathered into one here to give his unbaptized baby force to leap to Heaven" (*Run* 252). He turns and Janice's face "dumb with grief" blocks the light. "'Don't look at *me*,' he says, 'I didn't kill her.'…'*She's* the one.'…. [It's] just the simplest factual truth" (*Run* 253). Surely, it is the way God must see it? Even his protective mother is horrified.

He runs up Mt. Judge away from the cemetery and their accusing eyes, dodging Eccles' grasping hands—and, like an anti-Moses, walks down the other side of the mountain to Ruth, his pagan fertility goddess. In the wake of the baby's death, Coach Tothero, half paralyzed by strokes, had disabused him of reverence for the Laws: "Right and wrong aren't dropped from the sky. We. We make them. Against misery" (*Run* 240). Old man Springer has reinforced the lesson: "The question I always ask myself in a bad situation is, How do we cut the losses from here on in?" (*Run* 246). The Laws are merely utilitarian, of a piece with Mouseketeer Jimmie's proverbs. Eccles

---

or may not speak to us, however hard we listen for him. The nether hole of a woman ["vagina"] is blindly sought by a sightless "eye" cloaked with a feeling skin, never out of contact, a sure thing, i.e., a substitute for God or at least for death. As Jack Kerouac once summed up his friend Neal Cassidy's quest: "sex was the one and only holy and important thing in life." (Steven Watson, "Beat Generation: Neal Cassidy," *Waiting for the Sun,* archives.waiting-forthe-sun.net/Pages/ArtisticInfluences/Beats/Beat-Bios/cassady_bio.html.)

blasphemously conflates Jesus' atonement for our sins with baby Rebecca's sacrifice: "I think marriage is a sacrament, and that this tragedy, terrible as it is, has at last united you and Janice in a sacred way" (*Run* 241). These revelations chill Rabbit: "He wants to believe in the sky as the source of all dictates" (*Run* 241). Maybe, it all *is* just a roadmap—if you know where you want to go.

At least, Ruth's arms are real. But she pushes him away as a rat and killer: "No, you don't do anything. You just wander around with the kiss of death" (*Run* 260). Harry is in love with life. He likes making things live: Nelson, Baby Rebecca June, old Mr. Smith's rhodies—for one last time—and now his and Ruth's baby in the womb. But to create life is to bring death into the world. From Adam and Eve on down. That's why there has to be more. Ruth threatens abortion. Divorce Janice or forget me: "If you can't work it out, I'm dead to you and this baby of yours is dead too" (*Run* 262). "The sensation he had counted on, of being by nature her mate, of getting on top of her, hasn't come" (*Run* 260). Nevertheless, "'You have it,' he coaxes. 'Have it.'...He loves women when they're first pregnant; a kind of dawn comes over their bodies" (*Run* 261). He'll feed her, make love to her, "I'll work it out" (*Run* 262). But, in spite of Tothero, Springer, Eccles, his father, all of them, he cannot imagine working it all out, the guilt, the responsibility, "the mere engineering of it" (*Run* 263). So, "he runs, Ah: runs. Runs" (*Run* 264). Updike commented in 1995 that "the book ends on an ecstatic, open note that was meant to stay open, as testimony to our heart's stubborn amoral quest for something once called grace."[41]

This is all very unsatisfying—maybe even outrageous. Its banal offensiveness is impossible to romanticize away. What *are* we meant to think of Rabbit? The question is inescapable—Updike insists that we ask it. Updike/Rabbit's fear of death and endless nothingness, "a jumble of horror" as his youthful protagonist calls it in "Pigeon Feathers,"[42] is one kind of rationale

---

[41] Updike, "Introduction," *Rabbit Angstrom*, x.

[42] "Without warning, David was visited by an exact vision of death: a long hole in the ground, no wider than your body, down which you are drawn while the white faces above recede. You try to reach them but your arms are pinned. Shovels pour dirt into your face. There you will be forever, in an upright position, blind and silent, and in time no one will remember you, and you will never be called. As strata of rock shift, your fingers elongate, and your teeth are distended sideways in a great underground grimace indistinguishable from a strip of chalk. And the earth tumbles on, and the sun expires, and unaltering darkness reigns where once there were stars."

for his desperate and despicable behavior. Poor dumb mutt Janice will scarcely suffice to keep time at bay. Nature's springing mandate to erotic passion is another kind of rationalization: *Penis erectus non conscientiam habet.*[43] Time momentarily fulfilled and obliterated in corporal climax—and renewed in corporal generation. However, Rabbit is surrounded by people judging him at every step of the way, from dime store audiences to his mother/father/priest. Every woman who arouses him judges him: Janice, Ruth, and Eccles' wife Lucy. In lieu of judging himself, he runs and runs—to nowhere. So, how does Updike the author judge him? As William Deresiewicz concludes after reviewing Updike's lifelong work and reputation, "Updike watches, but he doesn't judge. He doesn't judge Rabbit's unbreakable narcissism, his inability to love anyone except himself, including his children.... That he doesn't judge has been the hardest thing for readers to accept, both then and now."[44] As Updike himself warns in his "Introduction" to the Everyman's Library publication of the entire tetralogy in 1995, "Rather than arrive at a verdict and a directive, I sought to present sides of an unresolvable tension intrinsic to being human. Readers who expect novelists to reward and punish and satirize their characters from a superior standpoint will be disappointed."[45] Michial Farmer offers a crucial insight into this diffidence, but may miss the larger import:

> All of this points to the dialectical ethics of Updike's fiction—what he calls in a famous interview its "yes, but" quality.... That dialectic results in one of the more frustrating aspects of Updike's fiction for some readers, which is that his characters do really atrocious things and he refuses to judge them. The novels are moral novels in the sense, that, as he once put it, they ask the reader, "What is goodness?"—but that's just a matter of presenting the dialectic rather than settling on side or the other, and rather than coming to some sort of synthesis/

---

John Updike, "Pigeon Feathers," *The New Yorker* (19 August 1961) www.newyorker.com/magazine/1961/08/19/pigeon-feathers.

[43] Shakespeare concludes his Sonnet 151: "No want of confcience [pun on French *con*-science, i.e., cunt-science] hold it that I call, / Her loue, for whofe dear loue I rife and fall."

[44] William Deresiewicz, "'A Great Symphony of American Junk': What David Foster Wallace misunderstood about John Updike," *The New Republic* (8 September 2014) newrepublic.com/article/119200/updike-reviewed-william-deresiewicz.

[45] Updike, "Introduction," *Rabbit Angstrom*, xi.

> conclusion. The question is always open: Rabbit is both a spiritual striver and a terrible person, and you can't have one without the other.[46]

Which is the "yes" and which the "but"? Neither seems like an acceptable solution. A spiritual striver (who has not quit trying, as Ruth says) but immature and selfish and driven by lust (as Eccles judges him). Or, as Robert Detweiler describes him, "Irresponsible, undependable, and gutless, Rabbit is the quintessence of the nonhero. That Updike has not made him an entirely despicable man but has instead cast him in the ironic mold makes the portrayal all the more effective."[47] On a quest but screwed up—with the possibility of a comedy of redemption? Or screwed up but with intimations of something more—with tragic despair or mere degradation at the end? But Updike actually takes this dialectic a radical step further. Would we want to have one without the other? Would God want one without the other? Are we onto something beyond discursive resolution?

All of this is even more delicately balanced than Farmer or Detweiler indicate. The interlude gardening for Mrs. Smith on her formerly elegant estate introduces an Edenic and cosmic perspective:

> SUN AND MOON, sun and moon, time goes. In Mrs. Smith's acres, crocuses break the crust. Daffodils and narcissi unpack their trumpets. The reviving grass harbors violets, and the lawn is suddenly coarse with dandelions and broad-leaved weeds. Invisible rivulets running brokenly make the low land of the estate sing. . . . and the earth itself, scumbled, stone-flecked, horny, raggedly patched with damp and dry, looks like the oldest and smells like the newest thing under Heaven. (*Run* 117)

And so on and on—beautifully evocative. This lends extra weight to acerbic Mrs. Smith's final encomium: "You kept me alive, Harry; it's the truth; you did. . . . That's what you have Harry: life. It's a strange gift and I don't know how we're supposed to use it but I know it's the only gift we get and it's a good one" (*Run* 192). This more than balances Ruth's accusation of Harry's "kiss of death" or—better—encompasses it. But, even more significantly,

---

[46] Michial Farmer, "On Updike: An Interview with Michial Farmer on Updike in the Contemporary Moment," *Former People* (8 April 2017) www.formerpeople.wordpress.com/2017/04/08/on-updike-an-interview-with-michial-farmer-on-updike-in-the-contemporary-moment/

[47] Detweiler, *John Updike*, 38.

Harry's three months in the blooming Garden opens a perspective for us that has no roadmap. Its autochthonous variety and vitality escapes conventionality, swells the richness of life, from the singularity of the Bianchi rhododendron to the great profusion of Horace Smith's overgrown, "rhododendron plantation."[48] Against the tired little rules for human behavior in 1950's Mt. Judge, the whole of the human imaginary looms in this riotous profusion. At the same time, those habitual and prudential conventions are revealed as truly exotic, as exotic as "the single big flower Oriental temptresses wear on the sides of their heads on the covers of the paperback spy stories that Ruth reads" (*Run* 118). From this anthropological perspective, the dregs of Janice's Old Fashioned perched in front of the Mickey Mouse Club TV show is as astonishing as the San-Graal paraded before Perceval in the hall of the maimed Fisher King![49] All quests are not equal, but all are equally quests. We with Perceval must ask the right questions. But what are they? From what perspective *are* we to judge Harry and Janet?? The point seems to be deepening the reader's disorientation—not resolving it.

In his 1968 *Paris Review* interview, explicating his "yes, but" quality of storytelling, Updike makes the astonishing claim that a guilt-free character, a guilt-free Rabbit, would cease to be a person: "Unfallen Adam is an ape.…I feel that to be a person is to be in a situation of tension, is to be in a dialectical situation. A truly adjusted person is not a person at all—just an animal with clothes on or a statistic."[50] A spiritual striver who was a good person, a person of perfect faith, must in the world's eyes be a holy fool, a Don Quixote, a Candide, a Houyhnhnm, a King of the Jews, a martyr surrounded by faithful pagans. We can see that such a character would be useless to the storyteller except for satiric or didactic purposes. But might not God prefer that we all be such? Certainly, God would not prefer Rabbit Angstrom to St. Francis of Assisi, would He? Updike seems to have stumbled into a mare's nest of illusion and confusion—no wonder we wish he had simply judged Rabbit for us and been done with it.

---

[48] One can hardly refrain from thinking of Manderley's profusions of overgrown, blood red rhododendrons, tokens of the drowned and famously promiscuous Rebecca in Daphne du Maurier's 1938 novel of that name and Alfred Hitchcock' s first Hollywood movie (1940) winner of his only Best Picture Academy Award. Updike was a precocious eight years old.

[49] This is what James Wood gets so badly wrong about Updike's "high lyric kitsch."

[50] "Updike," *Paris Review.*

Here, context is all. We must try to make a distinction where it necessarily eludes us. First, how does Updike as the human author think about these things? Certainly, over the next decade—as his marriage (in 1953) to Mary Pennington dramatically falls apart (in 1962), comes back together as mildly resentful and mutual infidelity, and finally ends (in 1976)—he does not go easy on himself and his personal guilt and regret. The deeply autobiographical novel, *Marry Me*, lay buried in a bank deposit box for fourteen years because it would have been too hurtful to those who had been close to him and half a dozen stories about unhappy adulterers, intended for *The New Yorker*, were at his request put on "the shadow bank" by his editor—to be held until time had cooled their offense a bit. As Begley wonderfully elicits, the bottom line for these artful sublimations of suffering is consistent; the misery of carnal love thwarted is—in Updike's writerly mind—equally a matter of conscience and timidity, duty and cowardice.[51] As Updike judges himself, so must he judge his alter-ego, Rabbit. If anything, his treatment of Rabbit puts his character on the hook even more keenly. This is no mere preemptive *mea culpa*—much less in the style of Philip Roth, *épater la bourgeoisie*. So, what *are* Deresiewicz and Farmer pointing to—or better yet, what is Updike *pointing to*? Paradoxically, it is Rev. Eccles who orients us by getting it exactly wrong: "'The truth is,' Eccles tells him with womanish excitement, in a voice embarrassed but determined, 'you're monstrously selfish. You're a coward. You don't care about right or wrong; you worship nothing except your own worst instincts'" (*Run* 115). No. It is nothing so easy to identify nor so easy (on paper) to fix or condemn as this suggests. It's not a matter of what you worship or what moral roadmap you follow. Later, Fritz Kruppenbach makes the crucial second distinction for us as he chastises Jack Eccles: "What do you think now it looks like to God, one childish husband leaving one childish wife? Do you ever think any more what God sees? Or have you grown beyond that?"[52] How *does* God think about these things? This is the context in which spiritual striving must be authenticated—to even get to the "yes, but." This is the scrambled question for Updike, as much as for Rabbit. The personal imperfectly, fatally mixed with the religious, echoes "the melancholy, long, withdrawing roar" of "Dover Beach" of a century before, now

[51] Begley, *Updike*, 227–55

[52]For Kruppenbach, the issue isn't the run-of-the-mill Angstroms and Springers, it's Eccles—God's self-anointed little fixer. After all, "'If Gott wants to end misery, He'll declare the Kingdom now'" (*Run* 146).

ebbing at last on the shores of Updike's Ipswich,[53] its once envisioned restoration in a Puritan "City upon a Hill."[54] So scrambled, the question must be approached indirectly, metaphorically, suggestively.

There is a simple but profound conundrum here. If we could figure out God's own judgment of us (from scripture, conscience, priest, revelation, reason, whatever), then God's judgment would be nothing but a species of (privileged) human judgment. But, if we *cannot* figure out God's judgment of us, how can it even be relevant to how we live? The Levinasian solution to the conundrum is simply that with every look, every face, every regard, we know we have been judged and found guilty—before we have done anything—which is enough, maybe too much! It's not the content of the judgment that matters or its casuist application; it's the vertical dimension it opens in Being: the Sacred. Updike defeats every attempt to bring Rabbit within the ordinary gambit of right and wrong—without abandoning him to the worship of his own worst (or best) instincts. *He keeps him on the hook.* As Rabbit himself laments, "It disgusts him to feel the net of the law slither from him. They just won't do it for you, they just won't take you off the hook" (*Run* 246). He is on the hook before the face of God. The BIG hook. The only hook that is not just human power, prejudice, prudence, or propaganda in disguise. Let us see how he wiggles.

---

[53] The Sea of Faith "Retreating, to the breath/Of the night-wind, down the vast edges drear/And naked shingles of the world." Matthew Arnold, "Dover Beach," begun in 1849 and first published in 1867.

[54] John Winthrop, *City upon a Hill*, 1630. "For we must Consider that we shall be as a City upon a Hill, the eyes of all people are upon us; so that if we shall deal falsely with our God in this work we have undertaken and so cause him to withdraw his present help from us, we shall be made a story and a byword through the world, we shall open the mouths of enemies to speak evil of the ways of God and all professors for God's sake; we shall shame the faces of many of gods worthy servants, and cause their prayers to be turned into Curses upon us till we be consumed out of the good land whether we are going." Ipswich was founded by John Winthrop the Younger, Governor Winthrop's son, in 1634.

## *Rabbit Redux*.[55]

Ten years later, the ecstatic openness of *Rabbit, Run* has been replaced with a "stale peace" (*Redux* 271), about to be disturbed, shattered, reinvented. Time scabs over all wounds—or almost. They all still dance a little around the baby's death and Harry's betrayal, as if the wound were deep, but the narrator tells us that Harry "has become sole heir to the grief" (*Redux* 297). Although maybe at this point, they are simply recirculating the dance of avoidance, kicking the can of *meaning* on down the road to be dealt with later. Time is again the deep plot of the novel, but now it is the future crashing in on them, unexpected, disorienting. Offering Rabbit a second chance—Rabbit *redux, restored*—perhaps. Second chance at what? In 1959, Updike could not, of course, have imagined the Sixties—although arguably Jack Kerouac already had anticipated them as the founder of the Beat Generation in the midst of those Eisenhower years. But that helter-skelter decade was ready made to let Rabbit try on another skin—and Janice too. This time around Rabbit will try it Kerouac's way: drugs and beatific, apocalyptic visions, with Skeeter—skinny, Black Jesus—as Rabbit's motor-mouth Neal Cassidy.[56] Unfortunately, for Nelson—the promised and only one—emerging into adolescence, his skin will shrink, mummifying him before his time. Not for him, the ecstatic openness of his father—he is cursed, as Mom Angstrom insists, with those small Springer hands. (Even his eventual wife, Teresa/Prudence, is an inch taller than he will be.) What if anything can redeem the even bigger mess Rabbit creates this time? Where's the grace when we *really* need it?

*Redux* also gives Updike a chance to respond to the large questions left gaping by *Run*. Is being a yearning, hyper-narcissistic *Schussel* enough to redeem life from its end in death, is straining hyper-articulately toward the inarticulable Beyond enough to sacralize your existence? Is Rabbit the only one truly alive in *Rabbit, Run*? On the other hand, suppose Rabbit had followed the advice he received? Suppose he had become dutiful and docile and followed the roadmap laid out for his momentary, inconsequential existence? Suppose the people around him are the real people and he's the ghost? What *were* his alternatives? These are usually not relevant questions for a work of

[55] Updike began writing *Rabbit Redux* February 7, 1970 and the first draft was completed December 11, 1970. The fictional action of the novel takes place from July 16, 1969 to mid-October, 1969.

[56] Neal Cassidy died in Mexico at forty-one in 1968 of "systemic disintegration," Jack Kerouac aged forty-seven in 1969 of cirrhosis of the liver.

fiction—out of bounds, as it were. But here they become generative questions, not simply continuations of what was in the original novel. This is the genius of Updike's unique format of retrospective prospect. These questions become almost as real as life, or maybe even realer than life, questions.

Finally, it was his father, Earl, who became his role model. He's now a Linotyper like his Pop working for Verity Press. ("Verity Press" is a signal that we are to deal with a ham-fisted author this time, for whom print—the written book—is intrinsically immutable.) Rabbit's instinct for order is measured by ninety possible brass matrices and kept orthodox by the spacebands necessary to justify a rail of type—while nevertheless slinging molten lead. (As we will see, Updike considers setting type—making an order of words—a mundane first cousin to actually authoring the novel, slinging smoldering passions and hot sex.) Shared drinks at the Phoenix Bar in Brewer (a ham-handed signal of the fire out of which their marriage will reemerge) marks the end of an ink-stained working day before Harry catches the bus home to his recently acquired suburban "villa" and his son Nelson (Janice working until late at night at the Springer's new Toyota franchise) and his father rides the bus back around the mountain to his failing wife—Parkinson's Disease. Mim, the little sister who adored him, is a high-priced hooker in Vegas. The narrator tells us soothingly that Harry and his father, working together for ten years, "have grown into the love they would have had in Harry's childhood, had not his mother loomed so large between them" (*Redux* 270). However, within days, Neil Armstrong will set foot on the moon, and Harry will discover his wife is fucking Charlie Stravos down at the car lot. By the end of the novel, Harry's highly skilled job will be eliminated by new technology, and his new house will burn down. The road map isn't working out so good—these are all unprecedented destinations. The old story becomes a newly new story.

For one thing, it becomes Janice's story too. It is not so much Rabbit *redux*, as Janice *ducere*? Janice leading. This is the moment to redress the charge of misogyny. Misogyny is hatred, contempt, or distain for women—except as sex objects. The charge against Updike is that his fictions share a *worldview* that is misogynist, not just that the male characters in his fictions are misogynist but that the presumed narrators are misogynist as well. In *Rabbit, Run*, "dumb mutt" Janice epitomizes this denigrating perspective. Give Janice a break, give her an internal voice, give her at least as much humanity as Rabbit—please! Of course, when we do get to *Rabbit Redux*, we see

Rabbit/the narrator treating Skeeter (with his giant Afro) with even greater distain. Is it racism? Racism is hatred, contempt, or distain for people of color—except as objects of fear. Let us back up a step; the narrator clearly treats Rabbit as a feckless jerk, surrounded by other men just as foolish, ineffectual, and hen-pecked as he is. Maybe, we are in something bigger than mere misogyny or racism? Maybe Updike's worldview is full-blown misanthropy. Misanthropy is hatred, contempt, or distain for the whole human race—except as a mirror held up to God's face. There will be more about this below.

In *Redux*, Janice is treated as a newly set free, sexually liberated woman, outsmarting her husband at every turn, and admired—for a time—by an intelligent, interesting man who likes to talk to her as much as he likes to "sell her herself" as he licks her flesh. She has a hard time believing that she—small, dark, clumsy, bad-with-numbers Janice—is adorable. And she really, really likes the sex. Of course, she is not a hard driving, *au courant*, "lean in" striver. But neither is anyone else, male or female, in the novel. Successful, beautiful, cutting-edge people are not what Updike is writing about in the Rabbit novels—male or female. Deciding to leave her frail and overwhelmed lover in favor of the all-too-married husband, she leads Harry back to the connubial bed and her familiar curves of flesh, just as handily as Penelope puts Odysseus to the test of their rooted marriage bed—after long absence and extended dalliance. (Nelson, however, doesn't fare nearly so well as Telemachus, perhaps because Nelson didn't have the advantage of hero-worshipping distance from his father's shenanigans.) By the time Rabbit is ready to rest *at age fifty-five*, Janice will own the Toyota dealership and run the show. And he will muse on "That strange way women have, of really caring about somebody beyond themselves" (*Rest* 1327).

But, why bring back (redux) Rabbit, caught at last amongst the word salads of the Press, to register this "polluted and fractious time," as Updike recalls it in his memoir "On Not Being a Dove."[57] It is not just to give Janice

[57] Updike, *Self-Consciousness*, 115. Christopher Ricks observed at the time that *Rabbit Redux* "never decides just what the artistic reasons (sales and nostalgia are another matter) were for bringing back Rabbit instead of starting anew; its existence is likely to do retrospective damage to that better book *Rabbit, Run*." Christopher Ricks, "Flopsy Bunny," *New York Review of Books* (16 December 1971). Ricks's slur echoes Plato's famous slander that poets—unlike philosophers—have only the

her due. As sequel, the book is already over determined, especially with the formal symmetries Updike took delight in pasting into *Redux*. The setting transitions from Mt. Judge walk-up to Brewer suburban villa. His formidable mother goes from sharp-tongued protector to shuffling, mumbling invalid. This time it is Janice who leaves behind Nelson and moves in with her lover—and saves a life (her lover's) rather than loses one (her daughter's). This time it is Rabbit whose self-indulgence carelessly allows a girl to die (by fire in *Redux*, water in *Run*)—and allows the man (Skeeter) who left her to die in an upstairs bedroom to escape without consequence. Where Janice drank too much whiskey, Rabbit smokes too much dope. Eccles's half-hearted conventional (White) Christianity is replaced by Skeeter's grandiose (Black) apocalypticism as a possible answer to Rabbit's spiritual quest. In guilty passivity Rabbit loses the ability even to masturbate, while Janice unbuttoned and self-assertive discovers the joys of sex. Jazzed, Janice wears out her clever, Greek, car salesman lover, whereas Rabbit's Ruth becomes a fat, hard, chicken farmer's wife. The possibility of their hide-and-seek daughter, Annabelle, holds open the question of Rabbit as the kiss of death or as life giver. Put this bluntly, the book seems more plot mechanism than plot.

In short, those gaping questions left dangling by *Run* receive a curiously—but maybe necessarily—unambitious answer in the end. Facing the ruins of their crappy, burned-out "villa," recalling the ruins of their and the Fosnacht's marriages (wall-eyed Peggy Gring Fosnacht, whose bed and body Harry was sharing as his house and "virginal" Jill burned up), Harry and Janice end up at the crummy *Safe Haven Motel*. Too much, Updike, too much! It begins to sound like *Pilgrim's Progress*; maybe it is all an allegory after all?[58]

Rabbit as "Christian" everyman fits the parody. He is burdened with a Biblical sense of sin and been told (in that long ago Sunday school) that salvation/resurrection is promised. Unable to find his own way to the Celestial City of deliverance, instead he follows "a shining light" that only he sees and leaves his wife and children to pursue it. Along the way he falls into the Slough of Despond. When Jill first convinces him to shelter Skeeter, lest the

---

pleasure of their audiences (and perhaps their money) in mind, rather than the truth, i.e., they tell fascinating lies about the gods.

[58] John Bunyan's elaborate allegory, *The Pilgrim's Progress from This World, to That Which Is to Come* published in 1678, was one of the most influential pieces of Christian literature ever written—and, written in plain language, arguably one of the first novels in the European tradition.

pigs "crucify" him as a dope dealer, Rabbit feels the Black man as opening a cesspool under him "a pit of scummed stench impossible to see to the bottom" (*Redux* 447). As he explains to Janice, he could not stand to go back to Peggy again:

> "Couldn't stomach it, frankly. It wasn't her, she was great. But all this fucking, everybody fucking. I don't know, it just makes me too sad. It's what makes everything so hard to run." "You don't think it's what *makes* things run? Human things." "There must be something else." She doesn't answer. "No? Nothing else?" Instead of answering, she says, "Ollie is back with her now, but she doesn't seem especially happy." (*Redux* 611)

Like Bunyan's Christian, pilgrim Rabbit is again offered misleading advice to just follow the rules. The Mr. Worldly Wiseman, Mim, urges him to listen to Mr. Legality and his son Civility in the village of Morality:

> "Why don't you tend your own garden instead of hopping around nibbling at other people's?" Mim asks.... "I have no garden," he says. "Because you didn't tend it at all. Everybody else has a life they try to fence in with some rules. You just do what you feel like and then when it blows up or runs down you sit there and pout." "Christ," he says. "I went off to work day after day for ten years." (*Redux* 587)

No Grace, all Works. Mim knows what she is talking about, living in the desert with gangsters: "Gangsters are puritans. They're narrow and hard because off the straight path you don't live. Another rule they have is, Pay for what you get because anything free has a rattlesnake under it. They're survival rules, rules for living in the desert" (*Redux* 578). No Grace, all Works. The city of Vanity Fair and the silver mine of Hill Lucre that lie ahead will wait on the temptations and indulgences of *Rabbit Is Rich* (Rabbit and Janice making love on a pile of gold Krugerrands).

In the meantime, pilgrim Christian has already had the crushing burden of sin removed, conveniently rolled into Christ's empty tomb. With that, Updike ends his flirtation with Protestant Christian misanthropy—ends it in the Safe Haven Motel. Reuniting, sleepy and shy they snuggle naked in the afternoon motel bed, talking in desultory "spurts" (again, Updike, too much): "[her breasts'] presence near his lips drugs him. All sorts of winged presences exert themselves in the air above their covers." (*Redux* 617) Christian's three angels? Or is it the first ever—oh, so careful—docking of two extraterrestrial vehicles in Soyez 4 and 5 (the epigraph to the novel)? "'I feel so guilty.' 'About what?' 'About everything.' 'Relax. Not everything is your fault.' 'I can't accept that'" (*Redux* 618–619). Then limply nestling his prick along "the curved crevice between the polleny...orbs of her ass," his hand "comes upon the familiar dip of her waist": "He finds this inward curve and slips along it, sleeps. He. She. Sleeps. O.K.?" (*Redux* 619). Docked. As the epigraph quotes Lieut. Col. Shatalov in Soyez 4, "It took me quite a while to find you, but now I've got you." Asleep, original Adam and Eve, rescued from fallen despair in the crummy Safe Haven Motel. Is this the best we can do? A little bit of mutual forgiveness and mutual need, baby Rebecca and run-away Jill floating off as radiant debris, Janice's reassurance that Nelson will get over it (he won't), the comfort of the lost and newly found familiar, fucking not the *whole* story after all, and a 350 page book ended. O.K.?

Not O.K., says Christopher Ricks, as he proceeds to dismantle Updike's artifice. The elaborate parallelisms with the moon shot "too much solicit attention" without delivering corresponding elevation.[59] His gibberish errors on the Linotype machine, printed into the novel as if set in type for *The Vat*, reflect his fury and guilt too neatly, as if words failed the masterly author. The "oral hang-up" shared by Rabbit, Jill, and Skeeter shows up distastefully in the narrator's descriptions of the television "spurting" and the refrigerator door "sucking." According to Ricks, it's either inept or suggestive, and in the latter case "it blurs the distinction between Rabbit and his creator which admirers of the book are having to argue is scrupulously maintained." Rabbit's being canned at the very moment he is setting the type for the news report of the fire and Jill's death, Ricks reads as a cover up, a trumped-up punishment that is not too punishing—just as Rabbit was always let off at the last minute in *Run*: "We are to give a more than even break to this particular sucker and suckee." In an interesting piece of psychoanalysis, Ricks puts his finger—he thinks—on Updike's weakness. He is so enamored of Rabbit running, his first great success (and maybe, like basketball-playing Rabbit, anxious that it may be his only great success), that he will always let him off the hook, "all mercy and no justice," and thus leave him without the depth that interests the great authors and their readers. Curiosity is replaced by analysis and explanation. Quoting T. S. Eliot, Ricks concludes, "where the desire to understand and explain outweighs curiosity, the author restricts himself more and more; he confines himself to analyzing what he has put together; his

---

[59] Ricks, "Flopsy Bunny," *New York Review*. Sir Christopher Bruce Ricks is a connoisseur of poetic diction (former Professor of Poetry at Oxford University) and a master of practical criticism—W. H. Auden considered him the ideal critic for a poet. All quotations from Ricks are from this review.

characters become easily exhausted, because the writer can extract no more than he has deliberately put in."

Leaving aside the fact that *langue*, the deep structure of socially shared language, always imports more structurally into any individual text or *parole* than the author can intend,[60] Ricks is not wrong about the mechanics of *Redux*. He just has not taken his analysis far enough to see what may going on in the broader exchange between author and readers. Against the latter-day literary rules, Updike is vigorously signaling to the reader above the heads of his characters and narrator. In his *Paris Review* interview, Updike lamented that conventional criticism denigrated "the presiding, talkative, confiding, and pedagogic author,...[feeling] that something has been lost with this authority, with this sense of an author as God, as a speaking God, as a chatty God, filling the universe of the book."[61] *Redux* signals above all else that it is *written*, it is literally printed and—as he says in the interview—"there is some cerebral effort needed to turn a bunch of mechanical marks on a page into moving living images." In his memoir, "Getting the Words Out," he both expresses his bewilderment at the criticism that "I wrote all too well but had nothing to say" and traces his fascination with "The papery self-magnification and immortality of printed reproduction." In the case of his critical bewilderment, he insists that critics had it exactly backwards. He had "the whole mass of middling, hidden, troubled America to say,...that would take a whole lifetime to sort out, particularize, and extol with the proper dark beauty," whereas "My own style seemed to me a groping and elemental attempt to approximate the complexity of envisioned phenomena." In the case of his fascination with print media, starting in childhood with alphabet blocks and typewriter impressions and proceeding to cartoons and comic books, with their pen lines, cross-hatching, and benday, only very gradually did he come to conceive of the possibility of making *a book*: "I have trouble distinguishing between the functions of the publisher and those of the printer. The printer, in my naïve sense of the literary enterprise, is the solid fellow, my only real partner, and everyone else a potentially troublesome intermediary between

[60] The distinction of *langue* and *parole* is Ferdinand de Saussure's famous contribution to semiotics, see *Cours de linguistique générale*, published in 1916 after Saussure's death.

[61] "John Updike, The Art of Fiction," *Paris Review*.

him and myself.…To be in print was to be saved."[62] The key to reading Updike is to *read* him:

> My models were the styles of Proust and Henry Green…styles of tender exploration that tried to wrap themselves around the things, the tints and voices and perfumes of the apprehended real. In this entwining and gently relentless effort there is no hiding that the effort is being made in language: all professorial or critical talk of inconspicuous or invisible language struck me as vapid and quite mistaken, for surely language, printed language, is what we all know we are reading, just as a person looking at a painting knows he is not looking out of a window.[63]

So, let us briefly pick up where Ricks left off. The readerly *Redux* is all distance from naïve mimesis and naïve moralism—we are *not* looking through a window. Updike's parody of Bunyan's *Pilgrim's Progress* is only one among many parodies in the novel that press us back into the mind of the author. The "projected" copies of *Vat* articles in process of being typeset,[64] replete with typos and inversions (the matrices being read backwards by the operator), are joined by frequent imagined headlines that comment on the action—and seem to belong neither to the narrator nor the character: "CLINIC FOR RUN-AWAYS OPENED. *Fathers Do Duty On Nights Off*" (Redux 390), which pops up on the page as Rabbit massages and compliments Jill's breasts their first time in bed together. TV newscasts, including coverage of the York race riots occurring 50 miles away, and TV shows like *Laugh-In* are partially transcribed into the text. Then, there are the great chunks from classic abolitionist literature "read aloud" into the text: Theodore Parker and William Lloyd Garrison and Frederick Douglass. Both

---

[62] In the "Introduction" to the Tetralogy, Updike comments that the Linotyper "was the blue-collar equivalent of my sedentary, word-productive profession." Updike, "Introduction," *Rabbit Angstrom*, xiii.

[63] John Updike, "Getting the Words Out," *Self-Consciousness*, 103–108.

[64] Updike seems here to be rubbing our noses in readerly convention. The type has not been cast, inked, or printed (and will not be with the errors—usually shown as corrected and thus somehow fixed "in progress") but it is on the page as a distinctive font and isolated by generous whitespace from the rest of the text on the page of the book, an immutable printed fact, in fact, to which we can recur. We the readers—making a cerebral effort—have no trouble decoding this fantasy and placing it in Updike's fictive world, although ontologically never printed, corrected typos are a graphic impossibility.

Rabbit and Skeeter, with their inhuman nicknames,[65] are given eloquent set pieces—more or less out of character, neither are *that* articulate. Rabbit defends the Vietnam War to Charlie Stravos and Janice, just as Updike did in real life with Philip Roth and others.[66] Skeeter harangues and insults and unmans Rabbit in a kind of parody of "niggerization": "Chuck, you're learning to be a loser. I love it. The Lord loves it. Losers gonna grab the earth, right?" (*Redux* 533). In Skeeter's verbal world where "Mr. Charlie" (and "Miss Ann") were pejoratives for Whites reaching back to slavery, Rabbit becomes "Chuck" and Nelson "Babychuck," and they blend in with his stories of fighting Victor Charlie, "VC" the Viet Cong, in Nam. James Baldwin's *Blues for Mister Charlie*, produced and published in 1964, turns on a murdered Black man who had bragged on having sex with White women—and was inspired by the lynching of Emmett Till in 1955. Black Skeeter's living room sex with White Jill, spied on by the neighborhood children, finally leads to his attempted lynching, the firebombing of their home by irate neighbors. Other characters also come too neatly packaged verbally. Stravos, another "Charlie," is given an eloquent antiwar screed.[67] Nelson is allowed his only moments of eloquent pleading for care and love, flashes of his father's feeling that the carnal is not the last word. Even Pop is allowed to express some beautifully demotic racial prejudice.

From plot to parody and self-parody *Redux* is indeed over determined—the presence of the author is unmistakable from beginning to end. This upends the preferred illusion that the formally realistic novel is really happening—or *could* really happen. We are reminded again and again that the thoughts, feelings, and actions pretended to be the characters' and narrators' are nothing but the author's word pictures, which is to say that it is not the imagined characters' and narrators' task to make meaning of their world, each other, and themselves. It is the real-life author's purposes and interests that count: "As a phantom of my imagination, he [Rabbit] was always, as the

[65] In Rabbit's fascination with Skeeter, he contrasts blobby white faces with "The curious greased grace of his gestures, rapid and watchful as a lizard's motions, free of mammalian fat" (*Redux* 484). The overdone alliteration is surely Updike's self-parody?

[66] "I wanted to keep quiet, but could not. Something about it all made me sore. I spoke up, blushing and hating my disruption of a post-liberal socio-economic-cultural harmony I was pleased to be a part of." Updike, "On Not Being a Dove," *Self-Consciousness*, 126.

[67] In another parenthetical wink, Greek "stavros" is the "cross" on which Janice impales herself to find sexual redemption.

contemporary expression has it, *there* for me, willing to generate imagery and motion. He kept alive my native sense of wonder and hazard."[68] This double vision, within the story and above the story, is not just Updike playing God. By analogy, it is God playing God, regarding Adam and his descendants with a "native sense of wonder and hazard." Updike is retelling the sacred story, in an utterly mundane register, where transcendence is both absolute (as author) and relative (as mundane).

A story opens up the sacred by testifying to a radically transcending presence. But, as we have already noted, there is a conundrum concealed in this formulation that must be teased out by indirect means. In so far as the sacred transcends its representation, it is not present in it. That is to say, in so far as God is the author of all Creation ("And God said, 'Let there be light …'"), He is not a character/creature in it. Similarly, "In the beginning" is not God's beginning; it is the beginning of our inspired storytelling, *not* the beginning of the story itself, which always escapes us.[69] Updike addresses this conundrum in *Redux* by making the author a character in his own book.[70] Not a fictional "author" written into existence by the real author, but the real author doing *all* the writing, *all* the parodying, *all* the voicing of characters and narrator, *all* the wink-winking as texts by other writers/"printers" are inserted in a kind of inverse palimpsest. The metaphor being exploited here is not—as Updike proposed—the moon landing, it is storytelling itself. Teller, told, and implicit audience are held up explicitly as a kind of mirror in which we see ourselves transfigured by meaning: the teller's meaning (with all his confusions and evasions), the told's meaning (with all its vacuities and rabbit trails),

---

[68] Updike, "Introduction," *Rabbit Angstrom*, vii.

[69] In the "Philosophical Coda" appended to this study, I turn to Gabriel Josipovici's marvelous analysis (in *The Book of God,* 1988) to grasp how Genesis brilliantly fudges this issue rhetorically. See pp. 231–32.

[70] Updike is usually not thought of as playing postmodern games of author-author-who's-got-the-author. Certainly, he had no interest in competing with Philip Roth, for example, in that respect. But his first novel, *Poorhouse Fair*, was a futuristic fantasy, his third novel, *The Centaur*, was explicitly cast as mythicizing his father, and he loved casting himself into the mind of Bech, including having Bech interview "John Updike" for the *New York Times* and write the foreword to Updike's complete collection of Bech stories. In his own way, Updike was an experimentalist, a point that Bob Batchelor is eager to make: "perhaps it is not too much of a stretch to claim that he is an experimental novelist who also wrote suburban fiction, or one who wrote experimental fiction based on ideas at the heart of mainstream America." Batchelor, *John Updike*, 135.

and the meaning for the embedded audience(s) (with all their half-digested experiences, spotty memories, and incoherent thoughts). Why *write* about Rabbit? Why *read Rabbit*? Why bring him back as if he had a continuing existence, *Redux*? Telling the story changes the story, changes us. That the story is a word-picture—and not just a window on these worlds of meaning—makes this a funhouse of mirrors reflecting mirrors, artful picture revealing aspects beneath the surface of apprehended reality and critical interpretation throwing artifice into high relief. This quintupled[71] density of meaning points in the direction of the sacred, it points to an always receding transcendent—a meaning more and more strongly felt as pursued but never fully grasped. What *does* it mean that Updike is writing this for us and we are reading it for…what? It is not the straight and narrow way to the Celestial City; but it is Christian pilgrim's "light" pointing the way. Pointing. Only pointing. O.K.?

## *Rabbit Is Rich*[72]

In the fullness of time, this is as good as it gets. Health, hope, energy, and fulfillment prevail—made piquant by a few missed opportunities (a missed hook-up with his best friend's wife, failure as a father). In the tradition of the classic comedy, no one dies untimely, and the story hinges on a wedding. In the more homely tradition of American humor, Updike doesn't scant the ludicrous implications of the late twentieth-century American Dream. It is all social satire, delicious irony, and streets paved with gold (or at least new Toyotas). Updike considered it the happiest of the four Rabbit novels: "Buoyant."[73] Sex has become wife swapping (managed by the wives) and anal sex ("a void, a pure black box, a casket of perfect nothingness") (*Rich* 1000). With

[71]At least quintuple: i. Within the story, from the characters' points of view; ii. From Updike's point of view as author; iii. From our point of view as readers; iv. As forced to regard Updike as author and ourselves as readers, i.e., through the metaphor of storytelling; and v. Through our critique of what we see and how we come to see it, our interpretation of all of the above. Needless to say, most people read for the story—at the first level—and even sophisticated critics, like Ricks, can get stuck on reading for the moral of the first-level story ("all mercy and no justice") i.e., as if they were attending a hanging instead of reading a novel.

[72] *Rabbit Is Rich* is set from late June 1979 (and long lines at the gas pumps) to January 20, 1980, Super Bowl Sunday. He finished the first draft on April 19, 1980. He originally intended to for it to be *Rural Rabbit.*

[73] Updike, "Introduction," *Rabbit Angstrom*, xv.

his anal penetration of "dying from lupus" Thelma Harrison (wife of his old nemesis, playmaker Ronnie), Rabbit bottoms out. Awed by her offering (it is a first time for him), he listens as she confesses her love for *his* love of life. He pumps her for more praise and then trustingly confides "his sense of miracle at being himself, himself instead of someone else, and his old inkling, now fading in the energy crunch, that there was something that wanted him to find it, that he was here on earth on a kind of assignment" (*Rich* 1001). They end their connubially assigned night of violations and confidences by sprinkling each other, 'in the Name of the Father and the Son and the Holy Spirit, I piss on you and you piss on me.' This exchange of excretions and secretions in search of God is either outrageous self-parody or mordant self-analysis. It raises the issue, as David Foster Wallace put it, that with *Rabbit Is Rich,* "his characters seemed to become more and more repellent, without any corresponding indication that the author understood that they were repellent."[74] How repugnant is sin anyway, Mister—dear departed—David Foster Wallace? As the Second Letter of Peter reminded the faithful, false prophets who forsake the right way

> have eyes full of adultery, insatiable for sin. They entice unsteady souls. They have hearts trained in greed. Accursed children!...For it would have been better for them never to have known the way of righteousness than after knowing it to turn back from the holy commandment delivered to them. It has happened to them according to the true proverb, The dog turns back to his own vomit, and the sow is washed only to wallow in the mire.[75]

Or as Updike/Harry has it, "Where will his come go? Nowhere but mix with her shit" (*Rich* 1000).

The social satire[76] is scarcely more attractive. Fulfillment is voracious consumption; *Consumer Reports* is the new Bible. The malice hidden in all the fun is directed at Rabbit. In the midst of his "bourgeois bliss,"[77] his only legacy is his angry, stunted son. None of it is fun for Nelson, just breaking

[74] Wallace, "John Updike," *The New York Observer.*

[75] 2 Peter 2.14, 21–22.

[76] Cleverly, Updike has paced his nonhero through all the stages of bourgeois development, from itinerant tinsmith in *Run*, to Franklinesque printer in *Redux*, to established merchant in *Rich*, and—everyman's dream—to capitalist rentier in *Rest.*

[77] John Updike, *Higher Gossip: Essays and Criticism* (New York: Alfred A. Knopf, 2011) 456.

things.[78] They wish each other dead and gone. Rabbit muses at the end of the novel that maybe the gods no longer speak directly to us, maybe "God is in the universe the way salt is in the ocean, giving it a taste....mixing Coke and potato chips" (*Rich* 1040). Just so, Lot's wife is a pillar of salt guarding—by God's orders—the Salt/Dead Sea, the scene of her ruined home. Fritz Kruppenbach's question to Jack Eccles resonates here: How *does* God see all this? In 1980, America is Updike's Sodom and Gomorrah—there is no redeeming factor amidst the butt-fucking. A contagion of material happiness condemns spiritually rather than rewards. Who are the ten righteous left whose presence might preserve us in this generation? After debating it for a quarter century, in his final revisions for the Tetralogy in 1995 Updike restored "an omitted brief reappearance of Jack Eccles" to *Rabbit Redux*.[79] Call it a retrospective prolepsis, but the spokesperson for responsibility and God's purposes in *Rabbit, Run* (who according to Updike "almost became the co-protagonist")[80] is now outed in *Rabbit Redux* as a burly, smarmy homosexual: "His fluffed-up head seems huge" (*Redux* 438). Clerical collar and nifty wife and bishop father long gone, even God's own anointed ones are sodomites in the New Age Seventies.

*However*, at the very end of this sad, sad comedy, as Harry resettles himself in front of the TV in his brand-new home with its silvery-pink wing chairs to watch Terry Bradshaw win Super Bowl XIV in far-off Pasadena (the closest we get in this mundane world to a transcendent/*super*natural moment?), his new daughter-in-law softly lays his brand-new granddaughter, still nameless, in his lap. Foundling her tiny cranium, he thinks:

> Through all this she has pushed to be here, in his lap, his hands, a real presence hardly weighing anything but alive. Fortune's hostage, heart's desire, a granddaughter. His. Another nail in his coffin. His. (*Rich* 1045)

---

[78] Nelson is like a sore tooth in Updike's poor, ruined mouth (see the memoir, "On Not Being a Dove," *Self-Consciousness*, 154–63); he cannot quit worrying at it. His biographer makes the astonishing judgment that "the travails of Nelson and Rabbit are a nightmare extension of his anxieties about his feckless children, a product of the guilty sense that he himself was holding them back—that his single-minded and monolithic success was at the root of their aimlessness." Begley, *Updike*, 398. Like so much of Updike's own free indirect diction, it is hard here to tell if the bitter "feckless" is Begley's narrative judgment or his report of Updike's own judgment.

[79] Updike, "Introduction," *Rabbit Angstrom*, xxi.

[80] Ibid.

And God gives us, like Lot and his salacious daughters, another questionable pass. He, like all of us, seems to want to see what happens next.

So, the saga will continue, but the secular has had its day. With *Rabbit Is Rich,* Updike has definitively dismissed the modern world's answers to the leading questions originally posed by *Rabbit, Run.* Can words, however eloquent and celebratory, make shit a sacrament? Can desires, however imaginative and passionate, dignify sagging, mortal flesh? Is there any way to change the story, will better words or nobler actions flip the dreary outcome? (Come on—you're invited to try.) Or is all secular salvation just wishful thinking, a material fairyland that hardly charms for even a little while? At the ninth hour on the Cross, even the incarnate Jesus said it is not enough. Time is not enough to fulfill our mission on earth. Even Jesus needed God.

## *Rabbit at Rest*[81]

Harry is losing it. His memories have holes in them. Sometimes he realizes that he does not clearly know where he is. Distractedly, his intentions slip-slide away all on their own. He cannot communicate with those close to him even when he wants to. His appetites have become childish, Double Stuf Oreos and spiteful teasing—he has trouble remembering the last time he and Janice had sex. His cholesterol-stuffed heart rebels against hauling his increasing bulk around. His golf game is going to shit—he cannot even beat the *alter cockers* he plays with in Deleon, Florida. His wife, daughter-in-law, and mistress all keep a family secret from him that even his eight-year-old granddaughter is in on. He obsesses about the bombing of Pan Am Flight 103 over Lockerbie, Scotland, just before Christmas:

> Imagine sitting there in your seat being lulled by the hum of the big Rolls-Royce engines and the stewardesses bringing the clinking drinks caddy and the feeling of having caught the plane and nothing to do now but relax and then with a roar and giant ripping noise and scattered screams this whole cozy world dropping away and nothing under you but black space and your chest squeezed by the terrible unbreathable cold....Everything falling apart, airplanes, bridges, eight years

---

[81] Begun on January 12, 1989, the first draft of *Rabbit at Rest* was completed on September 30, 1989. With an almost journalistic contemporaneity, the timeframe of the novel is from December 28, 1988, to September 22, 1989. *Run* his spring novel, *Redux* fall, *Rich* summer, and *Rest* winter.

> under Reagan of nobody minding the store, making money out of nothing, running up debt, trusting in God. (*Rest* 1056)

Harry is losing the battle with time. What does he have left—before his heart bursts?

In *Rest*, Updike nudges Rabbit onto a larger stage, not just the evolving tragi-comic setting for his picaresque antics in the first three novels, but a secular world remorselessly molding him from the inside out (onion-flavored potato chip by onion-flavored potato chip) as he struggles nevertheless to shape a moral realm within his kingdom of self. Whatever it was in Rabbit that sustained Updike's attention over three decades and four novels rises toward a kind of tragic nobility as he grapples with his mortality and with his son, his only hedge against mortality. The gods that attend his *peripeteia* are pagan;[82] they spin out men's destinies, not promise their salvation. But, our sense of their presence is all the transcendence that we shall get in this modern world. For Updike, it seems that the Protestant gulf between God and man is finally too great to be bridged by the Cross; the Incarnation without its embodiment in the saints and sacraments and indulgences within the Great Chain of Being is just wishful thinking (but no less powerful for being so).

This bigger world that has provided the texture of his life and determined his range of choices revolves around politics and technology and economics—not fading religion! Reading a Christmas-present book on the Dutch role in the American Revolution,[83] Harry muses on what we do not know about the ambitions, forces, and contests that have shaped us: "The past glimmers like a dream at the back of Harry's mind,...that sinister mulch of facts our little lives grow out of before joining the mulch themselves, the fragile brown rotting layers of previous deaths, layers that if deep enough and squeezed hard enough make coal as in Pennsylvania" (*Rest* 1088). The Dutch

---

[82] The key moment in a tragic plot, according to Aristotle in his *Poetics*, is the moment of reversal or *peripeteia* where the hero, a remarkable man but flawed, gains the insight that crushes him to the ground. This is the moment of pity and terror that purges the audience (*catharsis*).

[83] In 1982, the Dutch government published commemorative materials celebrating the two hundredth anniversary of U.S. and Dutch friendship, Holland the second country (after France) to recognize the new Republic and the first to salute its flag. The book Rabbit is desultorily reading turns out to be Barbara Tuchman's *The First Salute* published in 1988—he swears to finish reading it even if it kills him (he's dead before he's done). The Dutch East Indies Company was the first great—absolutely ruthless—European trading empire (and first multi-national corporation) England's main rival for two hundred years.

were pushed out of Nieuw Amsterdam (New York City) by the English in the First Anglo-Dutch War in 1664 and lost their East Indies possessions (Kerala) as a consequence of the Fourth Anglo-Dutch War in 1780-84, launched because of the Dutch trading support for the rebellious American colonists. Winthrop's God-filled City on a Hill becomes the Battle of Bunker Hill and Harry marching at the head of the Fourth of July parade, dressed as Uncle Sam.[84] Visiting Thomas Alva Edison's botanic laboratory at his winter home in Ft. Myers, Florida (Henry Ford built next door), Harry and Janice—for the grandkids' sake—trade ginned-up amazement at the old inventor's persistent ingenuity: "'Oh,' [Janice] says, trying to join in. 'I guess the old movie machines. And the toaster and waffle iron. I hadn't realized he had invented those, you don't think of them as needing to be invented. You wonder how different the world would be if he hadn't lived. That one man'" (*Rest* 1138). Oh, they were inevitable, Rabbit opines, only the zipper the result of a unique genius (as he had read).[85] The old movie machines are now being displaced by the ubiquitous TV and the computer graphics of video machines. Playing "Annihilation," Harry and his four-year-old grandson, Roy, cannot hit a single space monster: "'Well, Roy,' he sums up, when he gets his breath back, 'if it were all up to us, the world would be taken over by space monsters'" (*Rest* 1146).

The real aliens who are taking over the sandy ancient sea-bottom and endless mangrove swamps of Southwest Florida are the retirees from Pennsylvania and New Jersey (once hopeful frontiers themselves) who continue to flood into the sun and flat emptiness. When Rabbit and Janice first bought into Valhalla Village in Deleon, they could see glimpses of the Gulf from their balcony. Since then, six-story pink condos have sprouted up closer to the water, and that is what they see: "Development! We're being developed to death" (*Rest* 1075–76). Since Ponce de Leon was felled by a poisoned arrow in 1521 near Deleon (pronounced *Deelyun* by the locals), Florida has come a long, long way.[86] Now, driving home with Nelson and his family (come for

---

[84] Rabbit has never been to Boston, Updike's chosen stomping grounds. In Rabbit's mind, Boston is farther away from Brewer PA than is Miami FL. The Celestial City, in Updike's mind, is even further—much further—away.

[85] The prototype for the zipper was invented by Elias Howe (inventor of the sewing machine) in 1841, but did not come into use on clothing until the 1930s.

[86] Florida was the first part of what is now the United States to be visited and settled by Europeans. It belonged to the Spanish off and on for 235 years, acquired by treaty by the U.S. in 1822, becoming a state in 1845. Until after WWII, Florida was the least populous Southern state. It's now the third most populous in the

a five-day winter vacation) in the Camry Deluxe wagon, Harry/the narrator thinks, "Of all the roads Harry has seen in his life, Route 41, the old Tamiami Trail is the most steadily depressing, lined with the repeating franchises selling gasoline and groceries and liquor and drugs all mixed together in that peculiar lawless way they have down here, low pale buildings cater especially to illness and age" (*Rest* 1075). They will eat their dinner in the Mead Hall, above the golf course's Club Nineteen in Building B, distinguished by that same lawless clutter. On the one hand, you won't be seated in the evening in shorts or without a jacket, but, while you dine on one side of the combination restaurant and function room on Wednesdays (Woden's—Odin's—Day), on the other side of the room they are calling out Bingo numbers. Their earthly battles done, living on pensions and Social Security, the retired warriors dining in the Mead Hall await their final defeat in an on-going American *Götterdämmerung*. No personal resurrection awaits them in Odin's Hall. What *do* the gods have in store for them, for Rabbit? Will Rabbit finally find out who he really is?

Nellie's attacks on his father and attachment to his mother (the only one who truly loves him—because he reminds her of *her* father), not to mention Rabbit's betrayals of his son, are deeply Oedipal.[87] The last time Harry speaks with his son before the final heart attack, he thinks to himself: "You're not a man in this world until you've got on top of your father" (*Rest* 1487). Janice clearly identifies the fatality in their conflict: "You're another man. Men have this territorial thing. You think of the lot as yours. He thinks of it as his" (*Rest* 1256). At the meeting of the Three Ways, King Laius attempts to force a young unknown man off the road and strikes him with his prod when he won't give way. The young man, the son he thought he had left to wither and die as an infant, strikes him back and kills him and most of his party. Nelson has his revenge for Becky and for Jill, children/sisters left to die. He snorts and smokes away $200 grand skimmed from the Springer Motor Company and provokes Mid-Atlantic Toyota to pull the franchise: "'No more,' Mr. Shimada states. 'Too much dog shit, Mr. Ank-strom'" (*Rest* 1407).

country. "Deleon" is a fictitious place made up in honor of Updike's mother, who for decades struggled to write and publish an historical novel based on the life of Juan Ponce de León, the "discoverer" of Florida.

[87] Updike covers his Sophoclean tracks with sly irony in *Rabbit Remembered*, just enough backtracking to insure that we are all in on the joke. When at their first meeting Annabelle alludes to Nelson's feelings toward their father, Nelson responds: "That Oedipal crap, you mean? Freud is fun to read, but in the workplace he doesn't hack it. Nobody in the business uses Freud anymore." (*Remembered*, 260)

Continuing on his way and coming into Thebes, Oedipus relieves the city from the siege of the chanting Fury with her riddle. In Apollodorus her question was, "What is that which has one voice but becomes four-footed and two-footed and three-footed?" This has been the riddle of Rabbit from beginning to end of the tetralogy. What is that sense of himself as unique that persists through all the unanticipated, negligible stages of his life? As Athenaeus glosses the Sphinx's riddle, "So mutable a thing is none that moves in earth or sea or sky." Updike sums it up in the Introduction to the Tetralogy: "An adult human being consists of sedimentary layers. We shed more skins than we can count, and are born each day to a merciful forgetfulness. We forget most of our past but embody all of it."[88]

Welcomed as a savior and prophet, Oedipus beds the widowed Queen—his mother. This forbidden sex invites a fateful plague, destroying crops, livestock, and babies in the womb alike. Prudence, Rabbit's son's wife, opens her thighs to a recovering Rabbit because procreative sex has become death; she fears contagion from Nelson. His gay friends and fellow cokeheads down at the Laid-Back are dying of AIDS, our late twentieth-century plague. For Rabbit it is his last taste of Paradise, as Pru, whose long, knuckle-reddened hands remind Rabbit of his mother's hands, screws him (and comes twice). When this quasi-incest and last questionably vicious betrayal of his disappointing son is revealed, Janice in tears on the phone, speaking to him for what none of them know is the penultimate time, laments "Oh, Harry. How *could* you? Your own daughter-in-law. Nelson's *wife*....Now you've done something truly unforgivable....I mean, Harry, what you've done is the kind of perverted thing that makes the newspapers. It was *monstrous*" (*Rest* 1443–44). Pagan Oedipus, earth-bound, swollen-footed, contrasts with Christian Rabbit, whose last act on earth is a leap up—in his new *Nikes* (goddess of Victory)—toward the basket, toward a final victory and its laurels: "The hoop fills his circle of vision, it descends to kiss his lips, he can't miss" (*Rest* 1510). A winner, he collapses into the red dust of the basketball court. The surgeon tells Janice that his whole left ventricle is shot, angry that Harry had resisted his advice to have a bypass instead of the angioplasty, as angry as "a golfer who has missed three short putts in a row" (*Rest* 1512).

Following Aristotle (for whom Sophocles' *Oedipus Rex* was the paradigm of tragedy), we can now ask where is the reversal, the *peripeteia*, and what is the *hamartia*, the flaw, that bring Harry to grief? Rabbit's flaws and faults are numerous, some of them he owns, some of them own him. With Oedipus,

---

[88] Updike, "Introduction," *Rabbit Angstrom*, xxi.

Rabbit has a grand overestimation of his ability to control his fate—or at least not to be caught. What appears to be blinding arrogance in Oedipus is more a fantastic romanticism in Rabbit. He feels himself uniquely alive, not accountable to anyone else, on a special calling to get to the cosmic heart of life. But without this spiritual pretension there's nothing to Rabbit, just his pretty little skin—as Ruth accused him. Unlike Oedipus who could have easily dialed it back a few notches and still been the King, a lukewarm quest for the sacred meaning of life would almost be worse than overweening spiritual pride. Lukewarm Puritanism is no Puritanism at all—might as well just stick to the stagey state religion. His spiritual pride is not the thing that brings him down; it is the thing that keeps him going, fitfully, ineptly, insensitively going.

The flaw that brings him down lies much deeper, far, far beyond his control, far, far beyond anyone's control. It is what makes Rabbit truly an everyman. At the same time, what makes him special is that he—unlike most of us and unlike Oedipus—knows he has this flaw. And like a good Protestant he tries to fight it. In the end gravity brings him down. In the end the Rice Krispies of grease in his right coronary artery bring him down. In the end dead matter brings him down: "Something tragic in matter itself, the way it keeps watch no matter how great our misery. He went back to the apartment that day after Becky died and nothing was changed. The water in the tub, the chops in the skillet" (*Rest* 1352-53). Sitting in Thelma and Ronnie's no-brand-name church listening to a lame eulogy for the woman he had illicitly loved for ten years, he pricks up his ears when the minister shares Thelma's religious take on her long, chronic illness: "a minor misunderstanding,...a matter of some tiny wires in her system being crossed....Perhaps God was responsible only for what we ourselves could experience and see, and not responsible for anything at the microscopic level" (*Rest* 1389). Even God must concede the victory to matter. As Janice still sometime reflects, God could not even pull the plug on that hateful, fatal bathtub full of water and soap and shit and her baby daughter. Dust to dust. Rabbit now knows he is human, just a bag of guts, about to be part of "the fragile brown rotting layers of previous deaths."

After Thelma's funeral, out in the rutted red earth of the church parking lot, Rabbit speaks to Cindy Murkett, whose swagging breasts he never got to fondle on that long ago Caribbean holiday. Run to fat now, glaring at Webb's new little blond wife, she expresses her sympathy for the loss of Thelma. Rabbit tells her that he's had some physical problems lately "and they give me the feeling I've walked through my entire life in a daze" (*Rest* 1391). Matter not only condemns him; now he grasps that matter has betrayed him. The merest traces of his existence will be left, like the worn places on Mom Angstrom's kitchen table, the grimy spots on his wall-to-wall rugs at the doorways, the skim of skin oil on the edge of the bedroom bureau that is a touch point for navigating to the bathroom. Everything that loomed as so solid and portentous growing up is disposable:

> Rabbit feels betrayed. He was reared in a world where war was not strange but change was: the world stood still so you could grow up in it. He knows when the bottom fell out. When they closed down Kroll's, Kroll's that had stood in the center of Brewer all those years, bigger than a church, older than the courthouse, right at the head of Weiser Square there, with every Christmas those otherworldly displays of circling trains and nodding dolls and twinkling stars in the corner windows as if God himself put them there to light up this darkest time of year....Rabbit realized the world was not solid and benign, it was a shabby set of temporary arrangements rigged for the time being, all for the sake of money....If Kroll's could go, the courthouse could go, the banks could go. When the money stopped, they could close down God Himself. (*Rest* 1469)

Turning into Valhalla Village after his last run for it, he reflects "Now Springer Motors is *kaput finito*. Down the tubes just like Kroll's. Nothing is sacred" (*Rest* 1472). Everything he had counted on, everything he had resisted, everything he had run from, everything he had run to, is diaphanous. You can't even trust the stolidity of matter. In *Rabbit Remembered* Nelson tries to tell Annabelle about their father "but when he holds out his hands the dust pours through them, too fine and dry and dead to hold. Time has turned the spectacular man to powder, in just ten years" (*Remembered* 266).

Oedipus blinded, ruined, becomes a sacred monster; what about Rabbit with his coronary arteries, those slippery sea-cunts,[89] occluded? We know from Sophocles' *Oedipus at Colonus* that wandering Oedipus—the gates of every *polis* shut against him and his pollution—is finally granted a divinely promised rest and that he successfully defends his moral innocence in the midst of despicable deeds, all set in motion by forces beyond his control and,

[89] As Harry—under local anesthetic—watches his angioplasty on the X-ray monitor screen, he/the narrator reflects that "The mechanically precise dark ghost of the catheter is the worm of death within him. Godless technology is fucking the pulsing wet tubes we inherited from the squid, the boneless sea-cunts" (*Res*t 1298).

indeed, before his birth: "blind, unknowing, I, I came to this."[90] Rabbit, adrift, alone in Valhalla, and soon to be Rabbit at Rest, thinks "So he and Pru did fuck, once. What are we put here in the first place for? These women complain about men seeing nothing but tits and ass when we look at them but what are we supposed to see? We've been programmed to tits and ass....One thing he knows if he had to give parts of his life back the last thing he'd give back is the fucking" (*Rest* 1478). Could Oedipus have done differently? He tried to avert the prophecy of his parricide and, thereby in his profound ignorance, brought it to pass. Could Rabbit have done differently and still been Rabbit? Trespassing on the holy precincts of the Eumenides, in their grove outside of Athens, Oedipus asks only a pittance, "It's little I ask and get still less, but quite enough for me. Acceptance—that is the great lesson suffering teaches, suffering and long years, my close companions, yes, and nobility too, my royal birthright."[91] Rabbit, wrestling all his adult life with the nothingness of death, responds for the last time to his son's needs: "'Don't *die*, Dad, *don't*.'...'Well, Nelson,' he says, 'all I can tell you is, it isn't so bad.' Rabbit thinks he should maybe say more, the kid looks wildly expectant, but enough. Maybe. Enough" (*Rest* 1516). Acceptance, acceptance of all we have experienced and done and all that has preceded our experiencing and doing. Acceptance even of the world that cruelly will continue without us and soon enough obliterate all our struggles and triumphs (the sad, faded newspaper clippings on the showroom walls, "Angstrom Scores 42").

Oedipus, at the end, knows that the present strife all about him, his sons at war with each other, one defending, one attacking Thebes, his brother-in-law Creon abducting his daughters, will all pass—like Lockerbie, AIDS, Bart Giamatti dead at 51,[92] Hurricane Hugo, Jim Bakker's fall from grace, the British atrocities around Williamsburg (*"a pregnant woman was found murdered in her bed...written [in her blood] above the bed canopy: 'Thou shalt never give birth to a rebel.'"*) (*Rest* 1504). The prophesized good that Oedipus will do his hosts, the Athenians, is unthinkably in the future. He shares the mystery:

---

[90] Sophocles, *The Three Theban Plays*, trans. Robert Fagles (New York: Viking Penguin, 1982) 317.

[91] Ibid., 283.

[92] If I have to tell you who Bart was, it proves my point. He was Yale's youngest President ever and had, sadly, a very short tenure as the Commissioner of Baseball before his early death.

> Oh Theseus, dear friend, only the gods can never age, the gods can never die. All else in the world almighty Time obliterates, crushes all to nothing. The earth's strength wastes away, the strength of a man's body wastes and dies—faith dies, and bad faith comes to life, and the same wind of friendship cannot blow forever, holding steady and strong between two friends, much less between two cities. For some of us soon, for others later, joy turns to hate and back again to love."[93]

Rabbit remembers the sneak attack on Pearl Harbor, the Bataan death march, monkey-robot fanatics who had to be torched out of their caves with flame-throwers. Mr. Shimada remembers "As boy during Occupation, rooked up to big GI soldiers, their happy easy-go ways. Enemy soldiers, but not bad men. Powerful men." (*Rest* 1403) Toyota began modestly, made something people wanted and was affordable. It succeeded by following the American way, working hard, rebuilding for the future, democratically. Now, however, United States acts like little brother, crying and complaining about competition: "But in new times America make nothing, just do mergers, do acquisitions, rower taxes, raise national debt. Nothing comes out, all goes in—foreign goods, foreign capital. America take everything, give nothing. Rike big brack hole" (*Rest* 1404). Like the big black asshole Rabbit spotted once on the rear end of an attenuated old tall guy in the Valhalla locker room that seemed to flow down into the entire long space between his legs—"a fleshy chasm" (*Rest* 1482). Insulting. Pacemakers, crutches, wheelchairs, impotence, drooping assholes, America being called dog shit by short, little, conquered people. Death—and nothingness. Insulting, all insulting.

So, we say goodbye to Rabbit, regretfully—against all expectation. With Janice we want him back, "his desertions and Pru and Thelma and all whatever else are washed away by the grandeur of his lying there so helpless, so irretrievable"[94] (*Rest* 1515). The big cheese, the man in charge, the Maestro, the Rabbit who does not ever want to be caught or squeezed, who knows how decisively to seize the moment, who refuses to disown his choices and passions, who remembers to the very end the grace that had once been his—going one-on-one against the Black kid, Tiger, as "He bursts from within;...feels something immense persistently fumble at him, and falls unconscious to the dirt" (*Rest* 1510–1511). The King is dead.

---

[93] Ibid., 322.

[94] Although, of course, she also thinks, "Now, I can sell the house." Tucked away in Penn Park, it's the only house Rabbit has ever loved.

## *Rabbit Remembered*[95]

The Biblical impulse to ask "what's next?" is very strong. How are all these folks going to get along without Mr. Charlie to keep them hopping? When Creon takes the reins in Thebes and vows to return the realm back onto the paths of righteousness, he runs head on into his even more self-righteous niece, Antigone, and ends by sacrificing his own son. In "Rabbit Remembered," against all probability Updike honors dead Rabbit by restoring a sister, Annabelle (Ruth and Rabbit's love child), to Nelson and, through the protectiveness this inspires, giving Nelson a new start with his alienated family, with his alienating work, with his own sense of exile from his father's love: "It's like she's something my father left me to take care of, and I don't have a clue how to do it" (*Remembered* 322). Finally, the story is not a tragedy, even if it isn't a transfiguration. At a key moment, literally passing into the new millennium (time opening up in a new 000 beginning) *at a crossroad*, a revitalized Nelson—like his father before him—acts recklessly and decisively to avoid being squeezed. Updike stretches reality just a tad by having Nelson sense Rabbit's aura hovering in the back seat of his little off-white Corolla as he plays chicken with a huge black-and-silver Ford Expedition. Escaping a collision by an inch, his passengers are cheering, Pru is hugging him, "Oh honey, that was great, the way you made that asshole chicken out. I think I wet my pants.' 'Me, too, almost,' says Annabelle. 'It's funny about death,' Billy [Fosnacht] contributes from the back seat. 'When you actually face it, it's kind of a rush'" (*Remembered* 368). Rabbit would have been proud. Nelson used to be good only at *wrecking* cars.

---

[95] In his Introduction to the Tetralogy, Updike confessed that he decided to pull the string on Rabbit in 1989 because he wasn't sure that he—Updike—would be alive and fully functioning at the millennium to write another chapter of Rabbit's life. But, when the time came and he was, he wrote the novella *Rabbit Remembered*, picking up key survivors and inheritors of Rabbit's 56-year-long run—ten years later. Then, as I have already noted, ten years after that Updike himself was dead of lung cancer. Poetry written in those last few years was published shortly before his death as *Endpoint* (New York: Alfred A. Knopf, 2009). One poem of twelve lines, entitled "Requiem" under the heading "Light and Personal," concludes: "For life's a shabby subterfuge, / And death is real, and dark, and huge. / The shock of it will register / Nowhere but where it will occur" (*Endpoint*, 93). While this may be an unblinking judgment by Updike on his own life and death, it is given the lie—as I shall shortly conclude—by the five Rabbit books. He loved his creation more than he loved himself. Narcissism turned inside out.

In order to live, every new generation has to break the spell of those looming parents. As Pru complained to Harry about whiny Nelson—as they maneuvered each other into their act of quasi-incest—"I thought he'd grow, I never dreamed how enmeshed he was, with you two. He's still trying to work out what you two did to him, as if you were the only parents in the world who didn't keep wiping their kid's ass until he was thirty." (*Rest* 1362) Sophocles and Freud had it right, but their gods were just too primitive and vengeful—all Id and no Ego. Our fading Christian God, however, is far too sophisticated and inscrutable, playing games, peek-a-boo, an iron glove on a velvet fist, Roman torture featured as Christian love. However, Updike the author as God (both primitive: a stag among housewife does [as he remembers]—and sophisticated: the author of a half-million word *magnum opus*) makes his protagonists repulsive, but still loves the heck out of them. In the end, he takes care of Nelson. His parents ("collaborator[s] in this immense accidental enterprise of bringing another human being into the world") (*Remembered* 325) must be got out of his way. Updike shuffles Rabbit off this mortal coil before he must shrink and shrivel in his son's eyes. He waltzes dumb mutt widow Janice into even dumber mutt widower Ronnie Harrison's arms (with three dumb mutt sons/step brothers). Janice's betrayal of his father with Ronnie lets him finally escape her fumbling, loving talons.

With *Rabbit Remembered*, Updike comes full circle back to the formal realism of the Puritans. Delicately, insightfully, he traces the multiple circumstances, character traits, and local accidents that shape Rabbit's son after his death. He's not going to pull any rabbits out of the hat. But he does pull off a sort of secular redemption. The reader can easily track the path of redemption in this Secular City; it is almost like one of Nelson's social-worker case studies in dysfunction and its cure. I leave it to you, the reader, to ferret out the details. If the author is signaling anything over the characters' heads here, it is that these fragile, recalcitrant lives can be made to fit together more or less. I imagine Updike attending his little world with a slight smile on his face, like the *Mona Lisa* but not so smug.

That is it for now with *Updike* remembered. When we look back over the five novels, it has been a bravura performance. *Rabbit, Run* mythicized Rabbit, made him larger than life through his elevated diction, his mobile refusal of the straight and narrow,[96] his existential heroism above the law, his sense of the ineffable transcendent seeking him—as he sought it in sex, in

[96] It is a refusal in the grain of Herman Melville's "Bartleby, the Scrivener" (another producer of words on paper) but much more dynamic.

church, in living and making things live, in not giving up. The insistent parody of *Rabbit Redux*—exploring the farther edges of the American universe—presented us with a metaphor of ultimate transcendence and a final whisper of unmerited forgiveness. The satire of *Rabbit Is Rich* forecloses on the American Dream. Mere time is all we've got, and it is not enough for a lifetime, no matter how much fun we have. But an unlooked-for granddaughter may buy us time, as we have confirmed for us when we get to *Rabbit Remembered*. The mundane tragedy of *Rabbit at Rest* is unexpected, almost impossible to pull off. Who knew that Rabbit had it in him to be *monstrous*? Who knew that his losing battle with time would inspire him instead to defy death in pursuit of remembered glory, *sic transit gloria mundi*. Like Pheidippides, he falls dead declaring victory, as earth bound finally as ever was limping Oedipus—but not defeated!

We see here why it matters that we have followed Rabbit through all his briar patches of time. The desire to rise above mere matter is the key. As Levinas profoundly grasps in the epigraph to our "Philosophical Coda" below, "To be human means to live as if one were not a being among beings."[97] In *Rabbit Remembered*, glory is irrelevant. It is not victory, the classical tragic aspiration, that ultimately distinguishes us in the face of almighty obliterating Time. Only continuity, the covenantal promise, can make time our ally in transcendence.[98] Nelson sees the Angstrom in Annabelle, which allows him for the first time to see the Angstrom in himself—and his son Roy will be *tall*. Thus, in returning to formal realism, his essential métier, Updike also strikes a note of Biblical realism. It is not the New Covenant, Jesus summoning anonymous fishers of men to follow him to find new life and eternity; it is the Old Covenant, God pledging to stay with Abraham and his descendants through all of time to come, time everlasting, time out of mind. Nelson finally says, as Rabbit said, as Abraham said, "Here am I."[99]

---

[97] Emmanuel Levinas, *Ethics and Infinity: Conversations with Philippe Nemo*, trans. Richard Cohen (Pittsburgh PA: Duquesne University Press, 1987) 100.

[98] See "Philosophical Coda," 268–70 for Levinas's notion of sacred time as *diachrony*—not synchrony.

[99] As Levinas—the critic—would say, God is present as testimony, not representation.

## Secular Puritans

In a material world that seems to be just one damn thing after another, we nevertheless search time for the plot that gives meaning to our lives. This spiritual challenge describes both author writing and character "running" in Updike's "Rabbit" tetralogy. Passion Week, the point of temporal departure for *Rabbit, Run*, poses the same problem for God the Creator and for Jesus and his disciples, stunned by the insensate turn of events from triumphant processional to deep betrayal to empty tomb to temporizing promise. *What's going on?* In responding to this fundamental question, Rabbit Angstrom is an exceptional everyman, thoroughly shaped by secular context and contingent event but preserving an inwardness, an incorrigible spiritual narcissism that is selfish, feckless, and—in a sense—saintly in its unwillingness to settle for the world as it is. This caricature of the subjective Protestant conscience—no authority but God's own Presence—means that while Rabbit flounders Updike withholds judgment. Moral diffidence may be the only trace of transcendence left in a prosaic world.

4

# Morrison's Re-Membered Slaves

*"The cultural mechanics of becoming American are clearly understood. A citizen of Italy or Russia immigrates to the United States. She keeps much or some of the language and customs of her home country. But if she wishes to become American—to be known as such and to actually belong—she must become something unimaginable in her home country: she must become white."*
*—Toni Morrison*

For more than half a century, Toni Morrison engaged in a singular and in some ways paradoxical project. At the least, what she was *trying* to do and what she actually *accomplished* do not seem to quite match up—and not just in terms of her success. In fact, her success immediately presents us with a puzzle. Surely, the recipient of a National Book Critics Circle Award (1977), a Pulitzer Prize (1989), the Nobel Prize in Literature (1993), the National Book Foundation's Medal of Distinguished Contribution to American Letters (1996), and a Presidential Medal of Freedom (2012) is a successful writer, an accomplished writer. Essentially, she says that that's all well and good, but irrelevant—or even misleading—as to what she is trying to do: "I don't like to find my books condemned as bad or praised as good, when that condemnation or that praise is based on criteria from other paradigms. I would much prefer that they were dismissed or embraced based on the success of their accomplishment within the culture out of which I write."[1] Or, as she explained again a decade later,

> It's very important to me that my work be African-American; if it assimilates into a different or larger pool, so much the better. But I shouldn't be *asked* to do that. Joyce is not asked to do that. Tolstoy is not. I mean, they can all be Russian, French, Irish or Catholic, they write out of where they come from, and I do too. It just so happens that that space for me is African-American; it could be Catholic, it

---

[1] Toni Morrison, "Rootedness: The Ancestor as Foundation," *What Moves at the Margin: Selected Nonfiction*, ed. Carolyn C. Denard (Jackson MS: University Press of Mississippi, 2008) 60; "Rootedness" originally published in 1984.

> could be Midwestern. I'm those things too, and they are all important.[2]

Morrison just wants—in the first place—to be a Black writer, like Tolstoy is a Russian writer and Joyce is an Irish writer.

Interestingly, all three of these ethnic/national identities remain contentious, right up to the present moment—but enormously powerful nonetheless. What is it to be Russian—an aristocratic Christian anarchist like Tolstoy? Tolstoy believed that serfdom was at the heart of Russian patriarchal identity and that its abolition would threaten his own life (as a landowner) and the spirit of family that he prized above all else. As he wrote in his diary in 1854, two years before Tsar Alexander II announced the need for emancipation of the serfs: "It's true that slavery is an evil, but it is an extremely lovable evil."[3] What is it to be Irish—an apostate Catholic and self-imposed exile to continental Europe like Joyce? The Gaelic revivalists, like Yeats, who tried to gather an Irish audience and Irish theater, were as Stephen Daedalus described it in Joyce's *Ulysses*, "a symbol of Irish art. The *cracked lookingglass of a servant.*" The eminent Irish critic Declan Kiberd pungently observes that "Like all colonised peoples whose history is a nightmare, the Irish have no choice but to live in the foreglow of a golden future. For them history is a form of science fiction, by which their scribes must rediscover in the endlessly malleable past whatever it is they are hoping for in an ideal future."[4] Immemorial Russian serfs, simian servile Irishmen, and Black American slaves are paradoxically both identities and denials of identity—identities whose history is a nightmare. What does Morrison make out of this nightmare? What is it to be Black like Toni Morrison?

---

[2] Elissa Schappell, "Toni Morrison, The Art of Fiction No. 134," *The Paris Review* 128 (1993) www.theparisreview.org/interviews/1888/toni-morrison-the-art-of-fiction-no-134-toni-morrison. Morrison's ready recourse to paranormal spirituality as metaphor and fantasy is identifiably Catholic as well as reflecting Black folklorist supernaturalism and voodoo mysticism. Her settings are often Midwestern (*The Bluest Eye*; *Beloved*) encompass transplanted Midwesterners (*Jazz*), or replicate tropes of the Midwestern frontier (*Paradise*). And she insists realistic settings are a key to her mixed style: "… you can be as imaginative as you like. Provided you have the accuracy and the legitimacy and the authenticity of place." Margaret Reynolds, "Interview with Toni Morrison," in Louisa Joyner, *Toni Morrison, the Essential Guide* (London: Vintage, 2003) 17.

[3] Anne Hruska, "Love and Slavery: Serfdom, Emancipation, and Family in Tolstoy's Fiction," *The Russian Review* 66.4 (2007) 627.

[4] Declan Kiberd, "Anglo-Irish Attitudes," *Field Day Pamphlet, No. 6* (1984) 17.

Unlike Malamud, O'Connor, or Updike, Morrison came to her vocation as a writer gradually and unexpectedly. She was born in 1931 and raised in Lorain, Ohio, a favored mill-town destination for African-Americans (and Eastern European and Mexican immigrants) during the Great Migration of Southern Black people north and west following World War I. Her mother was from Alabama and her father from Georgia. She was an avid reader in her childhood and converted to Catholicism at the age of twelve, taking Anthony as her baptismal name (hence "Toni" as the nickname she eventually adopted—born Chloe Ardelia Wofford).[5] She graduated from Howard University in 1953 with a degree in English (the first in her family to attend college). Her time in Washington, D.C. was, she reports, her first real experience of racial segregation (including color cliques within the African-American student body at Howard). After earning a Master's degree from Cornell University (her thesis was on Virginia Woolf and William Faulkner), she taught English for eight years at two Historically Black Colleges and Universities (HBCUs): Texas Southern University and her alma mater, Howard. With her divorce in 1964 and two young children, she began working in publishing, eventually becoming the first Black woman senior editor in fiction at Random House in 1967. In that role, she was instrumental in bringing forward African, Caribbean, and African-American writers and poets at Random House. Her signature project at Random House was a kaleidoscopic compendium documenting 300 years of Black life in America, *The Black Book* (1974).

[5] Conversion to Catholicism at puberty and renaming herself "Toni" in college suggest some conflicting motives. Her mother's strong African Methodist Episcopal (AME) faith was a statement of racial solidarity and independence (the first church founded on racial rather than doctrinal grounds) while Catholicism—even when there are Black and white parishes—is doctrinally one and universal, global in perspective. Her taking and keeping her husband's name, "Morrison," while insisting that neither the marriage nor the divorce had any lasting significance for her, is also suggestive of a paradoxical effort to become who you are by changing who you are. She told Terri Gross in a *Fresh Air* interview in 2015 that "I never felt like anything other than Chloe"—and that she had made a last minute attempt with the publisher to get her maiden name on her first book. "'I Regret Everything': Toni Morrison Looks Back on her Personal Life," *Fresh Air* (24 August 2015) ///F:/Book/Morrison/'I Regret Everything'%20 Toni Morrison Looks Back On Her Personal Life%20%20 NPR.htm.

Having begun writing fiction while teaching at Howard, she published her first novel *The Bluest Eye* in 1970 at 39.[6] A Nobel-prize winning career lay before her. Her third novel *Song of Solomon* (1977) won the National Book Critics Circle Award. In 1983, she left the publishing industry to focus on her writing, including literary criticism. She published the celebrated *Beloved* in 1987, which won the Pulitzer Prize for fiction in 1989 (and was made into a movie in 1998 produced by and starring Oprah Winfrey). In 1993, she was awarded the Nobel Prize in Literature, the first Black woman of any nationality to receive this recognition. During this period, she also continued her teaching at a number of institutions, retiring finally from the Robert F. Goheen Chair in the Humanities at Princeton University in 2006, after seventeen years in the post (including from 1997 to 2003 also serving as an Andrew D. White Professor-at-Large at Cornell University). She died in 2019, writing and working well into her eighties.

Morrison sets out to write as an African-American for African-Americans in a much stronger sense than Malamud writes as a Jew, O'Connor as a Catholic and a Southerner, or Updike as a Protestant. They, unlike Morrison, always had their eyes on the largest and most elite audiences for their work—they refused to be ghettoized.[7] Thematically, they honored and examined their inherited identities from an ironic distance. This makes particularly telling the criticism of Morrison by some African-American writers and critics that with her powerful focus on the past "she has written herself into a literary ghetto," irrelevant to White audiences who are curious about the disabilities of contemporary Black life, irrelevant to Black audiences who want to know simply how to escape them—individually or collectively. As the writer and

---

[6] She only published one short story, "Recitatif" in *Confirmation: An Anthology of African American Women* (1983) which was an exercise in writing about two protagonists, one white and one Black, in such a way as to make it impossible to identify who was which race.

[7] Reviewing Morrison's second novel *Sula*, Sarah Blackburn noted the rather uncritical early praise for *The Bluest Eye* by readers influenced by the women's movement and opined that, on the evidence of *Sula*, Morrison needed to "address a riskier contemporary reality....And if she does this, it seems to me that she might easily transcend that early and unintentionally limiting classification 'black woman writer' and take her place among the most serious, important and talented American novelists now working." *The New York Times Book Review* (30 December1973) reprinted in *Toni Morrison: Critical Perspectives Past and Present*, eds. Henry Louis Gates, Jr. and K.A. Appiah (New York: Amistad Press, 1993) 8.

philosopher Charles Johnson, author of *Middle Passage*,[8] put it, "I don't want to say she's beating a dead horse, but she probably feels more comfortable writing about that period as opposed to something more contemporary. I do think clearly that slavery-era stories and segregation-era stories are stories about the past."[9]

What this charge misses, I believe, is an irony intrinsic to her intentional identity as African-American. She accepts—and even embraces—the traditional separation of Blackness in America but denies that her protagonists were defined by that separation. "There was a time" she tells us, "There was a time, heretical as it sounds, when we knew who we were."[10] In essence, she is insisting that Black people in America should not look to White people either to love them or to free them—Blacks in America are neither just White folks' brothers and sisters under the skin (ethnic racial difference *per se* is *not* a fiction for Morrison) nor simply victims of racist prejudice (the will to work and press toward excellence was always within the private power of Black people).[11] At one time, *they* knew who *they* were. Even more paradoxically, she argues strongly that the canonical White American writers who created our national literature were actually the ones shaped by *Blackness*: "a real or

---

[8] Johnson, reflecting back on his National Book Award in 1990 for *Middle Passage*, identified the Eighties as "a time when black male writers were mothballed in order to promote black women authors." John Williams, "Charles Johnson Discusses 'Middle Passage' at 25," *New York Times* arts blog (10 July 2015). This observation comes, of course, after Morrison's *Beloved* had failed to receive the National Book Award in 1987 (as one of five finalists) prompting a protest petition from forty-eight Black writers. Johnson thinks black thinkers, at this point in time, are wasting their energies worrying about race. They should turn to the unsolved mysteries of the universe. Race is so over.

[9] Rachel Kaadzi Ghansah, "What Toni Morrison Saw," *New York Times Magazine* (12 April 2015) 56.

[10] Morrison, "Rediscovering Black History," *What Moves at the Margin* 50. This is her review of *The Black Book*, originally published in the *New York Times Magazine* (August 1974).

[11] "I remember when black people refused to let the enemy—'the man'—get to them, down there in that private place where we lived and where we exercised skill and power, be it over biscuit dough or quilts, railroads or levees, architecture or baskets. That was the whole point. White people never got to us *there*." Ibid., 52. She tells us that her father would sign the "perfect seams" he welded for WWII ships at U.S. Steel. Tessa Roynon, *The Cambridge Introduction to Toni Morrison* (Cambridge: Cambridge University Press, 2013) 6.

fabricated Africanist presence was crucial to their sense of Americanness."[12] In *Playing in the Dark*, she proposes to turn the tables and examine the impact of racism—not in terms of its consequences on its victims but in terms of its impact on "the mind, imagination, and behavior of masters." Critics' attention to the national literature of the United States is marked not just by their neglect of African-American texts but by their evasion of "the thunderous, theatrical presence of black surrogacy…in the literature they do study." How can they not pay attention to the imaginative and moral presence of "one of the most resilient Africanist populations in the world—a population that has always had a curiously intimate and unhingingly separate existence within the dominant one?"[13]

All of this goes to sharpen the questions. What does it mean for Toni Morrison *to be African-American*? What does it mean for her to write *as an African-American*? What does it mean for her to write *for African-Americans*?[14] In her Nobel acceptance speech, she tells us: "What moves at the margin. What it is to have no home in this place. To be set adrift from the one you knew. What it is to live at the edge of towns that cannot bear your company."[15] Slaves and their descendants were strangers in a strange land, like Moses' firstborn son, Gershom, internally exiled to a parallel history.[16] This

[12] Toni Morrison, *Playing in the Dark: Whiteness and the Literary Imagination* (New York: Random House, 1992) 6.

[13] Ibid., 12–13.

[14] As she forthrightly confessed in her Tanner Lecture in 1988, "The question of what constitutes the art of a black writer, for whom that modifier is more search than fact, has some urgency. In other words, other than melanin and subject matter, what, in fact, may make me a black writer? Other than my own ethnicity—what is going on in my work that makes me believe it is demonstrably inseparable from a cultural specificity that is Afro-American?" Toni Morrison, "Unspeakable Things Unspoken: The Afro-American Presence in American Literature," *The Tanner Lectures at the University of Michigan* (7 October 1988) tannerlectures.utah.edu/_documents/a-to-z/m/morrison90.pdf, 146.

[15] Toni Morrison, "The Nobel Lecture in Literature," *What Moves at the Margin* 207; originally delivered in Stockholm, Sweden, on December 7, 1993.

[16] Gershom (meaning "I have been a sojourner in a foreign land," Exodus 2.22) was a half-breed Midianite, whose rough and ready circumcision by his mother stays God's hand and saves Moses' life on his way back into Egypt (Exodus 4.24–26). His son Jonathan and Jonathan's sons became the priests of the tribe of Dan, destined to a parallel history to that of the Hebrews, stealing as their own the forbidden molten and graven gods from Micah in the hills of Ephraim, conquering a land for their own from the Phoenicians at Lalish (renamed Dan) in the Northern Kingdom. As long as

parallel history at the margin inevitably raises difficult issues of authenticity when you try to represent it. Nothing can be taken for granted—it is all typically shaped and misshaped by the White male gaze, as she says. So, to be blunt, is she the real deal, writing transformatively from her heart for a people whose murky identity as Americans she shares?[17]

Authenticity has a fourfold meaning here: existential (from the heart), integral (true to kith and kin and self), insightful (to the heart of the matter), and apposite (an original literary voice that illumines its subject). As Tim Parks points out, the question whether or not a piece of fiction addresses real—convincing—concerns of the author can only be answered across several works each "telling quite a different story that is nevertheless driven by the same urgent tensions."[18] That is, "authenticity" in the first place requires that life and work connect, however imaginatively the story is told—otherwise the novel's energies are just a pretext for a text (that will sell or dazzle or dismay). What are the deepest concerns that shape Morrison's writing? In *The Origin of Others*, she tells us flat out that her purpose is a determination "to de-fang cheap racism, annihilate and discredit the routine, easy, available color fetish, which is reminiscent of slavery itself."[19] She has no interest in

---

Shiloh housed the Ark of the Covenant, Dan stood as its great rival as a center of worship for Israel.

[17] The changing nomenclature for slaves and the descendants of slaves in America is one marker of this elusive identity (sliding, in addition, depending on audience and speaker): originally almost universally "nigger" or "nig" from the Latin for black ("niger") or still offensively "darky," partially replaced by "Negro" or "colored" among the self-consciously educated and genteel, which were succeeded post-Civil Rights movement by "Afro-American" and "black," now also commonly "African-American" (with or without the hyphen) in polite circles (a misnomer according to many prominent American Blacks and almost all immigrant Africans) and "nigga" or "niggah" in Black slang (often in defiant embrace of the negative identity fostered by white racism). "Nigger" is now deeply tabooed in officious public settings (where other hot-button vulgarities like "fuck" have become commonplace) and is euphemized as "the N-word."

[18] Tim Parks, "In Search of Authenticity," *New York Review of Books* (4 February 2015) www.nybooks.com/daily/2015/02/04/novels-search-authenticity/.

[19] Toni Morrison, *The Origin of Others* (Cambridge: Harvard University Press, 2017) 53.

living in some gauzy colorblind world,[20] but she hates living in a racist world that makes her color a pretext for oppression and contempt.

When you set out to represent a people who have themselves been segregated from the dominant culture, the existential question becomes more pointed. Are you writing from what you know in your bones because you are them? Or are you writing about "them" from an outside or superior position? At first glance, Morrison seems unequivocal here: "I didn't want it to be a teaching tool for White people. I wanted it to be true—not from outside the culture, as a writer looking back at it.…I wanted it to come from inside the culture, and speak to people inside the culture. It was about a refusal to pander or distort or gain political points. I wanted to reveal and raise questions."[21] However, this is an exceedingly tricky issue; without some distance intervening you are writing testimony, not a novel or even a memoir. In fact, her credo is that "The ability of writers to imagine what is not the self, to familiarize the strange and mystify the familiar, is the test of their power."[22] Growing up, Morrison's aspiring, working-class family (her mother "a Church woman, and a Club woman") may have known families like Pecola's in *The Bluest Eye*, but she herself did not grow up in any such. Her first novel is a work of considerable imagination, not least in its formal deviations from the conventions of storytelling. As she says in an early interview, "what I did is what every writer does—once you have an idea, then you try to find a character who can manifest the idea for you. And then you have to spend a long time trying to get to know who those people are, who that character is."[23] In her *Paris Review* interview, she is very direct about this distancing: "I never use anyone I know. In *The Bluest Eye* I think I used some gestures and dialogue of my mother in certain places, and a little geography. I've never done that since. I really am very conscientious about that. It's never based on anyone. I don't do what many writers do." [24] She suggests that this is not just

[20] As she says, "A criticism that needs to insist that literature is not only 'universal' but also 'race-free' risks lobotomizing that literature, and diminishes both the art and the artist." Morrison, *Playing in the Dark*, 12.

[21] Hilton Als, "Ghosts in the House: How Toni Morrison fostered a generation of black writers," *The New Yorker* (27 October 2003). www.newyorker.com/magazine/2003/10/27/ghosts-in-the-house.

[22] Morrison, *Playing in the Dark*, 15.

[23] Robert Stepto, "Intimate Things in Place: A Conversation with Toni Morrison," *Conversations with Toni Morrison*, ed. Danielle Taylor-Guthrie (Jackson, MS: University Press of Mississippi, 1994) 11, 15.

[24] Schappell, "Toni Morrison," *The Paris Review*.

idiosyncratic, but culturally necessary at this time, where public and private life "exist to exclude and annihilate each other." Using the very interesting example of "shouting" in Pentecostal Black churches, she reflects that "There must have been a time when an artist could be genuinely representative *of* the tribe and *in* it; when an artist could have a tribal or racial sensibility and an individual expression of it.... To transfer that [shouting] is not possible. So I just do the obvious, which is to keep my life as private as possible; not because it is all that interesting, it's just important that it be private. And then, whatever I do that is public can be done seriously."[25] She is of it but not in it; she herself is willingly Black but not defined by it. She insists on her freedom, not just from the White male gaze, but from the expectations of her own people, her own tribe. They may not totally approve or understand her work as African-American, but she will not be limited by the conventional categories of Blackness.

This desire to escape the defining gaze of an Other (the American White male, the American Black community, perhaps the Jamaican architect husband she did not really need telling her what to do) echoes the famous "double consciousness" identified over a century ago by W. E. B. Du Bois or, as he called it, "the strange meaning of being black":

> this sense of always looking at one's self through the eyes of others, of measuring one's soul by the tape of a world that looks on in amused contempt and pity. One ever feels his two-ness,—an American, a Negro; two souls, two thoughts, two unreconciled strivings; two warring ideals in one dark body.[26]

This was not simply the internalization of the contempt of a dominant class; for Du Bois it was also a fact of inferiority. As he put it in *Dusk of Daw*n in 1940, "every colored man living today knows...that by practical present measurements Negroes today are inferior to whites."[27] Even while insisting that this inferiority (criminality, poverty, ignorance) was historically contingent ("Negroes are not inherently ugly or congenitally stupid"), Du Bois admitted that the educated, cultivated Negro upper crust avoided contact with the poorest classes of Negroes for fear of being mistaken for them: "This exaggerates, at once, the secret shame of being identified with such people and

---

[25] Morrison, "Rootedness," *What Moves at the Margin*, 56–57.

[26] W. E. B. Du Bois, *The Souls of Black Folk* (Boston: Bedford Books, 1997) 38; originally published in 1903.

[27] W. E. B. Du Bois, *Dusk of Dawn: An Essay Toward an Autobiography of a Race Concept* (New York: Schocken Books, 1968) 173.

the anomaly of insisting that the physical characteristics of these folk which the upper class shares, are not the stigmata of degradation."[28] Thus, color becomes a fetishized marker not just for "whites" but for superior coloreds, informally codified as "the paper bag test" (no darker than a brown paper bag) for acceptance in elite Black clubs, churches, and drawing rooms (which so offended Morrison at Howard University, "off-putting and silly"[29]). At even the most common level, skin tone marked desirability and presumed superiority. In fact, green eyes and a high-yellow complexion were enough to make you "the white girl."

Interestingly, this internalization of public demeanor was sometimes turned on its head, as with Morrison's matriarchal great-grandmother Millicent MacTeer. Morrison recalls MacTeer's first visit from Michigan to visit family in Ohio. She was tall, straight-backed, and "tar black"—"the wise, unquestionable, majestic head of our family." MacTeer took one look at chocolate-brown Chloe and her sister playing on the floor and announced, "These children have been tampered with."[30] From her father's side of the family, the gaze was flipped again. This time it focused on the souls of White folks. Morrison calls it "racial vertigo." Her Grandfather and then her Father despised, feared, and distrusted all White people. Her paternal Grandmother and then her Mother believed that faith and reasonableness could prevail in reforming/redeeming White viciousness, indifference, and duplicity.[31]

This sense of an elusive, confounding, ramifying doubleness in the question of African-American identity has even deeper roots than the self-confounding gaze of the Other. The African-American cultural dilemma is itself a darker shadow of the classic American cultural dilemma. In his famous oration to the Harvard College Phi Beta Kappa Society in 1837, Ralph Waldo Emerson hopefully proclaimed "Our day of dependence, our long apprenticeship to the learning of other lands, draws to a close. The millions that around us are rushing into life cannot always be fed on the sere remains of foreign harvests. Events, actions arise, that must be sung, that will sing

[28] W. E. B. Du Bois, "On Being Ashamed of Oneself: An Essay on Race Pride," *Crisis* 40 (9 September 1933) 199–200.

[29] Ghansah, "What Toni Morrison Saw," 43.

[30] Morrison, *The Origin of Others*, 1–2.

[31] Morrison, "A Slow Walk of Trees (as Grandmother Would Say) Hopeless (as Grandfather Would Say)" *What Moves at the Margin,* 3–7; originally published in 1976 in the *New York Times Magazine.*

themselves."[32] What would it mean to write and create and think as an American, culturally distinct from the European traditions that gave birth to the country and originally shaped its intellectual, artistic, and spiritual life? Emerson insists that his is the moment of cultural birth, surpassing the revolutionary moment of the nation's founding when old and new still admitted of being compared. It is also, he envisions, the world-historical moment when the ordinary man, "the familiar, the low," will emerge from the herd as a democratic individual and universal man: "we will walk on our own feet; we will work with our own hands; we will speak our own minds." He charges the emerging generation with discovering and celebrating "the sublime presence of the highest spiritual cause lurking, as it always does lurk, in these suburbs and extremities of nature."[33] In the eyes of educated Europeans, American were provincials, materialistic and crudely democratic, importing what culture they possessed from European models in fashion, art, music, literature, architecture, politics, philosophy, and science. Emerson calls for a cultural revolution to flout this demeaning gaze.

If this were true of White Americans, then it was even more thoroughly the case for Black Africans kidnapped and brought to America as slaves—and their descendants. The Sub-Saharan Africans sold into slavery in the Americas by Arab and Black marauders and European/American slavers over the course of three centuries had only oral cultures. This lack of literacy was taken as evidence (along with their paganism and lack of industrial and scientific development) that they were metaphysically inferior in "race" and, thus, morally fit to be enslaved to the superior "white" race. If these slaves and their descendants were ever going to prove their status as "fully human," then they must become literate. The ideological/economic threat of this prospect is evident in the laws in the colonial South forbidding teaching slaves to read. The impulse to literacy and literature amongst American slaves has been traced by Henry Louis Gates, Jr., for example, to Phillis Wheatley, a fourteen-year-old girl brought as a slave as a child of seven in 1761 to Boston, Massachusetts Colony, and taught to read English and Latin by her master and his family. After an examination of her poetry by eighteen worthies (including John Hancock and both the governor and the lieutenant governor of the Colony) and an attestation by them of her knowledge of classical poetry, she eventually became the first published African-American poet. Or was she? Her poem

[32] Ralph Waldo Emerson, "The American Scholar," *Essays and English Traits*, The Harvard Classics, Vol. 5 (New York: P.F. Collier & Son, 1909) 5.

[33] Ibid., 21–23.

"On being brought from Africa to America" gives thanks for her enslavement: "Twas mercy brought me from my *Pagan* land, / Taught my benighted soul to understand / That there's a God, that there's a *Saviour* too: / Once I redemption neither sought nor knew." The language, meter, and sentiment of the poem have nothing distinctively African-American about them—nor African, for that matter.

The materials out of which a genuine African-American literary tradition could be forged lie elsewhere, as Gates insists: in its distinctive storytelling and demotic eloquence, in survivals of its pagan religion (Wheatley's poetry clearly betrays the influence of sun worship) and in its ecstatic embrace of a prophetic Holy Ghost Christianity, in its celebration of its distinctive food, costume, dance, and song, in its extended sense of community and family under conditions of intentional disruption and repression, in its dangerous sexuality and the shaping and misshaping of gender roles under the pressure of institutionalized rape of Black women and the public torture and murder of Black men and women alike—and, certainly, in the continuous resistance of slaves and the disenfranchised against their condition. In this sense, nothing should be more distinctively American than the Black quest and struggle for freedom. Instead Morrison argues, nothing could be more American than having to struggle for that freedom—in the heart of the democratic experiment. Slavery might have eventually self-destructed except that these slaves were marked not just by social status (as were Russian serfs and colonized Irishmen): "These slaves, unlike many others in the world's history, were visible to a fault. And they had inherited, among other things, a long history on the meaning of color."[34]

This absurd skin-deep exclusion from the American Dream—and White America's dedication to enforcing this exclusion—goes deeper than economics, deeper even than colonial ethnocentrism, deep enough to incite eventually a great, bloody war between brothers, with riots, repressions, and assassinations continuing for a hundred and fifty years thereafter. Morrison sees it as the dark side to Emerson's call for a new man for a new country. The cultural identity being given shape by the new nation's literature, she argues, "did not look solely to Europe to establish a reference for difference. There was a very theatrical difference underfoot. Writers were able to celebrate or deplore an identity already existing or rapidly taking a form that was elaborated through racial difference."[35] Autonomy and authority—American

[34]Morrison, *Playing in the Dark*, 49.
[35] Ibid., 39.

individualism—are modeled by the slave owner, as is his mastery over the raw, half-savage land he and his slaves wrest from the wilderness: "It was this Africanism, deployed as rawness and savagery, that provided the staging ground and arena for the elaboration of the quintessential American identity."[36]

Toni Morrison's instinct is that sovereignty—or some important part of genuine self-ownership—is to be forged in language and self-representation. It was true for "White" America, now—she thinks—it must become true for Black America. With tremendous intellectual ambition and more than a little naiveté, she sets out to become a contributor to an African-American literary canon that will have the power to illustrate for a new generation, for the post-Civil Rights generation, "what their responsibilities [are] and who and where [are] evil, where [is] good."[37] In mid-career, she observes that the novel from its seventeenth-century beginnings functioned to educate a newly emergent (middle) class "how to behave in this new world, how to distinguish between the good guys and the bad guys. How to get married. What a good living was. What would happen if you strayed from the fold." Similarly, as Negro tillers of the Southern soil moved North and West in the Teens, Twenties, and Thirties to industrialized cities, as the legal restraints on their citizenship and access to services were removed in the Fifties and Sixties, as opportunities for achievement, mobility, wealth, and celebrity multiplied in the Seventies and Eighties and Nineties, how were they to live? The connection to place and land was lost, their sustaining music was no longer their own,[38] the family

---

[36] Ibid., 44.

[37] Morrison, "Rootedness," *What Moves at the Margin*, 58

[38] "For a long time, the art form that was healing for Black people was music. That music is no longer exclusively ours; we don't have exclusive rights to it. Other people sing it and play it; it is the mode of contemporary music everywhere. So another form has to take that place." Ibid. Almost 200 years ago, Frederick Douglass recalled while still a slave that "they would sing, as a chorus, to words which to many would seem unmeaning jargon, but which, nevertheless, were full of meaning to themselves.... I did not, when a slave, understand the deep meaning of those rude and apparently incoherent songs. I was myself within the circle, so that I neither saw nor heard as those without might see and hear. They told a tale of woe which was then altogether beyond my feeble comprehension; they were tones loud, long, and deep; they breathed the prayer and complaint of souls boiling over with the bitterest anguish. Every tone was a testimony against slavery, and a prayer to God for deliverance from chains." Frederick Douglass, *Narrative of the Life of Frederick Douglass, an American Slave*, (Boston: The Anti-Slavery Office, 1845) 11–12.

and the church were no longer the primary source of archetypical stories, and the wisdom of the ancestors was past and passé. How *were* they to live? "It seems to me," she writes, "that the novel is needed by African-Americans now in a way that that it was not needed before—and it is following along the function of novels everywhere."[39]

She proposes, thus, to walk around the dark dilemma for the African American, which often seems to be a choice between assimilation to White America as the cultural goal ("race suicide," as Du Bois called it) or being left to wander through opposing worlds, sometimes absorbing the worst of both, maybe at best in the name of an often fatuous and trivializing multiculturalism or while searching for exotic Africanist foundations or yearning for race-free utopian futures. Instead, "These questions, which have engaged so many, have troubled all of my work. How to be both free and situated; how to convert a racist house into a race-specific yet nonracist home. How to enunciate race while depriving it of its lethal cling?"[40] She admits that her refusal to be caught by this dark dilemma means that other Black authors may not admire or be interested in her writing—nor is she asking them to: "After decades of trying to write powerful narratives portraying decidedly Black characters, they may wonder if I am engaged in literary white-washing."[41] This is a crucial question, and we shall return to it when we read *Paradise*.

As an editor and emergent writer, Morrison evolved her own aesthetic. She is acutely aware that writing about Black people for Black people requires a unique tonality—and that the pervasive doubleness of Black life in America poses a unique problem and temptation for Black writers. Who is writing for whom? The question "Who are they really?" is inseparable from the question "Who truly represents them as they are?" As Gates makes clear in his groundbreaking work of critical theory, *The Signifying Monkey*, this is precisely what is at issue in a still emerging African-American literary tradition. For Gates, the battle is fought over employing modes of representation that are either universal to Western literature or, by contrast, forged from indigenous oral traditions for which no established literary voice exists (and which struggle to create what they "represent"). He credits Ishmael Reed's novel *Mumbo Jumbo* (1972), with its parody and pastiche of previous Black writing, as the inspiration for his theory of autonomous African-American literary criticism.

---

[39] Ibid.

[40] Toni Morrison, "Home," *The House That Race Built*, ed. Wahneema Lubiano (New York: Pantheon, 1997) 5.

[41] Morrison, *The Origin of Others*, 53.

Culturally, the stakes could not be higher. He argues that either the persistent creative indeterminacy and unaccountable marginality of African-American life fall outside the canons of integrity and closure of the Western tradition or else the ultimate metaphysical wholeness of "a transcendent black subject" is a given, always already "available for literary representation in received Western forms as would be the water dippered from a deep and dark well."[42] Indigenous and always becoming—to be sung by its own song by its own poets. Or an exotic type—to be sung iconically whether by a Mark Twain or a Jean Toomer?

I believe that Morrison brilliantly navigates her way toward home between this Scylla of indeterminacy and Charybdis of subjection. She captures the deep difficulty of Black life without being captured by it. Her instinct to go back and retell stories that are bitter, complex, and joyous recovers—and, yes, invents—the self-aware African-American subject in the midst of deformity and loss. She enacts transcendence in immanence—not in some merely hoped for future. Authenticity at this level need not be given nor can it be withheld—although it can't be guaranteed. And even at its most elusive, Morrison struggles to re-member it. As she put it in her 1974 review of *The Black Book* for the *New York Times Magazine*, "The point is not to soak in some warm bath of nostalgia for the good old days—*there were none!*—but to recognize and rescue those qualities of resistance, excellence and integrity that were so much a part of our past and so useful to us and to the generations of Blacks now growing up."[43]

To put it as simply as possible, her paradoxical challenge as an author is to both *be* Black (as personal and social identity) and not to be *Black* (as regarded by the White world). She struggles to "[create] figuratively logical narrative language that insists on race-specificity without race prerogative."[44] How do you tell an engrossing story that is racial without being racist? She admits that the freedom to create and originate that she first felt in writing fiction was to some extent illusory: "It became increasingly clear how language both liberated and imprisoned me. Whatever the forays of my imagination, the keeper, whose keys tinkled always within earshot, was race."[45] How can she paradoxically *write* her way out of the prison house of language,

---

[42] Henry Louis Gates, Jr., *The Signifying Monkey: A Theory of African-American Literary Criticism* (New York: Oxford University Press, 1988) 218.

[43] Morrison, "Rediscovering Black History," *What Moves at the Margin*, 42.

[44] Morrison, "Home," 5.

[45] Ibid., 1.

the prison house of four-hundred-plus years of racist English language? She tells us that she borrows from the African-American oral tradition "To make the story appear oral, meandering, effortless, spoken—to have the reader *feel* the narrator without *identifying* that narrator...to have the reader work *with* the author in the construction of the book."[46] At the same time, she knows she must negotiate a fine line between incorporating Black dialect and syntax in print and parodying it or sentimentalizing it as "eye dialect."[47] Nineteenth-century Negro ballads, coon songs, and minstrel songs, as Michael Cohen—for example—analyzes them, were "constituted by the deployment of racist caricatures that used conventional sets of malapropisms, misspellings, and mispronunciations to represent Black speech as a degraded form of standard English; the aural conventions of minstrel speech and song worked in tandem with the visual orientation of blackface performance to produce the racial, social, and cultural politics of minstrely."[48] Morrison is challenged to create narratives that sabotage literary English without turning it into blackface:[49] "My effort to manipulate American English was not to take standard English and use vernacular to decorate it, or to add 'color' to dialogue. My efforts were to carve away the accretions of deceit, blindness, ignorance, paralysis, and sheer malevolence embedded in raced language so that other kinds of perception were not only available but were inevitable."[50]

In her "Foreword" to the 35th Anniversary Edition of *The Black Book* (2009), Morrison gave thanks for its staying power and concluded: "Its new life is more than a welcome gift; it is a requirement for our national health." From beginning to end, her work as an editor and writer and critic has been political in purpose. She couldn't be more adamant about it: "If anything I do, in the way of writing novels (or whatever I write) isn't about the village

---

[46] Morrison, "Rootedness," *What Moves at the Margin*, 59.

[47] "Eye dialect" is as you see it in print—not as you hear it. As Morrison explains, it is "the dialogue of black characters...construed as an alien, estranging dialect made deliberately unintelligible by spellings contrived to disfamiliarize it." Morrison, *Playing in the Dark*, 52.

[48] Michael Cohen, "Paul Laurence Dunbar and the Genres of Dialect," *African American Review* 41.2 (2007) 248.

[49] How fine the line may be is indicated by her lament for the demise of *Amos 'n' Andy*, one of radio's most popular "blackface" shows (1928-1960): "Sapphire, Kingfish, Calhoun and Mamma were not hideous stereotypes but 'characters' for whom we had much affection." Morrison, "Rediscovering Black History" *What Moves at the Margin*, 39.

[50] Morrison, "Home," 7.

or the community or about you, then it is not about anything. I am not interested in indulging myself in some private, closed exercise of my imagination that fulfills only the obligations of my personal dreams—which is to say yes, the work must be political. It must have that as its thrust....The problem comes when you find harangue passing off as art. It seems to me that the best art is political and you ought to be able to make it unquestionably political and irrevocably beautiful at the same time."[51] What does she mean? Of course, the settings for her work are the crime of slavery and Jim Crow, the damage done to generations of dark-skinned African descendants in America, the refusal of White America to do what is necessary to set it right or even acknowledge the debt, the continuing assaults on the integrity and equality of Black Americans, and the responses they have made and can make to these assaults, including glimpses of a true liberty. But, to our surprise a close reading of *The Bluest Eye* and *Paradise* reveals that Morrison does not just explore this now familiar setting; she *explodes* it. Anything less is mere harangue. She sees this work as essential not just for Black people going forward, but for the nation as a whole. The final paradox may be that her real accomplishment is neither political nor aesthetic—she works to restore our souls to ourselves.

As she told Rachel Ghansah, she counted her editorial work bringing forward Black writers as her contribution to the Civil Rights movement, but her call at the American Writers Congress in 1981 for "a heroic writers' movement: assertive, militant, pugnacious" went unanswered. As Ghansah concluded, "What we know now is that the inclusive, empowered revolution that Morrison raised a battle cry for has failed to come to pass." She quotes Junot Diaz, the Dominican-American writer, "The literary world has tripled down on its whiteness." "Who," Ghansah asks, "will tell the stories we don't tell ourselves?...What will happen to the next generation of authors who are writing from the margins?"[52] After the tremendous upheavals of the Sixties, Morrison saw the Seventies as a time of retreat and disappointment: "most of us are plagued by a sense of being worn shell-thin by constant repression and hostility as well as the impression of being buoyed by visible testimony of tremendous strides."[53] Or, more bitterly, as Ghansah reports her saying forty years later, "the killing of young black men has never changed all that much, with or without hoodies." The young—young Blacks—now bewilder her, their shallowness, their lack of fear, their absorption in mass media and

---

[51] Morrison, "Rootedness," *What Moves at the Margin*, 64.
[52] Ghansah, "What Toni Morrison Saw," 54.
[53] Morrison, "The Slow Walk of Trees," *What Moves at the Margin*, 8.

consumption, their truncated, deracinated futures cut off from a vision of "a shared and mutually responsible society." Even time seems to no longer have a future, she argues. But, as unlikely as it seems now, literature and our past may be the key to a reopening of history:

> I know that literature no longer holds a key place among valued systems of knowledge; that it has been shoved to the edge of social debate; is of minimal or purely cosmetic use in scientific, economic discourse. But it is precisely there, at the heart of that form, where the serious ethical debates and probings are being conducted. What does narrative tell us about the crisis in diminished expectation?...When the power and brilliance of many late twentieth-century writers focus on our condition, they often find a rehearsal of the past to yield the most insightful examination of the present and the images they leave with us are instructive. [54]

She concludes, "I believe I am detecting an informed vision based on harrowing experience that nevertheless gestures toward a redemptive future. And I notice the milieu from which this vision rises. It is race inflected, gendered, colonized, displaced, hunted....[History] is about to take its first unfettered breath."[55] Far from making political progress or despairing of it, Morrison prophesizes a spiritual rebirth. But first we must go back into the harrowing—fettered—history and tell the beginnings of a very different story, in a very different language. Paradoxically, the future depends on the past and on the visionary, new/old stories we can tell of it—of awakening from the nightmare of the past to a new judgment day. How does Morrison contribute to this transformative retelling?

The secret she claims is "To take away the gaze of the White male. Once you take that out, the whole world opens up."[56] Take away Whiteness and you take away both the color fetish and the spirit forged in response to it. Perhaps, you are left with the Transcendentalists' universal man, a particle of

---

[54] Toni Morrison, "The Future of Time: Literature and Diminished Expectations," *What Moves at the Margin*, 176; originally published as the 1996 Jefferson Lecture in the Humanities, sponsored by the National Endowment for the Humanities.

[55] Ibid., 185–86.

[56] Ariel Leve, "Toni Morrison on Love, Loss, and Modernity," *The Telegraph* [UK] (17 July 2012).

the Over-soul,[57] a low flame and feeble hope indeed. I think from the beginning, Morrison proposes a much more radical transcendence, not just that Blackness should be accepted and celebrated in itself, *but that whiteness should disappear as the phantom it is.* But, Morrison's first novel—*The Bluest Eye*—seems at first glance to be about the impossibility of transcendence of the color fetish. The White gaze is its metaphoric motive and the inescapabilty of Blackness is its resolutely immanent plot. Transcendence here must be approached through the spirit's backdoor and spring from subterranean rhetorical sources—amphiboly deepened to self-parody.[58] A very slender, hackneyed story becomes, in Morrison's subversive telling, a ramshackle *tour de force.*[59]

## *The Bluest Eye*

The story is simple, although the people in it are complex—as complexly interwoven as are their social circumstances and tangled histories and personal virtues or vices. The narrator is a neighbor and kind of childhood friend of Pecola Breedlove. Now grown up, she sums it up at the end: "So it was. A little Black girl yearns for the blue eyes of a little White girl, and the horror at the heart of her yearning is exceeded only by the evil of fulfillment."[60] The horror is living in a world that tells you over and over again that you are ugly and unlovable just because you are you and not someone, something, else. The evil is the only loving you get befouls and betrays you and drives you

[57] "... that Unity, that Over-soul, within which every man's particular being is contained and made one with all other; that common heart." Ralph Waldo Emerson, "The Over-Soul," *Essays and English Traits*, 133.

[58] As she says in praise of Faulkner's delineation of racism in *Absalom, Absalom!* "the structure is the argument. Not what this one says or that one says...it is the *structure* of the book." Schappell, "Toni Morrison," *The Paris Review*.

[59] Its selection for the Oprah Winfrey Book Club gave it a second life. As Morrison says in the afterword to that new edition in 1993, "With very few exceptions, the initial publication of *The Bluest Eye* was like Pecola's life: dismissed, trivialized, misread. And it has taken twenty-five years to gain for her the respectful publication this is." John Young, "Toni Morrison, Oprah Winfrey, and Postmodern Popular Audiences," *African American Review* 35.2 (2001) 193.

[60] Toni Morrison, *The Bluest Eye* (New York: Washington Square Press, 1970) 158; all references to *The Bluest Eye* will be from this edition and indicated parenthetically in the text.

pitiably mad, a madness that seems to make you what you aren't. But, importantly, the story does not quite begin with this story.[61]

The implied author[62] begins the story by indirection, with a strong narrative voice *but not the narrator's voice*—and with an implicit question. The question is "What is a story?" The epigraphic text begins with fourteen lines of text echoing the subject matter and short sentences and repetitions of the Dick and Jane basal readers. This text is then repeated without punctuation or capitalization and then a third time without spacing. It is both highly structured and disorienting. The question it raises is both abstract and concrete—but also invites the reader to ignore the issue. Which raises the coeval question: "Who is the reader?" Who is the reader who can read for what is "hidden" in plain sight? Which is itself a trick question, since no text has a meaning in and of itself—all texts, however plain and simple, reveal their meaning only to their *readers.* Readers are precisely the people who can recognize alphabets, pictograms, glyphs, or characters as signifying and grasp their hidden signification for a community of users: Russian, English, Chinese, Hindi, Mayan, or Greek, as words, sentences, paragraphs, figures of speech, characters, plots, and meanings.

---

[61] I am unsure whether Morrison is concealing this narrative stutter from *us* or from *herself,* when she claims that "in *The Bluest Eye*...the book [stands] exposed, before the cover is even touched, much less opened, by placing the complete 'plot' on the first page—and finally on the cover of the first edition." Morrison, *Tanner Lecture*, 151.

[62] I am using the concept of an "implied author" here more narrowly initially than in Wayne Booth's classic formulation (*The Rhetoric of Fiction* 1961). Booth used it to denominate the character, perception, and evaluations that inform the meaning of a work as a whole (i.e., the sensitive mind implied in the textual communication and decoded by the sensitive reader) and he insisted we can distinguish this "titular" author from what we may know of the person who actually wrote the text. In Booth's sense, we read the story to become acquainted with its implied author, not to discover something about the (perhaps squalid or humdrum) inner life of the actual author. More narrowly, what I want to draw attention to here at the beginning of *The Bluest Eye* is the explicit intrusion of a presumed authorial voice within the narrative, i.e., neither the voice of the actual author talking above the book nor the voice of the *narrator* of the story talking within the book. We have seen this sort of implied "authorial" intrusion at moments in Malamud, O'Connor, and Updike as well, when a perspective *inconnu* trumps the narrator's perspective, but never as strikingly executed as here—and at the beginning of the book before either narrator or shaping authorial character have any foothold in our imagination. As the novel unfolds, the implied author in Booth's broader sense reveals *and conceals* herself.

The trick question gets trickier, however, when a text is given a double meaning for a special audience—as if it were not only encoded in language but written in code. The implied author is *not* simply quoting from the Scott Foresman basal reader series[63] featuring an idealized American family, Dick, Jane, Mother, Father, Baby (Sally), and Spot the dog, she is *signifying* on it or, as Gates distinguishes it, Signifyin(g).[64] Signifyin(g) is the characteristic way that the Black vernacular tradition undermines White discourse by repeating it with a difference that mocks or criticizes the original text subliminally:

> Free of the white person's gaze, black people created their own unique vernacular structures and relished in the double play these forms bore to white forms. Repetition and revision are fundamental to black artistic forms, from painting and sculpture to music and language usage.... Whatever is black about black American literature is to be found in this identifiable black Signifyin(g) difference.[65]

The mockery is—as it must be—deniable. It is there for those with ears to hear, the Black audience. Yet it remains deniable to those whose ears should hear it only very faintly, a sly murmur—quasi-backtalk—for the White audience. Gates describes it as "the (political, semantic) confrontation between two parallel discursive universes,...between two separate and distinct yet profoundly—even inextricably—related orders of meaning.... The black vernacular discourse proffering its critique of the sign as the difference that blackness makes within the larger political culture and its historical unconscious."[66]

> Here is the house. It is green and white. It has a red door. It is very pretty.

---

[63] The series was used extensively through the Thirties, Forties, and Fifties to teach sight-word recognition reinforced by repetition. Catholic versions with "John" and "Jean" replacing "Dick" and "Jane" as saints' names were introduced in the Forties and in the Sixties multi-ethnic versions emerged. Popular competing series included a Row, Peterson and Company version featuring Alice, Jerry, and Jip the dog—referenced on pages 40 and 156 of *The Bluest Eye* as a "blue-eyed" totem for Pecola.

[64] For Gates, the capital "S" distinguishes this rhetorical mode from the straightforward signification of sign and concept and the elided "g" recalls the vernacular origins of the form in the dropped final consonant of spoken Black English.

[65] Gates, *Signifying Monkey*, xxiv.

[66] Ibid., 45.

> Here is the house it is green and white it has a red door it is very pretty
> Hereisthehouseitisgreenandwhiteithasareddooritisverypretty

The White child reading *Fun with Dick and Jane* reads a different text from the one a Pecola Breedlove reads. On one level it is meaningless as a possible story for *her* life, gibberish:

> Hereisthehouseitisgreenandwhiteithasareddooritisverypretty

On another level it condemns her actual life to meaninglessness, the picture of the "real" life she will never have:

> Here is the house. It is green and white. It has a red door. It is very pretty.

The simple charm of Dick and Jane's blue-sky family disturbingly harbors a bitter and toxic joke—the truly American story in a nutshell: "two separate and distinct yet profoundly—even inextricably—related orders of meaning."

What *is* a story? "Dick and Jane" is as minimalist a story as is possible: "Who will play with Jane?" At the same time it is the archetype of a story: an authoritative narrative voice and a clearly normative universe where things happen: "Run, dog, run." Moreover, it is as primal a story as possible, used to create readers of stories, to teach them to read. Certainly, for most adult readers it would be the most negligible of stories. What does it have to do with the real story of *The Bluest Eye* beyond a general sociological reference?[67] Why beat it to death by extensive "quotation" and deconstruction? A child would not question it, but we know it is not real. But then no story is real. What are we supposed to get out of this unlikely narrative opening? And, who is "we?" Maybe it is not enough to read English to read this story within a story. Maybe we who cannot read beyond the writin' are the ones being made fun of for not trying hard enough—or for trying too hard? What is a story? Who is its reader? Who is its teller?

After this confounding beginning, the confiding voice of the first words of the italicized "preface" that follows this epigraph come as a shock: "*Quiet as it's kept, there were no marigolds in the fall of 1941*" (9). It is knowing, cosmic in reference, and takes us in three paragraphs from the narrator's childhood and growing up to the death of her innocence and eventually to the

---

[67] In his review of *The Bluest Eye*, L.E. Sissman notes the "unnecessary and unsubtle irony" of the Dick and Jane frame. "Beginner's Luck," *The New Yorker* (23 January 1971) reprinted in *Toni Morrison: Critical Perspectives*, 5.

most profound of questions: "*There is really nothing more to say—except why. But since that is difficult to handle, one must take refuge in* how" (9). This unitalicized "how" at the end is a heavy wink from Booth's implied author. And the unanswerable "*Why?*" will resonate throughout *The Bluest Eye* and all of Toni Morrison's subsequent fiction.

The winking, implied author and the highly self-conscious narrator are all over the subsequent text, "like white on rice" as they say. The cumulative effect is inordinately clumsy and disorienting—it displaces the focus of the story away from Pecola and the Breedloves and their fractious family and toward, instead, the narrator, the implied author, and the complicit reader, who is giving the narrator a free pass and the implied author what she wants. As Haskel Frankl put it in an early review, "Miss Morrison has gotten lost in her construction." The crucial scene between Pecola and Soaphead Church comes too late, Frankl says, and Claudia (the narrator) and her sister Frieda "serve little purpose beyond distraction."[68]

Once again, what Morrison is trying to do and what she actually accomplishes do not quite match up. Not only does Frankl miss the point, Morrison seems to misunderstand it as well.[69] As she explained years later, "I thought I was telling a tale untold": "I felt what I was doing was so unique that I didn't think a man could possibly understand what the little girl in *The Bluest Eye* was feeling. I did not think a White person could describe it."[70] Instead,

---

[68] Haskel Frankl, *New York Times Book Review* (1 November 1970) reprinted in *Toni Morrison: Critical Perspectives*, 3.

[69] OK, how could Morrison "misunderstand" her own work? We scarcely need William Wimsatt and Monroe Beardsley's notion of the Intentional Fallacy and all of its more radical post-structuralist (under)minings of the lacunae, evasions, and unsayings of the text to grasp this. No writer knows why something stirs her imagination, where the ideas and the next words will come from, why revisions are necessary, whether the text before her actually captures some elusive sense. Does Morrison understand her own book? Of course she does—just not fully. She kept writing and revising, revising, revising until it felt done (enough) whatever *done* was in reality done. Remarkably, when she functions as her own critic, even that *done* is not absolutely done. In her Tanner Lecture, she closely analyzes the openings of several of her novels. Her reconstruction of her authorial intentions blurs into her interpretation and judgment of the finished texts. As she ruefully concludes in the case of the first four pages of *Sula*, "Perhaps it 'worked,' but it was not the work I wanted to do." Morrison, *Tanner Lecture*, 154.

[70] Claudia Dreifus, "Chloe Wofford Talks About Toni Morrison, *New York Times Book Review* (11 September 1994).

Morrison *untells* a tale dismally old and too often retold. As Jerry Bryant observes in a generally positive review of *Sula*,

> It is true that Morrison operates within many of the racial commonplaces. First in *The Bluest Eye* (1970), now in *Sula*, she has staked out an area of the Midwest made familiar to us by Sherwood Anderson, the small Ohio town governed by a rigid moral prudery that dampens spontaneity and twists natural appetites. She focuses on the black sections of those towns, and, to the middle-class hypocrisy attacked by Anderson, she adds the racial prejudice of the whites. But this is the weakest strain in her novels, for it is virtually impossible to do anything fresh with a vein that has been mined to exhaustion.[71]

But Bryant also spots unexplored territory amidst this familiar landscape of oppression and victimhood: "Writers like Toni Morrison, like Ed Bullins and Alice Walker, are subtly making our old buildings unsafe. There is something ominous in the chilling detachment with which they view their characters. It is not that their viewpoint is amoral—we are asked for judgment. It's that the characters we judge lie so far outside the guidelines by which we have always made our judgments."[72] How does she *untell* our "Dick and Jane" morality? How does that unanswerable *"Why?"* displace all our familiar judgments? What story are we in?

After all this elaborate narrative throat-clearing and a decorous page with the Latinate section-heading "Autumn" (decorated with conventional editorial fleurons), Morrison gobsmacks us with an opening straight out of a good "bad Hemingway" write-alike contest: "Nuns go by quiet as lust, and drunken men and sober eyes sing in the lobby of the Greek hotel. Rosemary Villanucci, our next door friend who lives above her father's café, sits in a 1939 Buick eating bread and butter." (12) What in the world? "Nuns go by…" sounds like a sentence (or two) that a wannabe writer has polished and cherished for years waiting for an opportunity to use it, somewhere. Morrison worked on *The Bluest Eye* for over a decade before it was published—her first published work of fiction. For the last three years of this extraordinary incubation period, she worked as a senior editor for fiction for Random House. This pretentious, opaque, arty, opening sentence is no novice mistake. It would have been the first thing she would redline in a manuscript submitted to her for publication. Her care for the right word in the right place is

[71] Jerry H. Bryant, "Something Ominous Here," *The Nation* (6 July 1974) reprinted in *Toni Morrison: Critical Perspectives*, 9.

[72] Ibid., 9–10.

legendary. In her symposium contribution "Home," she describes (over the course of ten paragraphs) the issues, disputes, struggle, and anxiety about changing *one* word in the penultimate sentence of *Beloved*—on the advice of her editor:

> The trouble it takes to find just one word and know that it is that note and no other that would do is an extraordinary battle. To have found it and lost it is, in retrospect, infuriating. Well, what does it matter? Can a book really fall apart because of one word, even if it's in a critical position? Probably not. But maybe it can.... [According to my editor] it stood out like a sore thumb....I was eager to find a satisfactory replacement, because the point that gripped me was that even if the word I had chosen was the absolute right one, something was wrong with it if it called attention to itself—awkwardly, inappropriately—and did not complete the meaning of the text, but dislodged it.[73]

"Nuns..." is a purposeful sore thumb, meant to dislodge—at least in part—the meaning of the text.

"Nuns go by..." is not a novice misjudgment; it is an intentional, sly parody of that Great White Male, Ernest Hemingway. Hemingway parodies go back to the twenties.[74] Dwight McDonald's *Parodies: An Anthology from Chaucer to Beerbohm—and After* was published by Random House in 1960 and included Hemingway's own parody of Sherwood Anderson (*The Torrents of Spring*). Morrison is Signifyin(g) on Hemingway, a much admired adversary. She has taken his aesthetic to heart and delved deeply into the brilliant tensions his terse fictions conceal. As a recent title suggests, "Toni Morrison Is More Hemingway than Hemingway Himself." In his book *Nabokov's Favorite Word Is Mauve*, Ben Blatt documents that—of all award-winning English-language authors—the only one who used even fewer (–ly) adverbs per 10,000 words than Hemingway was Toni Morrison.[75] Hemingway fascinates

[73] Morrison, "Home," 6–7.

[74] As Louis Menard notes, "Hemingway parodies, of course, are a buyer's market. They are like zucchini in August; you cannot give them away." Louis Menard, "Parodies Lost: The Art of Making Fun," *The New Yorker* (20 September 2010). James Thurber's "A Visit from Saint Nicholas (In the Ernest Hemingway Manner)" appeared in *The New Yorker* in 1927 and E. B. White's "Across the Street and Into the Grill" appeared there in 1950 (the same year as Hemingway published *Across the River and Into the Trees*).

[75] Blatt statistically compares classics, fan-fiction, best sellers, and award winners in terms of adverbs, clichés, similes, and favorite words. Hemingway, notorious

Morrison both as a self-conscious embodiment of American White masculinity and its anxieties and as a writer for whom forbidden and hidden desires motivate life—and death (thank you, Dr. Freud). From the perspective of an Africanist presence in American literature, she sees him as an unusually "pure" case—neither an ideological racist nor a postmodern multiculturalist. In other words, he neither conceives of nor cares about African-Americans—except imaginatively.[76] In her subtle analysis of two Hemingway novels, she explores Hemingway's use of "an imagined Africanist persona to articulate and imaginatively act out the forbidden in American culture,"[77] specifically, in *The Garden of Eden* "the transference to blackness of the power of illicit sexuality, chaos, madness, impropriety, anarchy, strangeness, and helpless, hapless desire."[78] As she concludes,

> Ernest Hemingway, who wrote so compellingly about what it was to be a white male American, could not help folding into the enterprise of American fiction its Africanist properties. But it would be a pity if the criticism of that literature continued to shellac those texts, immobilizing their complexities and power and luminations just below its tight, reflecting surface. All of us, readers and writers, are bereft when criticism remains too polite or too fearful to notice a disrupting darkness before its eyes.[79]

---

for his admonition to cut the "fat," i.e., adverbs and adjectives, uses only 81 (–ly) adverbs per 10,000 words. Fan-fiction inspired by billionaire author J.K. Rowling weighs in at 140 per 10,000. Among the award winners, only Morrison beats Hemingway at 76 per 10,000. She is also at the top in short first sentences. Ben Blatt, "Toni Morrison Is More Hemingway than Hemingway Himself," *Literary Hub* (17 March 2017). Blatt's book detailing his findings was published by Simon & Schuster in 2018.

[76] "My interest in Ernest Hemingway becomes heightened when I consider how much apart his work is from African-Americans. That is, he has no need, desire, or awareness of them either as readers of his work or as people existing anywhere other than in his imaginative (and imaginatively lived) world." Morrison, *Playing in the Dark*, 69.

[77] Ibid., 66.

[78] Ibid., 81.

[79] Ibid., 90–91.

Playing the dozens is one of Gates' key examples of a "rap of misprision."[80] In this rhetorical trope, competitive, escalating "yo mamma" taunts illustrate Gates' distinctive African-American aesthetic, repetition with creative misrepresentations: "Yo mamma so fat when she turned around it was her next birthday." Obviously, playing the dozens does not require that the mamma in question actually be fat. Neither does "Nuns go by as quiet as lust" require that the nuns be quiet. What is Morrison signaling here? Not to be too polite or fearful, let this critic hazard a presumptively unlikely but suggestive hypothesis.[81] *Sotto voce*, Morrison is mocking story-making convention here, particularly the story-telling pioneered by Hemingway's breakthrough laconic—one damned thing after another—voice. "Papa" Hemingway's aesthetic is just a tricked-up version of Dick and Jane's "see and tell" style—it is all about the story line, no emotion, no reflection, just take it as it comes. In *The Bluest Eye*, by contrast, at the deepest level the story is *not* the thing—the mamma doesn't actually need to be fat. We don't even get to ask how fat the momma really is; it's irrelevant. Ultimately, it doesn't matter how blue the eyes are; it is not about the eyes. This fiction is *not* deeply about the characters, what they do, and what happens to them in consequence. This is storytelling closer to Fielding's *Shamela* than Richardson's *Pamela*, a sendup of right-thinking writing, the sabotage of Dick and Jane storytelling.

*The Bluest Eye* gives readers more than enough stereotypic story to keep them reading and nodding (or shaking) their heads, while immersing them in covert, playful, digressive, transgressing funk. In short, Morrison is also Signifyin(g) on the too easy narrative of self-defeating Black victimhood, a sad-colored version of Dick and Jane storytelling. If—instead—we go with the funk, Pecola turns out to be as much tragic hero as she is victim: Oedipus and his inescapable incestuous fate. Claudia becomes the griot as traducer, singing her legendary song with plenty of malice. And the implied author is more interested in covering her tracks than pointing the way forward. As Morrison admitted, "And for me, the alarm. There is always the threat of not being taken seriously, of having the work reduced to social anthropology, of

---

[80] Gates, *Signifying Monkey*, 52.

[81] As I stretch my prerogative as a critic, let me express my gratitude for the "textual spaces" Morrison intentionally leaves open for "the ruminations of the reader and his or her invented or recollected or misunderstood knowingness." Or, as she puts it, "[the] egalitarianism which places us all (reader, the novel's population, the narrator's voice) on the same footing." I also very much take her point that "when one writes, as critic or as author, all necks are on the line." Morrison, *Tanner Lecture*, 157, 163.

having the politics of one's own language, the politics of another language bury, rather than expose, the reader's own politics."[82] The social anthropology is strong; she hits all the right notes.[83] It is more than enough to keep you reading right past the funk. But let's listen for the mumble and scat of the funk and see where it takes us.

The narrator is a problem and has a problem. She seems to be Claudia MacTeer all grown up into a very sophisticated analyst and commentator trying to voice and present herself as the youngest and most naïve participant in the saga of Pecola and her obsession with blue eyes. She now knows way more about herself than she would possibly have been able to recognize at the time, much less articulate:

> Their conversation is like a gently wicked dance: sound meets sound, curtsies, shimmies, and retires. Another sound enters but is upstaged by still another: the two circle each other and stop. Sometimes their words move in lofty spirals; other times they take strident leaps, and all of it is punctuated with warm-pulsed laughter—like the throb of a heart made of jelly. The edge, the curl, the thrust of emotions is always clear to Frieda and me. We do not, cannot, know the meanings of all their words, for we are nine and ten years old. So we watch their faces, their hands, their feet, and listen for truth in timbre. (16)

This is poetry, as Wordsworth defined it "emotion recollected in tranquility," *recollected* thirty years later apparently. Very nice except that "truth in timbre" is another elegant sore thumb, *de trop*—one of many that could be cited almost at random. But this is like a hitchhiker's sore thumb, telling us—the readers who also must struggle to interpret the implied author's words—which way she wants us to go, that we must listen for the timbre, the overtones, the funk.

---

[82] Morrison, "Home," 7.

[83] See, for example, Koritha Mitchell's unguarded appreciation of all she learned from *The Bluest Eye* about how the world really works—and oppresses. Koritha Mitchell, "Belief and Performance, Morrison and Me," *Toni Morrison: Forty Years in the Clearing*, ed. Carmen Gillespie (Lewisburg PA: Bucknell University Press, 2012) 245–61. When I personally first started teaching *The Bluest Eye* to freshmen college students in 1975, I saw it just that way too. I—and a dozen of my fellow missionaries to the unenlightened—used *The Bluest Eye* to try to get self-satisfied, juvenile, Southern suburbanites to empathize with a radically different world that was literally and invisibly right across the railroad tracks from our campus.

Who is this grownup woman? Why is she telling this tale? Why is she telling it in this rhetorical mode of highly sophisticated quasi-naiveté? To whom is she speaking/writing? Very mysterious. And it needs to be, because, as Morrison already told us, she put the whole plot on the cover of the first edition. So, she seeds the story with open questions and semi-salacious hints to keep the imagination leaping. Within the first few pages: "she will cry and ask us do we want her to pull her pants down," "great carloads of slag [are] dumped, red hot and smoking," "The puke swaddles down the pillow onto the sheet," "Said he wanted a woman to smell like a woman," "Our shock was laced with delight," "Cholly Breedlove…had catapulted himself beyond the reaches of human consideration," "Remove the cold and stupid eyeball, it would bleat still," "only time to make curtains of soapy water careen down between the legs," "The truly horrifying thing was the transference of the same impulses to little white girls," "Then we both looked where Pecola was staring. Blood was running down her legs," "Then Pecola asked a question that had never entered my mind. 'How do you do that? I mean, how do you get somebody to love you?' But Frieda was asleep. And I didn't know" (12–29). That question dissolves into a short take from "Dick and Jane" again, except this time in all caps, bolded, and tailing off into meaningless repetition: "ITISVERYPRETTYPRETTYPRETTYP." (30)

But the problem goes deeper than maintaining an illusion of narrative suspense. Who is the protagonist here? As Morrison confesses, "The novel…does not in its present form handle effectively the silence at its center. The void that is Pecola's "un-being."[84] If there is anyone for whom *The Bluest Eye* is *not* written, it is the Pecolas of the world. So, finally we get beyond Claudia's obsessions[85] and try to enter Pecola's world—it will take much more than Claudia's recollections to get us *there*. A mighty omniscient narrator steps up the level of authority. We are given a wonderfully impressionistic picture of her setting, from a time "probably no one remembers longer, longer ago" before the time of the gypsies, the real estate office, the Hungarian baker, or the pizza parlor (30–31). Its human tonality, its timbre, is approached as

---

[84] Morrison, *Tanner Lecture*, 149.

[85] One of the cute touches the implied author blends nicely into this tale of obnoxious Whiteness is for Claudia to identify, not with Shirley Temple, but with Jane Withers, the older, brunette child actor who stole the show from Shirley in Shirley's break-through *Bright Eyes*, where Jane played her bullying nemesis, the bratty, spoiled, entitled, dark-eyed Joy Smythe (19).

medieval theologians approached God by the *via negativa*:[86] no one had ever lost a penny or a brooch in the sofa and reclaimed it, no one had given birth in the bed, no thrifty child had stuck gum under the table: "No happy drunk—a friend of the family, with a fat neck, unmarried, you know, but God how he eats!—had sat at the piano and played 'You Are My Sunshine'" (32). My, my, the implied author is working overtime, each one of these "no ones" another story, maybe even another book!

Then, with another dissolve into Dick and Jane: "THEYAREVERYH" (34), we finally get a story. Everything that is mean, ugly, deformed, and selfish about the Breedloves comes out; everything that has made them that way comes out. Surprisingly, it is not sordid—it is epic. "Their ugliness was unique....It was as if some mysterious all-knowing master had given each one a cloak of ugliness to wear, and they had accepted it without question" (34). They are troll changelings, human-not-quite-human, born with a caul (the "shroud" or "mask" that conceals, veils, eclipses Pecola) as the fairies' stolen tithe to Hell. The narrator has already told us "The only living thing in the Breedloves' house was the coal stove" (33). Now, it is morning and the coal stove is dead: "I said I need some coal. It's cold as a witch's tit in this house. Your whiskey ass wouldn't feel hellfire, but I'm cold. I got to do a lot of things, but I ain't got to freeze" (35–36). The ensuing hammer and tongs battle between Cholly (Devil) and Mrs. Breedlove (witch) displays "a darkly brutal formalism": "An episode of drunkenness, no matter how routine, had its own ceremonial close" (36). These quarrels gave "substance" to her days, allowed her to "display the style and imagination of what she believed to be her own true self," provided "the zest and reasonableness of life," and confirmed her calling to martyrdom: "She needed Cholly's sins desperately. The lower he sank, the wilder and more irresponsible he became, the more splendid she and her task became. In the name of Jesus. No less did Cholly need her....He poured out on her the sum of all his inarticulate fury and aborted desires. Hating her he could leave himself intact" (36–37). And, as always—according to the narrator—Pecola "struggled between an overwhelming desire that one would kill the other, and a profound wish that she herself could die" (38).

[86] In the Ninth Century, John Scotus Erigena explained, "We do not know what God is. God Himself does not know what He is because He is not any thing. Literally God *is not*, because He transcends being." According to the *via negativa*, we know this transcendent God by knowing everything he isn't.

"'Please, God,' she whispered into the palm of her hand. 'Please make me disappear'" (39). She could make almost all of herself disappear covered under the quilt in the aftermath of these titanic battles—except her eyes. And the eyes were the thing, the whole thing. Different eyes would make her beautiful. Different eyes would stop the bad things happening between her parents: "Each night, without fail, she prayed for blue eyes. Fervently, for a year she had prayed....only a miracle could relieve her" (40). Yet, she is already truly invisible—to White people. Mr. Yacobowski behind the counter of his grocery ("with the taste of potatoes and beer in his mouth, his mind honed on the doe-eyed Virgin Mary") looks toward her but not at her. In his face there is "The total absence of human recognition" which converts her Blackness to "static...dread" (42). The only characters who do see her are the three whores who live above the Breedloves' storefront apartment: China, Poland, and Miss Marie.[87] She loved these three weird sisters, who "[do] not despise her" but who "[do hate] men, all men, without shame, apology, or discrimination.... All were inadequate and weak, all came under their jaundiced eyes and were the recipients of their disinterested wrath" (47–48). These "Three merry gargoyles. Three merry harridans," (47) as our narrator names them, are an inversion of Shakespeare's already famous inversion with which he opens *Macbeth*: "Fair is foul, and foul is fair: Hover through the fog and filthy air" declare the three witches, tormenters of mankind. Now in Lorain, Ohio, it's "Foul whores are fair, and fair white beauty is foul." It does not get much funkier than this. Supernatural ugliness, miracles, martyrdom, titanic revenge, inhuman invisibility, and profound, darkling moral confusion, these are not small potatoes; they are the stuff of fairy tales, myths, classical tragedy. We are far beyond mere sociology here.

And so ends "Autumn."

"Winter" returns us to Claudia's reconstructed childhood self and introduces a nature goddess into the scene. Maureen Peal is a rich, high-yellow, dream child, with "a hint of spring in her sloe green eyes, something summery in her complexion, and a rich autumn ripeness in her walk. She enchanted the entire school." (52) Her "charming" dog tooth and six-fingered hands mark her as a true freak of nature. We witness a red-in-tooth-and-claw, sexually precocious episode where she seems to choose Pecola, briefly, as her

[87] China Poland hogs were the first breed originated in America, in Ohio in 1816, known for their large size and being typically black, sometimes with white patches. Miss Marie may be Maria Magdalene (*unrepentant* prostitute) counterpoint to Yacobowski's Virgin Mary, *Mater Dei*.

friend, before insulting her (and Claudia and Frieda): "I *am* cute! And you ugly! Black and ugly black e mos. I am cute" (61). It appears she was attracted to Pecola's status as sacrificial scapegoat (surrounded by Black boys chanting "Black e mo. Black e mo. Yadaddsleepsnekked. Black e mo" [55]).[88] And she is struck to learn her name: "Pecola? Wasn't that the name of the girl in *Imitation of Life*?" (57). Maureen's mother has seen the picture show four times already. The 1934 movie made from Fannie Hurst's novel had been a *cause célèbre*. It had partnered Claudette Colbert with the African-American actress, Louise Beavers, as single mothers each raising a daughter and building together a very successful international business selling "Aunt Jemima" pancakes. The most daring idea in the film was casting Fredi Washington, a mulatta, as Beavers's screen daughter *Peola* and making her desire to pass as White the linchpin of the drama.[89] As Fay Jackson wrote in the *Pittsburgh Courier* at the time,

> In "Imitation of Life," Fredi Washington...utters a cry. "I want the same things other people enjoy... ." [T]hat found an echo in the hearts of 12 million smoldering Negroes throughout the United States and probably has since their so-called emancipation from chattel slavery. Actress though she be, Fredi Washington expresses the desire for freedom and equal justice in this picture that is more convincing than any mere performer could have voiced.[90]

---

[88]The adult Claudia tells us now that "They seemed to have taken all of their smoothly cultivated ignorance, their exquisitely learned self-hatred, their elaborately designed hopelessness and sucked it all up into a fiery cone of scorn that had burned for ages in the hollows of their minds—cooled—and spilled over lips of outrage, consuming whatever was in its path. They danced a macabre ballet around the victim, whom, for their own sake, they were prepared to sacrifice to the flaming pit" (55).

[89] Hollywood censors considered it implicit miscegenation and would have been more comfortable with a white actress playing a mulatta trying to pass as white. How times do change.

[90]Anna Everette, "'I Want The Same Things Other People Enjoy': The Black Press and the Classic Hollywood Studio System, 1930–40," *Spectator* 17.1 (1996) cinema.usc.edu/assets/099/15965.pdf. The wave of Afro-American intellectual enthusiasm for *Imitation of Life* crashed after Sterling Brown, a legendary professor at Howard University—and one of Chloe Wofford's teachers there—published "Imitation of Life: Once a Pancake" in *Opportunity Magazine* in March 1935. Brown attacked the film as an accommodationist compromise filled with the old stereotypes and presumptions. As Everette glosses it, "Delilah [Beavers's character] and Peola are constructed in such a way that the white masters do not have to exert their racial

So, now we have three "White" goddesses of the silver screen in the story: Shirley Temple, Jane Withers, and Fredi Washington, and one subterranean Black girl, Pecola Breedlove. Before we are done, this ugly duckling will also molt into a beautiful swan—in her own mind.

Then a dissolve through Dick-and-Jane: THEKITTENWILLNOT-PLAYPLAYPLAYPLA" (67) to the omniscient narrator again, who picks up on the subdued criticism of *Imitation of Life*. All those "plain brown girls" from Southern homes with porch swings and pots of flowers, going to refined Black colleges, learning the lesson: "how to behave. The careful development of thrift, patience, high morals, and good manners." Now the narrator—or is it the implied author?—really goes after them: "They fight this battle all the way to the grave. The laugh that is a little too loud; the enunciation that is a little too round; the gesture that is a little too generous. They hold their behind in for fear of a sway too free; when they wear lipstick, they never cover the entire mouth for fear of lips too thick, and they worry, worry, worry about the edges of their hair." What are they fighting? Funkiness. The funkiness of passion, nature, emotions: "Wherever it erupts, this Funk, they wipe it away; wherever it crusts, they dissolve it; wherever it drips, flowers, or clings, they find it and fight it until it dies" (68). Well, all right, everyone to their own taste. But, no, this fair is foul indeed.

Without a hint of irony or melodrama, the implied author lays it out. Geraldine, guilty of quasi-bestiality, being a cold-hearted wife and mother, raising a nascent monster of abuse. When her son Junior was not covertly torturing her cat (which he resented as his mother's favorite [and her secret sex toy]), he was bullying White girls: "It was easy making them scream and run. How he laughed when they fell down and their bloomers showed. When they got up, their faces red and crinkled, it made him feel good" (72). Now, we get down to it, all the way down to the bottom of these plain brown girls' souls. Junior invites Pecola, crossing the school playground, to see his kittens. His ma's out and his father's at work. At first she is entranced by the beautiful

privilege because the black characters police their own racial boundaries and act accordingly." As Delilah explains in the film, God must have had a reason for making them black. After Brown's review appeared, supporters of the film like Zora Neale Hurston withdrew their approval; Hurston had traveled in Canada as Fannie Hurst's private secretary when Hurst conceived of the novel originally. In the novel, Peola successfully passes as white and disappears permanently from her mother's life. In the film, she breaks her mother's heart and after her mother's death returns to her "black" college and her own "blackness." In real life, Fredi Washington proudly *chose* to be a Black woman and was a civil rights activist.

house: "a big red-and-gold Bible," "Little lace dollies," "Potted plants," "A color picture of Jesus." Then Junior flings the cat in her face and laughs delightedly at her fear and pain. He won't let her leave and holds the door shut against her tears and banging. Then the cat rubs against her legs; its bluish green shining eyes hold her attention. Junior, curious at the silence, opens the door, sees the cat, and seizes it by a hind leg and whirls it around his head. Screaming, Pecola tries to intervene and her dress rips—and Junior flings the cat against the window: "It slithered down and fell on the radiator behind the sofa. Except for a few shudders, it was still. There was only the slightest smell of singed fur" (74).

At this moment, Geraldine opens the front door. "'What is this?' Her voice was mild, as though asking a perfectly reasonable question. 'Who is this girl?'" (74). These are indeed the two most fundamental questions in all of metaphysics. Geraldine will never have a clue to the answer to the first question—she is way too fearful of the world to dare ask it. It is, however, Toni Morrison's question from beginning to end: "What *is* this?" But Geraldine is absolutely confident she knows the answer to the second—she has always known in her bones the answer to the second question. She picks up the cat and looks at Pecola. What follows deserves to be read in full; it is a world-class rant—all in Geraldine's mind (as only the omniscient narrator could know it)—against all of her world's funkiness in the person of this little ugly, unseen Black girl. "'Get out,' she said, her voice quiet. 'You nasty little black bitch. Get out of my house'" (75). Fair is foul indeed. It turns out that a witch can be "[a] pretty milk-brown lady in [a] pretty gold-and-green house"[91] (76). At this point, we should be getting very uneasy about who the hell the implied author will turn out to be in this story? Let's stay with the funk.

And so ends "Winter."

"Spring" is ominous from beginning to end. Forsythia is for switching. Frieda's budding breasts are for illicit touching and her potential "ruin." The culprit is their roomer Mr. Henry, but Soaphead Church also gets his first slight mention. The MacTeer girls and other little Black girls in Lorain are already

---

[91] We might note here that Jerry Bryant's observation (see fn. 71 on p. 178 above) that Morrison "adds the racial prejudice of the whites" to "the middle-class hypocrisy" of the Midwest small town is not strictly accurate. Geraldine enforces *Black* racial prejudice: "The line between colored and nigger was not always clear" (70). Everything she despises about "niggers" is true enough. But her scorn and animus is generated by the fear that she might become such, or, more accurately, that she might be seen as such, whether by Black or White.

very familiar with Elihue Micah Whitcomb: "Why do I have to die? The little girls are the only things I'll miss. Do you know that when I touched their sturdy little tits and bit them—just a little—I felt I was being friendly?" (142). "Spring" is a series of case studies in how poisonous "Whiteness" is, sometimes reading literally as documentary case notes. The first case begins as comedy, almost blackface comedy in its conventions: Mr. Henry singing "Nearer My God to Thee," as Mama whales at him with a broom, until Daddy takes a shot at him and he jumps right out of his shoes and takes off running in his socks. Frieda not wanting to be *ruined* because that would mean becoming big and fat like the whore they call Maginot Line (Miss Marie). The only hope is to drink whiskey like China and Poland. They ain't fat because, according to Mama, whiskey ate them up. Pecola will know how to get whiskey because her father's always drunk. The sisters set out on a quest for this unlikely grail and come finally to the castle of their dreams in Lake Shore Park, where Pecola sits by the backdoor stoop. Mrs. Breedlove, Pauline, nicknamed Polly by the "affectionate, appreciative, and generous" White family (the kingly Fishers) for whom she kept house, lets them into the kitchen where a blueberry cobbler is cooling, "The purple juice bursting here and there through crust." She goes down in the basement to get the wet laundry for Pecola to haul home in her little wagon. The blond little Fisher girl walks in on them and is frightened and calls for Polly. The comedy turns vicious. Pecola touches the cobbler, and it tips over splattering her legs with hot syrup: "In one gallop Mrs. Breedlove was on Pecola and with the back of her hand knocked her to the floor. Pecola slid in the pie juice, one leg folding under her. Mrs. Breedlove yanked her up by the arm, slapped her again" (86). In disgrace, they are sent on their way, and the scene ends with "Polly" soothing the tears of the "pink-and-yellow girl" and promising her another pie. The Whiteness that has seduced Pauline Willams Breedlove is lovely, dainty, commodious, and in the perfect order she adores and keeps. As we are told in the backstory a few pages later: "More and more she neglected her house, her children, her man—they were like the afterthoughts one has just before sleep, the early-morning and late-evening edges of her day, the dark edges that made the daily life with the Fishers lighter, more delicate, more lovely" (101).

Having seen Pauline at her ugliest, virtually indistinguishable from Geraldine in her betrayal of Pecola, with another Dick-and-Jane transition (LAUGHMOTHERLAUGHLA), the implied author—that "mysterious all-knowing master"—whisks away the cloak of ugliness from Pauline and Cholly: "The easiest thing to do would be to build a case out of the foot. That is what she herself did. But to find out the truth about how dreams die, one should never take the word of the dreamer. The end of her lovely beginning was probably the cavity in one of her front teeth" (88). *The novelist*: note to self: she's had the drag foot[92] since she stepped on a nail at age two, but her lovely beginning was sustained at least through marriage and emigration: "Young, loving, and full of energy they came to Lorain, Ohio," (92) so "What could go wrong?" (93). The details scarcely matter, although the implied author and narrators work hard at imagining them (our omniscient narrator is joined off and on by Pauline's own out-of-any-context reminiscences, set off in italics: "*Cholly was thin then, with real light eyes. He used to whistle. And when I heerd him, shivers come on my skin*" [92]).[93] Her sense of aloneness in her large Alabama sharecropper family (Black to James Agee's White Alabama sharecroppers) is succeeded by religious yearnings ("Take my hand, precious Lord, lead me on"), yearnings satisfied by the appearance of Cholly Breedlove: "He came big, he came strong, he came with yellow eyes, flaring nostrils, and he came with his own music" (91). But from the beginning in Lorain she felt a new kind of alienation, too many white folks all around and the "*Northern colored folk was...no better than the whites for meanness*" (93). The beginning of the end is when only going to the movies gives her any pleasure. Our narrator primly remarks that in the movie house "Along with her idea of romantic love, she was introduced to another—physical beauty. Probably the most destructive ideas in the history of human thought" (97). The rotten tooth moment comes while watching Jean Harlow and Clark Gable—with

[92] A slant reference to Oedipus, with his pierced feet? The riddle of the Sphinx: What is man? may here be Soujourner Truth's cry: "And ain't I a woman?"

[93] One thinks of the style of James Agee's 1941 piece of fictocriticism *Let Us Now Praise Famous Men*, re-released in 1960 to considerable acclaim. Sometimes referred to as verbal montage, "fictocriticism" blends genres and muddles authorial control. It is applied variously to New Journalism, poststructuralist theory, and postcolonial anthropology. In essence, it means telling stories to make a point—with Montaigne as its putative progenitor. Morrison explains in her Tanner Lecture that in *The Bluest Eye* she was trying to sustain a "female expressiveness" that eluded her: "The shambles this struggle became is most evident in the section on Pauline Breedlove where I resorted to two voices; hers and the urging narrator's, both of which are extremely unsatisfactory to me" (Morrison, *Tanner Lecture*, 150). Oddly, she found it much easier to describe Cholly's "rape" by the white men (next up in our discussion) in feminized, passive language, deglamorizing Cholly's subsequent rape of Pecola. This narrative "shambles" is another excellent example of her accomplishing something different (as implied author) than what she set out to do (as author) (q.v. fn. 62 above).

her nappy hair put up in homage to Harlow's platinum wave over one eye. As she herself reports, "*There I was five months pregnant, trying to look like Jean Harlow, and a front tooth gone. Everything went then. Look like I just didn't care no more after that. I let my hair go back, plaited it up, and settled down to just being ugly*" (98). And to acquiring the virtues of an active church woman, a strict mother, and an indefatigable worker, twelve to sixteen hours a day to support her family (and the Fisher family). Even then there were moments with Cholly in bed after he comes and then touches her "*And it be rainbow all inside. And it lasts and lasts and lasts*" (104).

SMILEFATHERSMILESMILE. The Whiteness that poisoned Cholly Breedlove was not seductive, it was humiliating and emasculating. Abandoned to die by his mother as a newborn, he was saved and raised by his Great Aunt Jimmy and under the gentle tutelage of a drayman at the feed store, Blue Jack, a former slave. His tutelage by two White men was of a different sort. It also starts as a comic story. Aunt Jimmy has taken poorly, and Bible reading brought no improvement so the old root woman was summoned and diagnosed "you done caught cold in your womb. Drink pot liquor and nothing else." The narrator sings an extended threnody of admiration and lament for the old women caring for the dying woman: "And the lives of these old black women were synthesized in their eyes—a purée of tragedy and humor, wickedness and serenity, truth and fantasy" (110). Then feeling stronger, Aunt Jimmy ate a piece of peach cobbler—and died. The old women spruce up the remains and the survivor: "The funeral banquet was a peal of joy after the thunderous beauty of the funeral" (113). The narrator lays it on thick, choral strophe and antistrophe, stunned wonder, restored natural order, exaltation of physical frailty, a steep hunger for food. Still a thirteen-year-old boy, Cholly cannot fully grasp it. A slightly older cousin come from town says does he know some girls? They go out walking to a wild vineyard. The boys chase after and pelt the girls with half-ripe muscadines. Cholly and Darlene throw themselves down in the grass at the edge of the woods in the moonlight. She tickles him and laughs: "They were on top of each other in a moment" (116). His pants around his knees, "Just as he felt an explosion threaten, Darlene froze and cried out. He thought he had hurt her, but..." (116). Now the comedy is the "Blackest" of White mischief. Two white men (he could smell their whiteness) out coon hunting shine their lights on them, "'Hee hee hee heeeeee.' The snicker was a long asthmatic cough....'Get on wid it, nigger,' said the flashlight one" (117). Simulating coitus, he feels nothing but hatred for Darlene. The next day sorting through Aunt Jimmy's things, "he cultivated his hatred of Darlene" (119). The narrator explains that

Darlene was the witness to his impotence, that hatred of the hunters would have consumed him: "They were big, white, armed men. He was small, black, helpless" (119). (Later, hating Pauline would also become his psychic salvation.)

Fearing Darlene is somehow pregnant, he runs away with Aunt Jimmy's pitiful treasure stash—to find his runaway father, he hopes. He does, shooting craps in a back alley in Macon, Georgia. Samson Fuller is the antipode to Geraldine, he heedlessly destructive, she too carefully protective. He stands up from the game and "in a vexed and whiny voice shouted at Cholly, 'Tell that bitch she get her money. Now, get the fuck outta my face'" (123). Cholly backs away, stunned. Sitting on a box on the sidewalk, in the sun, trying not to cry, he soils himself. He runs and runs to hide and cleanse himself in the river. Later, three Macon whores invite him up into the warm dark, give him lemonade to drink from a Mason jar and "give him back his manhood, which he takes aimlessly" (125). Then our narrator does something very odd—or else the implied author simply takes over and implicitly undercuts the omniscient, gregarious, explaining narrator:[94] "The pieces of Cholly's life could become coherent only in the head of a musician....Only a musician would sense, know, without even knowing what he knew, that Cholly was free. Dangerously free" (125). (I guess we take her word for it and hum along.) Nothing mattered to him any longer but his own perceptions and appetites: "It was in this godlike state that he met Pauline Williams." But then the sameness of their marriage and the unaccountable intrusion of their children destroyed even that curiosity: "Nothing, nothing, interested him now....Only in drink

[94] Morrison makes good her intention "to have the reader *feel* the narrator without *identifying* the narrator" (see pages 169–70 above). Thus, amongst others, we have the implied author whose moral sensibility informs the telling, from epigraphic fragments to narrative voicings to mythic allusions to muffled parodies to rhetorical "sore thumbs." Sometimes, as in this passage, we seem to be directly addressed by this "author as God" (as Updike put it; see page 134 above). The classic omniscient narrator is also in fine fettle throughout and pretty reliable when she shows up. Claudia does yeoman work as the griot singing this tale but is considerably less reliable. And even Pauline, in all her misshapen innocence, gets in her extended (italicized) reminiscences (about as reliable as most memories). Soaphead Church does not have a lot to tell us, but when he finally appears, he adds a crucial new, superior, narrative voice—as we shall see. Whose story is it really? Why, it's Pecola's story, as she brokenly tells it at the very end of the novel—although it is much discounted by everyone except the implied author.

was there some break, some flood light, and when that closed, there was oblivion" (126).

So, he comes home reeling drunk one Saturday afternoon in the spring to find Pecola washing dishes at the sink. Hatred (of self, of whomever he cannot protect) boils; "Why did she have to look so whipped?...What could a burned-out black man say to the hunched back of his eleven-year-old daughter?" (127) A quiet, vulnerable gesture of hers dimly reminds him of his first meeting with Pauline. Tenderness mixed with the forbidden stiffens him. Creeping up behind her, he rapes her—and rapes her again when Pauline refuses to believe her—and gets her with child.

SEETHEDOGRUNR. The last bit of Spring's poisonous Whiteness comes courtesy of a long ago British nobleman settled on an island in the Greater Antilles. His line of mulatto bastards finally produced a Soaphead Church, so-called. Elihue Whitcomb, his grandfather a religious fanatic and founder of a secret sect, his mother half-Chinese and dead in childbirth, his father a schoolmaster of subtle cruelty, became a refined monster of self-deception, with "hard habits and a soft imagination" and "an invincible melancholy." (134) The griot devotes a great deal of nuanced anatomization to Soaphead, who seems a version of the Wizard of Oz, pitiably frightening and supposedly in charge of mysteries. The malice that attaches to almost all of the adults in the tale here becomes poisonous itself, or at least leads Pecola to poison Toto, so to speak, Bertha Reese's old dog Bob. It is a sign, Soaphead tells her, she will get her blue eyes. His deception supplies, he thinks, God's defect in the blue eyes department. He goes so far as to write God a letter rebuking Him: "You forgot, Lord. You forgot how and when to be God" (143). Thus, at the end of Spring we come back around to Morrison's fundamental question, not the anthropological "How?" but the theological "Why?" What after all is the difference between Soaphead's "God" and the Wizard of Oz?

Finally, briefly—forever—Summer. In Claudia's reconstructed sensibility (like Proust's evoked in a bite into...a strawberry) she imagines her mother in a pink crepe dress being nonchalantly swirled high in the sky by a summer tornado à la Dorothy: "The anticipation and promise in her lolling hand are not altered by the holocaust. In the summer tornado of 1929, my mother's hand is unextinguished. She is strong, smiling, and relaxed while the world falls down about her. So much for memory" (146). Indeed. Who the adult narrator Claudia is, why she is remembering these childhood days, how well she understood them then or now, and to whom she is speaking remain mysteries. Mysteries, sophisticatedly put forward as "the *Moirai* of our small lives"

(146). Claudia—the implied author—Toni Morrison—try—want to try—salving the situation: "All right. Only let me sing this time. You say the magic words" (149). They plant their seeds (in lieu of selling them to earn a bicycle) but nothing comes up. Nature ain't nearly enough. And nurture misses the point. *God* should have done better. And Morrison's magic words in the novel, her griot's song? Where are we in stretching "reality?" This is a novel of a kind, after all. This is a novel that reaches to be more than a novel, to touch the sacred.

PLAYJANEPLAY. Pecola's juvenile schizophrenia, triggered by her rape by her father (and surrounding traumas),[95] has apparently both rendered her psychogenetically "blind" and provided her with a typical doppelgänger, who becomes her sole "companion" both supporting her wish fulfillment and voicing her doubts about it. Their "dialogue" is not reported but merely transcribed. Is it only in her mind or is she talking to herself? Or is this what Claudia imagines is going on? Or is it the implied author sharing God's perception of Pecola's suffering? "So it was," concludes Claudia, who proceeds to excoriate herself and everyone else (with the exception of the Maginot Line and Cholly—foul is fair, fair is foul) for the self-serving harm they did Pecola. Enormous generalizations uncover our duplicity: "All of us—all who knew her—felt so wholesome after we cleaned ourselves on her. We were so beautiful when we stood astride her ugliness" (159). And so on and on for the last three pages of the book. Given Morrison's interdiction on harangues, this harangue must be intentional—and thus be beside the point? The End.

If this is not just a droopy-drawers quasi-slave narrative—if this is indeed Signifyin(g) on such—what must we listen for? Or, first of all, *who* are we listening to? It is not the White male gaze that is represented here after all; it is the Black female gaze, Claudia's gaze and Claudia's voice, as girl, daughter, sister and as a woman trying to unweave and reweave the threads of Fate as she sings this story. Additionally, Claudia (and Frieda) suffer from none of the disabilities of a Pecola. Outraged that no one would go even so far as

[95] Childhood schizophrenia is very rare (1/30,000). Avoidance of eye contact and arm flapping are symptoms and precursors, and Morrison emphasizes both of these characteristics. As Susan Willis points out, Pauline also lives out a kind of cultural schizophrenia: "As a housemaid in a prosperous lakeshore home…her marginality is constantly confronted with a world of Hollywood movies, white sheets, and tender blond children….Her emotions split, Polly showers tenderness and love on her employer's child, and rains violence and distain on her own." Susan Willis, "Eruptions of Funk: Historicizing Toni Morrison," *Toni Morrison: Critical Perspectives*, 310.

"'Poor little girl' or, 'Poor baby'" (148) and that everyone seemed simply to want her baby dead, the two sisters in Claudia's words "headstrong, devious and arrogant...with confidence, strengthened by pity and pride,...decided to change the course of events and alter a human life" (149). So, taking Claudia and Frieda MacTeer as stand-ins for both Chloe Wofford, author, and the implied author, whose game is still a bit of a mystery, we shall proceed on the assumption that that is exactly what this novel means to do: "to change the course of events and alter a human life." What *happens* may be unalterable but what it *means* is in the eyes of author(s) and readers. The territory we are now entering is closer to Greek tragedy than to the naturalistic novel.

The implied author has teased us with portentous metaphors and mythic allusions all the way through the story. She has also worked to disorient us and prevent us from adopting any particular point of view. The text is mixed up and alternative narrators abound. You might say that a thoroughgoing, unsystematic amphiboly is its (dis)organizing principle. So far, it is a textbook case of the uniquely creative indeterminacy and unaccountable marginality that Gates associated with an autonomous African-American literary sensibility. But in this case the "difference that blackness makes" between parallel discursive universes is pulled inside out. Blackness is the premise of *The Bluest Eye*, and the difference that *Whiteness* makes to this order of meaning is what is under discursive critique. The implied author does not leave it there. Let's remember Brer Rabbit got himself slung in that brier-patch so he could skip out the other side "des ez lively ez a cricket in de embers." The implied author has another hustle going on the side that will open up the text and cast seeds of doubt far and wide.

Soaphead Church provides the unlikely starting place for a subversive recasting of the novel. He is such an odd addition to the end of the story, a literalized *deus ex machina*. He is highly refined, self-reflective, very intelligent, learned, with a carefully constructed and rationalized persona (as a misanthrope). His animus toward adults mirrors the narrators' spite for: Pauline, Cholly, Geraldine, Samson Fuller, Mr. Henry, and at the end even Claudia herself all grown up. His exotic history, fondness for worn scraps of human meaning, and his sharp but fastidious sexual delight in little girls particularizes him and takes him out of the realm of stereotype. The implied author who has lavished this attention on him must mean something special by him. And he concludes his appearance in the novel with a long letter written to God—a strong new narrative voice.

If anyone knows the magic words "to change the course of events and alter a human life," it should be Elihue Whitcomb "[exposed] to the best minds in the Western world": Shakespeare, the Gospels, Gibbon, Dante, Dostoyevsky. But, he "read selectively, choosing the bits and pieces of other men's ideas that supported whatever predilection he had at the moment" (133–34). The saving words will *challenge, not reinforce,* our narratives of where we come from and where we are going. The problem is not that our words are mere lies or illusions; of course, they are. Every story we tell is just that: a story, an attempt to make sense of events. But Elihue puts his finger on it in his apologia to and indictment of God: "I told people I knew all about You. That I had received Your Powers. It was not a complete *lie*; but it was a *complete* lie. I should never have taken their money in exchange for well-phrased, well-placed, well-faced lies" (141). The problem is the completeness of the lie. Making it stick, leaving no way out, poisoning the rheumy-eyed old dog *and*, thereby, gifting Pecola with cobalt blue eyes. Our successful Dick-and-Jane / Hemingway / "poor little Pecola" stories—well-phrased, well-placed, well-faced—are not so much false as they are hopeless. They leave no way out.[96] Far from changing things, they mire us more deeply in the failed myths of our destinies: "*If we planted the seeds, and said the right words over them, they would blossom, and everything would be all right*" (9). The new myth cannot be sung until the old, stereotyped, haranguing, abolitionist myths are exploded. There is no freeing Soaphead—too, too much has gone wrong for too, too long. The griot's faithlessness is our only recourse. The best we can do is sabotage the too, too complete lie of "poor little Pecola."

(Let's take a critical moment before we plunge ahead. This is about to get a little far-fetched—*"yo mamma so fat ..."* I am going to go ahead and take the bait and re-think this as if it were alluding to Greek tragedy, i.e., as if Morrison's Pecola is a victim in the same general sense that Sophocles' Oedipus is a victim. This supposes that Morrison is Signifyin(g) on the "slave" narrative by leaning on a *universalist* Africanist/Greco-Roman rhetoric of tragedy. In support of this leap in perspective, we have Morrison's own expressed appreciation of Greek tragedy "in its similarity to Afro-American communal structures (the function of song and chorus, the heroic struggle between the claims of community and individual hubris) and African religion and philosophy.... [And] because *it* is masterly."[97] Morrison minored in Classics at Howard and is an avowed admirer of Martin Bernal's *Black Athena*,

[96] Nobel laureate "Papa" Hemingway—he-man—hated his mother and shot himself at 61, as did his father before him at 67 and his brother Leicester, a novelist, after him also at 67. Extreme Whiteness is a tar baby, too.

[97] Morrison, *Tanner Lecture*, 125.

with its thesis that Greece's efflorescence as the origin of European culture had *its* origin in its own "Egyptomania." As Tessa Roynon notes, "Since the mid-1980s there has been a quiet but consistent scholarly interest in Toni Morrison's engagement with the classical tradition."[98] On the other side of the equation, we have Morrison's adamant claim that "Well, in *The Bluest Eye*, I try to show a little girl as a total and complete victim of whatever was around her." Not a tragic hero? However, this claim from a 1976 interview happens to be accompanied by her admission "that it's a new idea to me—the emasculating black woman. It really is new—that is, in the last few years."[99] Yet Geraldine and all those other "plain brown girls" from respectable Southern homes were patently emasculating: "A sidelong look will be enough to tell him to smoke on the back porch....He must enter her surreptitiously, lifting the hem of her nightgown only to her naval" (69). Either Morrison knows a whole lot more than she knows she knows—or this interview is an authorial cat-and-mouse game. Or both. So, with these pretexts and caveats, let us proceed.)

Now, finally, to the "why?" The "why?" that escaped Claudia does not escape the implied author. Why was Pecola raped by her father? Why did Oedipus wed his mother? It is quite over-determined, which is what "Fate" is. It is suffering the self-interested malice of the previous generation. It is having the really bad luck of being in the wrong place at the wrong time. It is being targeted by the gods as exceptional, far above or far below the ordinary. It is being the product of a magnificently dysfunctional family. It is inheriting a destiny at the moment of birth that had really nothing to do with you—beyond your comprehension or control. Finally, it is possessing a fatal obsession and arrogance, his that he could set things right through his superior powers of interpretation, hers that she could set things right through the surpassing beauty of her eyes. They both, however, transcend their dismal fates by becoming sacred monsters. Oedipus emerges a tragic hero because he blinds himself and wanders the earth as a despised exile. Pecola because she gains her "blue eyes" and blindly paces the limits of her cage: "We tried to

---

[98] Tessa Roynon, "The Africanness of Classicism in the Work of Toni Morrison," *African Athena: New Agendas*, ed. Daniel Orrells et al. (Oxford: Oxford University Press, 2011) 381. Also see Tessa Roynon, *Toni Morrison and the Classical Tradition: Transforming American Culture* (Oxford: Oxford University Press, 2014).

[99] Robert Stepto, "'Intimate Things in Place': A Conversation with Toni Morrison," *Toni Morrison: Critical Perspectives* 384. This interview was conducted in her office at Random House.

see her without looking at her, and never, never went near.…So we avoided Pecola Breedlove—forever" (158). And to the (now) obvious point: *she pulled it off.* Pecola prayed every night for a year. She brought her small, shy self to the demonic Soaphead Church, having been rejected by everyone else, and asked for his help. She put herself in his hands, swallowed her fear and nausea, and approached God Himself with a sacrificial offering of old dog Bob. She believed with all her soul and created a self-sufficient world of her own. Whatta girl! Do any of us have the chutzpah to tell her she would have been better off sticking to a world full of Maureens, Geraldines, Paulines?[100]

Pecola cast her whole being on that one self-destructive desire to escape her fate, to own herself however monstrous it appeared to others. Our griot lovingly, admiringly, sings her fate while undercutting everything and everyone around her—even Claudia at the end. Only the three whores/witches survive the beat down—and Cholly: "He, at any rate, was the one who loved her enough to touch her, envelop her, give something of himself to her" (159). Fair must become foul, and foul must become fair if we are to sing a new song. The internalized Whiteness that poisons this whole world must be spewed out—and then? Then maybe we'll see what's on the other side of everything, the God's eye view, the transcendent view toward which our implied author gestures. The implied author of this textual mess may well be the stand-in for the putative Author of this whole messy world! As Morrison modestly said in her Jefferson Lecture, "I believe I am detecting an informed vision based on harrowing experience that nevertheless gestures toward a redemptive future."

## *Paradise*

We have barely scratched the surface of Morrison's literary worlds, a *deep* scratch but a bare scratch nevertheless. *The Bluest Eye* bent a griot's tale to begin to explode a set of racial commonplaces. *Paradise*, her seventh novel

[100] Jack and Jill of America, Inc. was founded by twenty middle-class African-American mothers in Philadelphia in 1938 "to bestow upon our children all opportunities possible for a normal and graceful approach to a beautiful adulthood." When queried at its sixtieth anniversary celebration about its elitist—and color-sensitive—character, one of the founders, Louise Truett, 87, replied: "We had a group of children from well-known, productive people in Philadelphia.…I didn't know a lot of dark-skinned people. I just didn't know them" (Marianne Rohrlich, "Feeling Isolated at the Top, Seeking Roots," *New York Times* (19 July 1998) www.nytimes.com/1998/07/19/style/feeling-isolated-at-the-top-seeking-roots.

written a quarter of a century later (1997), complicates and completes this demythologization[101] of the American Black experience. *Paradise* was the first novel she published after receiving the Nobel Prize; she conceived of it as completing the loose trilogy begun with *Beloved* (1987) and *Jazz* (1992). At the time, it was criticized for shallow characterizations, mystified, simplistic story lines, and inconsequential verbal lyricism.[102] These are, of course, the

---

[101] Paul Ricoeur's refined notion of "demythologization" insists on the necessity of a "foundational mytho-poetic nucleus of a society," which symbolically underlies the particular hierarchical structuring or distribution of the constituents of society (i.e., politics, nature, economics, art, religion, science, etc.). Contrary to Rudolf Bultmann (who introduced the concept of demythologization to modernize Christianity by stripping it of its New Testament cosmological "wonder world") no *logos* or rational analysis can do away with this irreducible, opaque kernel of symbolic meaning, because the *logos* and its cultural role in a society are themselves shaped, given meaning, and accredited through this mythical nucleus. Instead, the critical perspective of demythologization must be brought to bear when the *mythos* hardens into a literalistic, perverse reification, for example, the myth of absolute power in fascism or the myth of the sacrificial scapegoat in anti-Semitism and racism. Alternatively, when a community experiences a fundamental existential crisis, a "boundary situation" that threatens its destruction from within or without, it may be compelled philosophically "to return to the very roots of its identity": "The solution to the immediate crisis is no longer a purely political or technical matter but demands that we ask ourselves the ultimate questions concerning our origins and ends: where do we come from? Where do we go?" This is demythologization as critical resuscitation or historical reinterpretation of *genuine* myths, of "those myths which have as horizon the liberation of mankind as a whole." Paul Ricoeur and Richard Kearney, "Myth as the Bearer of Possible Worlds," *The Crane Bag* 2.1/2 (1978): 112–18. As Kearney explains, under those circumstances "time is made human through the interweaving of history and fiction—or more precisely through the 'refiguration' of time in historical and fictional narrative....Subjects, individual or communal, come to *imagine* and *know* themselves in the stories they tell about themselves." Richard Kearney, "Narrative Imagination: Between Ethics and Poetics," *Philosophy and Social Criticism* 21.5/6 (1995): 173–90. These stories open up possible worlds through which "we become aware of our basic capacities and reasons for surviving, for being and continuing to be what we are." Ricoeur and Kearney, "Myth as the Bearer of Possible Worlds" 114. This seems like a wonderfully apt description of Morrison's overall project.

[102] Michiko Kakutani in the *New York Times* compared it unfavorably to previous novels: "Whereas earlier Morrison novels like 'Beloved,' 'Song of Solomon' and 'Sula' fused the historical and the mythic, the mundane and the fantastic into a seamless piece of music, this novel remains an earthbound hodgepodge, devoid of both urgency and narrative sleight of hand. It's neither grounded in closely observed

same characteristics that told a double-voiced tale in *The Bluest Eye*. The myth in Lorain, Ohio, was that blue eyes were the paradigm of beauty. The myth in Ruby, Oklahoma, is that black skin is the paradigm of integrity; even one drop of White blood compromises the community. In terms of Paul Ricoeur's notion of demythologization, the reified myth of Black innocence—the innocence of the victim—is just the inverse of the perverse myth of white dominance and, more importantly, is inadequate to undergird the community in the face of the crisis of freedom.[103]

The *demand* for freedom, with its dialectic of rebellion and accommodation, diffidence and subversion, self-respect and humiliation, sustained the African-American community through the violence of slavery and segregation. Its resonance with Exodus, "Let my people go!" and with the New Testament ethic of love and transfiguration, "the first shall be last and the last shall be first," wed history with hope. Her first novel in the trilogy, *Beloved*, showed the almost incomprehensible depth of that demand for freedom, together with a glimpse of the incalculable cost of acting on it. Finally,

---

vignettes of real life, nor lofted by the dreamlike images the author has used so dexterously in the past to suggest the strangeness of American history; the novel's one surreal set-piece feels like a hasty afterthought, clumsily grafted on to try to kick the story to another level." Michiko Kakutani, "'Paradise': Worthy Women, Unredeemable Men," *New York Times* (6 January 1998) movies2.nytimes.com/books/98/01/04/daily/morrison-book-review-art.html. James Wood called it "sentimental, evasive, and cloudy": "in fact Morison loves her own language more than she loves her characters, and appears to view them as mere spokes of style who exist to keep her lyricism in motion." James Wood, "Toni Morrison's False Magic," *The Broken Estate: Essays on Literature and Belief* (New York: Random House, 1999) 214, 219. He accuses her of trading novelistic explanatory narrative for too easy myth, false magic, and parable. Wood assumes, of course, that Morrison aims (and misses) at a novelistic Dick-and-Jane narrative (the "how" of things) instead of—as I will argue—playing the dozens with the "why" of things.

[103] This is where someone like Stanley Crouch, brilliant Black jazz critic and controversial cultural commentator, gets Morrison so wrong. He accuses her (and others) of following James Baldwin's "new catechism": "Blessed are the victims…for their suffering has illuminated them, and they shall lead us to the light, even as they provide magnets for our guilt." He is brutal in his dismissal of *Beloved*: "For *Beloved*, above all else, is a blackface holocaust novel. It seems to have been written in order to enter American slavery into the big-time martyr ratings contest, a contest usually won by references to, and works about, the experience of Jews at the hands of Nazis." Stanley Crouch, "Literary Conjure Woman," *The New Republic* (19 October 1987) 38.

wholeness was unattainable within the rationalized, sadistic, Christian/criminal regime of Southern slavery. The unlived life can never be fully expiated—instead your thwarted love of the world will betray and haunt you.[104] The second novel, *Jazz*, explored a brief future of freedom: creative, cosmopolitan by fits, full of the imaginative drama of private lives, with their own myths, transgressions, conceits, and reconciliations. "History is over, you all, and everything's ahead at last."[105] Of course, in reality their bitter, brutal, resilient histories continue to shape and misshape their "freed" lives in unexpected ways. In the Roaring Twenties, the funk of the blues, the exuberance and playfulness of jazz, and an extraordinary stylization of passion and personality were the brilliant coming-out party for finally emancipated African-Americans. But, they were, perhaps necessarily, transitional. As we in fact know, the promising moment of the Great Migration, the Jazz Age, the Harlem Renaissance, the "New Negro Movement" melted away into the Great Depression, the disappearance of manufacturing jobs from the inner city,[106] post-war redlining, and the informal separation or *de facto* segregation of the races in Northern, Midwestern, and Western cities. The ghetto, "the projects," and failed inner-city schools replaced the slave quarters and tenant shacks. This is history that threatens to repeat itself over and over. Recompense for the original sin of slavery is not so easily paid forward.

By the time that Daniel Patrick Moynihan released *The Negro Family: The Case for National Action* in 1965 through the US Department of Labor, he could blame persistent Black poverty on the "tangle of pathology" within collapsing Black nuclear families, a deterioration capable of perpetuating itself—he thought—without the malevolence of the White world. Freedom in the event was as much a curse as a hope. The core myth of the demand for freedom had to be rethought, resuscitated, re-appropriated. Freedom at long last for slaves is a crisis, *not* in-and-of-itself a solution. *Paradise* wants to start over in a new Eden from which Satan is excluded—with the chance of getting it right this time. This mythic reification must be exposed as well; original sin infects the victim as well as the oppressor. In that difficult recognition may lie the seeds of a reconciliation of the "races" and the quietus of "Whiteness." Toni Morrison's apparent betrayal of racial solidarity may well be a salvific solvent allowing African-American "Black" to become eventually simply a

[104] Toni Morrison, *Beloved* (New York: Vintage, 2004).

[105] Toni Morrison, *Jazz* (New York: Vintage, 2004) 7.

[106] See William Julius Wilson, *The Truly Disadvantaged: The Inner City, the Underclass, and Public Policy*, 2nd ed., (Chicago: University Of Chicago Press, 2012).

distinctive ethnicity like "Russian" or "Irish"—or "Navaho" or "White Anglo-Saxon Protestant" (WASP). How *do* you get over on four hundred years of pervasive history that you are still part of? Does Morrison need to be more Black or less Black or beyond Black? Let's take a look at *Paradise*, where the failure of the self-willed future is prerequisite to transcendence.

Morrison refuses to cater to (White) readers by conducting them into her novels through a "safe, welcoming lobby" that lets them know as readers where they are in the moral scheme of things, as she says, "the line of demarcation between the sacred and the obscene, public and private, them and us."[107] Her insistence on an alien(ating) opening reaches an apogee in *Paradise*: "They shoot the white girl first"[108] (3). Every alarm goes off. "They" encompasses every monstrous power that ever lurked under your bed. "Shoot" makes it final with no chance of appeal or bargaining. Both "white" and "girl" violate whatever is left of middle-class security. And "first" promises ominous terror to come wherever and whenever we are at that present moment. You either shut the book right now or can't wait to read on—in either case anticipation is all you have to go on. Except for the epigraph. The epigraph is a very curious signpost indeed. It is both orienting and alienating in a much deeper sense.

Both *Jazz* and *Paradise* have epigraphs drawn from an ancient Coptic text that was among the Fourth Century Nag Hammadi codices discovered by accident in 1945 in upper Egypt and eventually deciphered and translated into English in the 1970s. This is unexpected, to say the least. These Coptic texts are translations of earlier Greek texts dating from the very beginning of Christianity, texts and ideas, so-called Gnosticism, that came to be considered heretical by later Christian theologians.[109] Elements of the syncretic mythos of Gnosticism persisted among some Jews, Christians, Muslims,

[107] Morrison, *Tanner Lecture*, 151.

[108] Toni Morrison, *Paradise* (New York: Vintage, 2014); all references to *Paradise* will be from this edition and indicated parenthetically in the text.

[109] Irenaeus, Bishop of Lyon, published *On the Detection and Overthrow of the So-Called Gnosis* in 180 CE. The contrast of his version of Christianity with Gnostic ideas did much to define what became orthodox Christian belief: Jesus' incarnation, death, and resurrection as salvific, four canonical Gospels telling his story, the unity and authority of both the Old Testament and Christian Scriptures, the unbroken line of apostolic authority and tradition in the bishops of the Church with its head in Rome, and creedal statements defining these core beliefs for the faithful. Until the discovery of the Nag Hammadi codices, Irenaeus and other heresiologists were the main source of our knowledge of Gnosticism through their attacks on it.

Zoroastrians, Buddhists, and Neo-Platonists until the late middle ages, with revivals of interest in the nineteenth century, including by the philosopher Arthur Schopenhauer and the psychologist Carl Jung. The discovery of the Nag Hammadi library, including new and startling "Gospels," reached a much broader audience with the publication of *The Gnostic Gospels* by Elaine Pagels in 1979, which was a bestseller and won both the National Book Award and the National Book Critics Circle Award. Pagels's controversial thesis was that early Christianity was much more various and contested than later orthodoxy suggests. But more than this rethinking of theological history, a number of the ideas in these Gnostic texts seemed shocking: separating the divinity of Christ from Jesus the man, rejecting the Old Testament God as the ignorant creator of this material world of pain and suffering, recognizing a multitude of subordinate deities, including Christ and Sophia the goddess of Wisdom, insisting that those who possess the *gnosis* (sacred knowledge imparted by Christ) can save themselves for eternal life as spiritual beings.

These ideas, which took many, many different forms according to the ancient heresiologists, were neither formal creeds nor philosophic rationalizations. They were of a piece with the mythologies of both the ancient Jewish world and the pagan Greco-Roman world. As Freud and Jung recognized, these myths express archetypes of the human situation in visionary and emotionally powerful stories. Orthodox Christianity and Gnosticism share a key mythos that distinguishes them from paganism: *the world we live and die in is corrupt*. For the ancient Greeks, the key mythos was the contrast between the deathless gods with their superhuman powers and the world of human strife, where "creatures of a day" are the playthings of divine favor and malice. The thwarted desire for human excellence and the cruelties and ironies of human endeavor simply are our fate as beings who die. It is a fundamentally tragic worldview. Christianity and Gnosticism, by contrast, envision a world where divine and human interpenetrate, in the former God can become man, in the latter man has a spark of divinity. In these religious visions, death need not be final. The difference between Christian and Gnostic is in the sense of corruption that condemns us to death—and its resolution. For orthodox Christianity, it is man's Fallen nature (sin and disobedience) that spoils Paradise, the good and plentiful world of God's creation. For Gnostics, it is the separation of some part of the divine from the ultimate Godhead that creates a Fallen world—the Creator God is an ignorant "Demiurge" or Designer of matter. In the Christian mythos, man requires redemption through Jesus' sacrifice on the Cross. In the Gnostic mythos, man requires enlightenment (*gnosis*) through Jesus' divinization on the Cross. If Jesus the wisdom teacher can become divine, then so can we when we grasp his insight, his intuition of himself as possessing the God within. The one holds out the promise of resurrection of the body, while the other envisions a transfiguration into pure and eternal spirit.

Morrison's epigraphs to both *Jazz* and *Paradise* are taken from the short Gnostic text "Thunder, Perfect Mind." As Elaine Pagels described it, "'Thunder, Perfect Mind' is a marvelous, strange poem. It speaks in the voice of a feminine divine power, but one that unites all opposites. One that is not only speaking in women, but also in all people. One that speaks not only in citizens, but aliens, it says, in the poor and in the rich. It's a poem which sees the radiance of the divine in all aspects of human life."[110] The speaker (perhaps Sophia, the personification of Wisdom) unites all division in the mundane world:

> Do not be ignorant of me. / For I am the first and the last. / I am the honored one and the scorned one. / I am the whore and the holy one. / I am the wife and the virgin. / I am the mother and the daughter. / I am the members of my mother. / I am the barren one and many are her sons.[111]

In some sources, Sophia plays a central role in the cosmic drama. Her unrequited desire for the ultimate Godhead, the Beyond the Beyond, leads her to descend into the material chaos of the Uncreated. From her womb comes the inferior Creator God, as well as all distinction and difference in matter and time—and the divine sparks of human spirituality. Her return to the presence of the Godhead will require Christ's intervention, becoming her missing bridegroom—and his revelation of himself will save with her those spirits possessed of *gnosis*, insight into the ultimate nature of Reality. At this remove, an inexact summary seems the best we will get.

What is going on here and does it matter? This is no entrance to a welcoming lobby; it serves up a phantasmagoria of colliding judgments. The action of the novel turns on 1) the exodus and radical self-segregation of the post-Reconstruction Black families who settled Haven, Oklahoma, and then Ruby; 2) the theological and social differences between the three Protestant churches in Ruby; 3) a generational dispute over the obscure meaning of a

---

[110] Elaine Pagels, "From Jesus to Christ," *Frontline* www.pbs.org/wgbh/pages/frontline/shows/religion/maps/primary/thunder.

[111] "Thunder, Perfect Mind," trans. George MacRae, *The Nag Hammadi Library*, www.gnosis.org/naghamm/thunder.

sacred object meant to last forever as the rallying point of the community; and 4) a lack of agreement on the part of the leadership on the limits and range of civic responsibilities (how far can individuals go in pursuing invidious personal goals and how concerned should the local community be about the larger society upon which their social and economic survival depends?). This discord comes to a head as 5) a conflict develops with a neighboring "cloistered" community that was a former Catholic convent and missionary school for assimilating Arapaho children (helping them forget who they are), which has become a womanist refuge for a diverse collection of wounded birds (each with her own conflicted history), seeking to heal them (helping them remember who they are) through a combination of Catholicism (blessed Mother Mary) and Brazilian Voodoo or Candomblé (all the other saints of the Catholic Church as personal spirits).[112] The ignorant and violent Black patriarchy that rules and preserves Ruby are 6) losing control of their children, their wives, and themselves and 7) feel that the strange but harmless women in the Convent are the cause of their decline—a source of corruption. 8) *They set out to lynch them*! Now, when you preface this stew of antagonisms and moral reversals with a leading allusion to Gnosticism and a female goddess of Wisdom who is "the designation of the division" of everything created, you stir it with a new spoon in a new way—or maybe in a new pot altogether.

Where is Morrison going with this? She is going nowhere. By the "end" of the novel, her characters are literally going, going, gone—maybe into a Gnostic heaven. What emerges is neither a perspective of a narrator or a character or an implied author nor some founding tradition nor some utopian ideology nor a New World religion.[113] On these levels, the novel doesn't hold together. It remains narratively open-ended. We do not know what story is being told. As Pastor Misner concludes listening to different stories of what happened, no one had "been able to formulate a credible, sermonizable account of it." (297) We don't know *what* to think—but we do get a lesson in *how* to think.

---

[112] See Jennifer Terry, "A New World Religion? Creolisation and Candomblé in Toni Morrison's *Paradise*," *Toni Morrison and the Bible*, ed. Shirley Stave (New York: Peter Lang, 2006).

[113] Jennifer Terry suggests that Morrison is contrasting "constructive and destructive religious practices" to explore "a positive model of New World creolisation." Ibid., 205, 192. This cultic take on Morrison misses the singular power of the novel in favor of tendentious amateur theologizing.

Instead of closure, *Paradise* displays the kind of imaginative deconstruction of vital existential oppositions that the anthropologist Claude Lévi-Strauss identified as the core of mythical thinking.[114] As his student Edmund Leach put it, "mediation between opposites is precisely what religious thinking is all about."[115] Where contrasting aspects of human life do not admit of reconciliation, mythic thought cobbles them together in apparently non-consequential stories that incorporate the quasi-mediation of other familiar oppositions or motifs: "mythical thought always progresses from the awareness of oppositions toward their resolution....Two opposite terms with no intermediary always tend to be replaced by two equivalent terms which admit of a third one as a mediator; then one of the polar terms and the mediator become replaced by a new triad, and so on."[116] Lévi-Strauss denominated this as *bricolage* or putting together in new ways events picked out of our concrete experience as significant and signifying.[117] He quotes Franz Boas with

---

[114] "Mythical" can mean many different things to us—besides "imaginary." The sense I take from Lévi-Strauss's exhaustive examination of native South American myths is different from the elevated (poetic, romantic, epic) "gaze" that knits together past and future, which Carolyn Denard identifies in Morrison. Carolyn Denard, "The Long, High Gaze: The Mythical Consciousness of Toni Morrison and William Faulkner," *Unflinching Gaze: Morrison and Faulkner Re-Envisioned*, eds. Carol Kolmerten et al. (Jackson: University Press of Mississippi, 1997). It is also different from the incorporation of mythological elements of the Bible and other discourses (e.g., Afro-American, Puritan, Beat, Roman, Yoruban) that Benjamin Burr argues Morrison employs in deconstructive juxtaposition to create a liminal space through which a non-privileged concept of salvation becomes possible. Benjamin Burr, "Mythopoetic Syncretism in *Paradise* and the Deconstruction of Hospitality in *Love*," *Toni Morrison and the Bible*, ed. Shirley Stave (New York: Peter Lang, 2006).

[115] Edmund Leach and D. Alan Aycock, *Structuralist Interpretations of Biblical Myth* (Cambridge: Cambridge University Press, 1983) 16.

[116] Claude Lévi-Strauss, *Structural Anthropology*, trans. Claire Jacobson and Brooke Grindfest Schoepf (New York: Basic Books, 1963) 224. Lévi-Strauss's triad is represented paradigmatically in his essay "Structural Analysis" as a vertical pole whose lower terminus is itself a polarity analogically replacing the original, unsurpassable opposition. Ibid., 49. Then, as he says, this new mediating term and a transform of one of the original oppositional terms can become the field for a new triad and an ever more fine-grained mediation. See schematic on p. 217.

[117] According to Lévi-Strauss, myth, magic, art, and ritual all share this concrete signification, signs of something more than themselves, addressing someone about something of experiential value to them. Comparing these modes of thought with those of the scientist or engineer, he insists that these "prior" sciences were no less

approval: "it would seem that mythological worlds have been built up, only to be shattered again, and that new worlds were built from the fragments."[118] This exactly fits Tessa Roynon's description of Morrison's "unifying impulse in her work—that of perpetually taking preexisting cultural structures apart and revising, rewriting, reenvisioning, or rebuilding them into new and better forms."[119]

According to Lévi-Strauss, this dream-like narrative complication proceeds until its richness and subtlety assuages—more or less—the angst of the provoking vital contradiction. Literally, the inexplicable mundane and its cognitive disturbance is transcended, not by going above, but by going below, deeper and deeper beneath the surface of the irreconcilable dimensions of the human world. Amphiboly surpasses narrativity. To put this more colloquially, Morrison is myth-making as much as she is story-telling.[120] She shatters the reification of Black victimhood and White racism while insinuating the power of racial memory to generate a new future for Black Americans—completing her demythologization of the American Black experience.

---

empirical and analytic, indeed that they undergirded the great vault into human culture: "It was in neolithic times that man's mastery of the great arts of civilization—of pottery, weaving, agriculture and the domestication of animals—became firmly established....Each of these techniques assumes centuries of active and methodical observation, of bold hypotheses tested by means of endlessly repeated experiments." Claude Lévi-Strauss, *The Savage Mind*, trans. George Weidenfield (Chicago: University of Chicago Press, 1962) 16–17. Modernity is scientific thought exploiting a more abstract (mathematical) and purely conceptual approach to the natural world, one that takes us far from any concrete or perceptual experience—but is powerfully predictive within its simplified realm. See my "Philosophical Coda" below for a critique of this purely instrumental approach to complex human realities.

[118] Ibid., 27.

[119] Roynon, *The Cambridge Introduction to Toni Morrison,* 12.

[120] Roynon draws the opposite conclusion from the same evidence. She sees the binary oppositions of the novel as the problem: "Morrison exposes the dangers of rigid binary thinking, or of action based on polarized thinking" and mythmaking as a danger: "*Paradise* is a novel about the dangers inherent in mythology and mythmaking." She and I completely agree that it would be a mistake to read these polarities as either "right" or "wrong," but she thinks Morrison is "more interested in the interactions between the Convent and Ruby than in their dissimilarity, in the (lost) potential for a mutually beneficial symbiosis than in the defeat of either one by the other." Ibid., 65–66. The idea of an ameliorative symbiosis sounds too good to be true or else smacks of Booker T. Washington's "Atlanta Compromise." Let's all just play nice, each in his/her place. The problem, as Ricoeur sees, is a *reified* mythos.

Morrison's fundamental conceit for the novel is a brilliant move. Ruby is an isolated, all-Black American town founded in the Forties by returning veterans. The novel traces the lives of two generations into the Seventies. This "bracketed" community allows her to focus on its racial character independently of the surrounding racist society battling through desegregation and Vietnam and assassinations, the Kennedys, Malcolm X, King. The problems and possibilities of the community are further bracketed by the interposition of a previous incarnation as Haven, formed by ex-slaves. Imaginatively, the racial character of the fifteen founding families of Ruby is as separated from white racism as it is possible to get, short of science fiction. To be precise, their character has been formed by white racism and their forefathers' resistance to White (and Black) racism. But white racism is no longer the context and challenge for them. They are their own best friends and worst enemies. As they own their past and seek their promised future, Morrison weaves the cross-currents of a critical resuscitation of the American Black *mythos*.

American racism predicated on color treats Black and White as irreconcilable; fantastically, even a drop of Black blood contaminates. The predominance of White blood elevates, particularly in the Black community. In almost every public domain that matters, White must dominate. And, to drive home this murderously enforced division of humanity, *Paradise* imaginatively reverses the judgments: even a drop of White blood contaminates, the blackest of black elevates, and murder enforces Black purity. On top of this riven sense of being American, Morrison layers a brutal patriarchy in Ruby and its opposite, a female sanctuary in the Convent. Within racism, femininity (as a mediating term) spans the racial divide.[121] White women could be wives and mothers and daughters; Black women were servants and concubines and chattel. Clearly—but unspeakably—absolute separation of the races was partially breached by the intimate services of Black women for Whites (cooks, housekeepers, nannies, and nurses)—and by the infusion of White blood in the offspring of slave women raped by masters and their sons. This unmentionable breach in American racism is compensated by a White male anxiety verging on panic that a Black man might impregnate a White woman—a taboo enforced by terror.[122]

[121] In Lévi-Strauss's terms, the unbridgeable opposition of American "blacks" and "American" whites is mediated by the polarity of gender, with the feminine pole becoming the "unspeakable thing," as Morrison calls miscegenation. Morrison, *Tanner Lecture*, 126–29.

[122] This reverse miscegenation is one of the prominent story lines in *Jazz*.

The town of Ruby is premised on denying this profoundly emasculating mediating connection, protecting with distance and guns the security of its women from White men—while staving off the threat of lynch mobs coming for the Black men. At the same time, these Black men emulate their former masters in insisting on the subservient status of their women and confining them to roles as brood mares and homemakers—"garden rivals." The mythos needs to deepen.

The servile intimacy of Black women gives us a way to re-construe "Blackness" as fundamentally Other in America. As Pauline Breedlove wonderfully illustrated in *The Bluest Eye*, serving a beautiful, blue-eyed family and child can consume nurture for one's own ugly Black child. In that case, "Us" by nurture trumps "Us" by blood. Her own chaotic family and burned-out husband become the "Them" she must punish and denigrate. In *Paradise*, this Otherness is no longer even tangentially a matter of White (by proxy) on Black. The Convent embodies and enshrines this gift/curse of Black, mongrel, female Nurture as the common denominator of their accepting, healing, celebrating community—including a token White girl. There is no other connection between these lost souls out in the middle of nowhere than their caring for each other. By contrast, the all Black community in Ruby is an exclusive community of blood and inheritance, fifteen families descended from the freedmen who first founded Haven. There is no us and them in the Convent; there is nothing but us versus them in Ruby. This sense of Alterity is so strong that even the Black women in the Convent become alien and threatening to them—as were the light-skinned Black people who turned away their darker fellow former slaves in the long exodus to Haven. The Otherness of blood is so strong that, when Deek Morgan and Consolata's carnal romance briefly bridges the divide between town and cloister (the image is of two intertwined fig trees), their delight in one another cannot survive her sanguine kiss—she bites his lip and licks up his blood. Them threatens to engulf Us; Nurture threatens to dilute Blood heritance; servility becomes assertive. The supposed Them of the Convent are so threatening that eventually murder is done. But this radical Alterity is mere fantasy. In spite of their ghost stories, when the lynch mob invades the Convent there is no Them there—just frightened women interrupted in their ordinary domestic tasks. As our epigraph to this chapter indicates, paradoxically the Us of Whiteness actually depends on the Them of Blackness. When the men of Ruby treat rapacious, murderous "white" men as Them, there is no them there either. Whiteness is neither blood nor nurture—whiteness *per se*, unlike Blackness, is not even potentially community.[123] It is all on the Black community now; the mythos moves into the roots of Blackness in America.

The Oven is a superb mythic symbol that mediates between community as Nurture and community as Blood. It stands in contrast to the gods and their powers, as manmade yet sacred. Black deliverance will not depend primarily on divine favor—however much one might argue about it. At its creation, the Oven immediately became the communal Hearth around which the new citizens of Haven gathered "for talk, for society, for the comfort of hot game." Deek and Steward's grandfather had chosen the words forged in iron on the Oven's lip, words that pointed up the narrow path of righteousness. Even as Haven was dying forty years later from the Depression and the Dust Bowl, "the Oven stayed alive" (15). Just so, the sacred fire of Vesta the Goddess of the Hearth, tended by Vestal Virgins for over a thousand years, was considered essential to Rome's continuity and security. (Among other powers, the Vestal Virgins could supposedly utter a prayer that rooted runaway slaves to the spot so long as they were within the city, and their mere presence could free condemned slaves.)[124] Returning from the War, Haven on its last legs, lessons learned over three generations "about how to protect a town": "like the ex-slaves who knew what came first, the ex-soldiers broke up the Oven and loaded it into two trucks even before they took apart their own beds" (16). The fire was extinguished. The grandparents were abandoned. Moving deeper into Oklahoma, they looked for the most remote spot "Out There."

The Oven as sacred Hearth and Nurture dies with Haven. These men and women now are not half the men and women their Old Fathers were with "their spectacular history...and cold-blooded obsession" (14). If the Old

---

[123] The stupidity and fatuity of so-called white supremacy is patent here. Nothing but a dog whistle for mendacious politicians and duplicitous provocateurs.

[124] Rhea Silvia was the legendary Vestal Virgin who, claiming that the god Mars impregnated her, gave birth to the twins Romulus and Remus. Their granduncle the King sought to kill them. They survived as feral children with a wolf for a foster mother and a god for a father (the ultimate in miscegenation). As young men, they restored their grandfather to the throne his brother had wrenched from him. Setting out to found a city of their own, they disagreed about which of the seven hills to choose as their site, and, each claiming the gods' favor, Romulus killed Remus—and went on to found Rome. Just so, Big Papa, Zechariah or "Coffee" to his twin brother's "Tea," chose to leave his truckling brother behind as he led the Old Fathers toward Haven, echoing the emphasis on uncompromising purity of the Biblical Zechariah.

Fathers were Father Abraham and his sons Ishmael[125] and Isaac on their exodus out of Harran toward a Promised Land, then Steward and Deek are Moses and Aaron still escaping the legacy of slavery and still trying to lead the way to that Promised Land. On this second exodus toward Paradise, the Oven thus becomes instead their Ark of the Covenant, preserving the holy tales of the elders, and meticulously recreated in Ruby. "A utility became a shrine" (103). However, crucial letters have been lost from its Holy Writ and no one remembers what they were. The (now) old and the young disagree about the admonition to righteousness. Even worse, the Oven has become a gathering point for rebellion and hellion for the young—and there are no tales from the adult generation to add to its memorials:

> Over and over and with the least provocation, they pulled from their stock of stories tales about the old folks, their grands and greatgrands; their fathers and mothers. Dangerous confrontations, clever maneuvers. Testimonies to endurance, wit, skill and strength. Tales of luck and outrage. But why were there no stories to tell of themselves? About their own lives they shut up. Had nothing to say, pass on. As though past heroism was enough of a future to live by. As though, rather than children, they wanted duplicates. (161)

The relentless individualism of America, even Steward and his twin Deek pulled apart by lust, avarice, and patrimony, destroys even the blood connection. The Oven as Hearth should have been the founding of a new Rome, to grow from its own strength, earned by its own strength. It was not—Haven withered away. This is not the mythos that, in the words of Paul Ricoeur, "[has] as horizon the liberation of mankind as a whole."[126]

Under its latter aspect as Ark of the Covenant, the Oven highlights the moral hazard inherent in the self-segregation of the Black community in Ruby. As Chosen or Covenanted—for better or for worse—the community would be responsive to something greater than themselves and their desires.

---

[125] Ishmael represents, perhaps, another path not taken by the freed slaves who founded Haven. Ishmael, the elder brother and scion of Abraham's miscegenation with his wife's African maidservant/slave, remains in Mecca, and his children's children are the progenitors of a great nation, as promised by God. He is the ancestor of Mohammad and thus of Islam and by extension the Nation of Islam with its call for a Black nation to be formed out of Georgia, Alabama, and Mississippi. Jim Crow laws, the Ku Klux Klan, and the sharecropping system all conspired to foreclose any Southern, homegrown route to Black independence and self-reliance.

[126] See fn. 101 above.

But, as self-determined and isolated from external consequences, there is no necessary check on egos and impulses. What feels like freedom can just as easily be license—and licentious. This would, in fact, be phenomenologically identical to the license and licentiousness of the Southern slave owner: "They think they have outfoxed the whiteman when in fact they imitate him" (306). When Steward leads the nine men of Ruby to attack the Convent and its five defenseless women, this is both to rally a community coming apart at the moral seams and, as Pat Best their chronicler "dispassionately" concludes, "because they *could*—which was what being an 8-rock[127] meant to them" (296–97). As Morrison notes, this same sense of unaccountable Privilege—because they *could*—underlay the casual degradation of slaves: "The danger of sympathizing with the stranger is the possibility of becoming a stranger. To lose one's racial-ized rank is to lose one's own valued and enshrined difference."[128] Even Steward's long-growing rage at his lack of control over family and community reflects the "gothic" sensibility of slave owners: "I am not a beast! I am not a beast! I torture the helpless to prove I am not weak."[129]

Haven and Ruby are attempts to escape from history, to leave the past behind, to start over on a different footing. But, severed from the Biblical promises of Exodus and the Gospels, Black hope is replaced by Black Exclusivity—and the fears it brings. The Future can be read either as Promise or as Threat. In Ruby, initial promise gives way to imminent threat. How do we lay claim to what is Ours when it is everywhere surrounded by what is Yours?[130] At its founding there was nothing allowed in Ruby that would attract or serve anyone from outside: "nothing to serve a traveler: no diner, no gas station, no public phone, no movie house, no hospital" (12). But Rev. Misner insists, "We live in the world, Pat. The whole world. Separating us, isolating us—that's always been their weapon. Isolation kills generations. It has no future" (210). The attempt at a safely separated "Ours" is mocked by the ghosts of the Arapahos who once hunted buffalo on these plains. It is mocked by all those "Black" towns that turned away the Old Fathers: "'They don't know we or about we,' said one man. 'Us free like them; was slave like

---

[127] "…eight-rock, a deep deep level in the coal mines. Blue-black people, tall and graceful, whose clear, wide eyes gave no sign of what they really felt about those who weren't 8-rock like them" (193).

[128] Morrison, *The Origin of Others*, 30.

[129] Ibid.

[130] Sargeant Person doubled his desire to eliminate the Convent women with a greedy eye for the pasture land he leased from them. The old joke: all a farmer covets is the bit of land that borders his own.

them. What for is this difference?'" (14). The threat to Exclusivity, the threat of contamination and corruption, becomes so overwhelming that signs of a malignant enemy are seen everywhere. Exclusivity makes live and let live impossible finally. The "moly" of the purply black, fiery peppers that could only be grown by the Convent ceases to work its prophylactic magic as a medium of exchange between Ruby and the Convent. The nine men of Ruby turn into the beasts ("I am not a beast! I am not a beast!") that their passion urged—the Circe myth is turned inside out.[131] The lynch mob strikes.

Finally, thus, it comes down to mortality. Who lives and who dies. What is life? What is death? From "the unacceptable, incomprehensible death" of Save-Marie, Sweetie and Jeff Fleetwood's damaged baby, who never got the chance to live, to Consolata saving by witchcraft Deek and Soane's teenage son, Scout, from a truck wreck—only for him to die in Vietnam. Her witchcraft is unable to keep Mary Magna, her savior from "shit-strewn paths," alive forever. And her witchcraft gives Steward Morgan his excuse to shoot her in the head. The polarity of life and death mediates between the threatening future as Corruption leading to Oblivion, and the power of Memories of Big Papa and his commandment to shape another Generation. Death is either decay of what has been or continuity for what will be.

The final mediating polarity is Corruption versus Generation. So, we come full circle back to the Gnostic myth. What is the corruption that threatens Black identity? What is the *gnosis*, the memory of a desire for wholeness, that might preserve it into the next generation? The easy answers have already been ruled out. On the one hand, this is not a matter of a brutal patriarchy or the assumption by the Morgans of unquestionable authority. On the other, it is not a matter of an all-accepting sisterhood and New Age healing rituals. Under the sign of Sophia, "the designation of division," there are no good and bad guys. The antagonisms that motivate the novel are equally real and equally at fault. This is *not* after all what Michiko Kakutani suggests in the title of her *New York Times* review of *Paradise*: "Worthy Women, Unredeemable Men." From a Gnostic perspective, the divisions themselves are at fault, but—of course—they are the divisions that in one form or another animate all human living. So, we start with the all-embracing attempt by the citizens of Ruby to escape the life-defining, life-denying division of Black and White in America, an escape to an all-Black, 8-rock Black, enclave. As Roynon

[131] In Homer's *Odyssey*, Hermes (at Athena's direction) gave Odysseus the magic herb "moly" to protect him from Circe's enchantment that had turned his men into beasts.

points out, this echoes the emigration of the Pilgrims, the Puritans, the Mormons. The charges that Roger Williams made against his fellow Puritans, their civic coercion of conscience and the displacement of Indians from their lands, could be echoed in Ruby. The fear of the Other that drove white cruelty is now Ruby's fear of the Other, of the Convent, of their own young, even of the men they have become over the past forty years.

"Feet" are the mythic element that brings the newly resuscitated *mythos* to its resting/launching point. Feet that anchor and root us to the earth; feet that allow us to move back and forth across the earth. The hegira out of Mississippi and Louisiana began when Big Papa took a bullet in the foot rather than dance to the White man's tune—leaving his brother behind. Now Deek Morgan, his grandson and a twin like Big Papa, walks barefooted to Rev. Misner to confess his sins: "It was Deacon Morgan who changed the most. It was as though he had looked in his brother's face and did not like himself anymore" (300). This is not about the White man anymore. These are his, his brother's, and his ancestors' own original sins. Even Big Papa was burying his own shame when he rejected his brother:

> "Lack of words," Richard said. "Lack of forgiveness. Lack of love. To lose a brother is a hard thing. To choose to lose one, well, that's worse than the original shame, wouldn't you say?" Deacon looked at his feet for a long time. Richard stayed quiet with him. Finally he raised his head and said: "I got a long way to go, Reverend." "You'll make it," said Richard Misner. "No doubt about it." (303)

The same shame attaches to those better provisioned, lighter-skinned Blacks who turned them away on their journey toward freedom. It is the shame before God that drove Cain to kill his brother Abel.

Shame, the shame of being descended from slaves, must give way to Deek's self-willed humility. In this recreated *mythos,* the memory is not of servility (and the desire for vengeance and/or escape) but of keeping faith with those who wore the yoke and prevailed. Thus, in repentance and resolution, American Blacks become their own archetypes—to work out their own destinies—to judge their own. To become your own judge and live by your own commandment—honoring and transcending the admonition of the Oven of the Old Fathers—is a fraught moral freedom beyond any mere existential freedom.

The Reverend Richard Misner, making his decision to stay "among these outrageously beautiful, flawed and proud people," concludes

> They think they have outfoxed the white man when in fact they imitate him. They think they are protecting their wives and children, when in fact they are maiming them. And when the maimed children ask for help, they look elsewhere for the cause.... Unbridled by Scripture, deafened by the roar of its own history, Ruby, it seemed to him, was an unnecessary failure. How exquisitely human was the wish for permanent happiness, and how thin the human imagination became trying to achieve it. (305)

For the last few pages of *Paradise*, Morrison's imagination thickens like clotted cream. Under the sign of Save-Marie and the life she never had, Morrison sketches people, places, and times that had no life in the novel but are the site of reunions, forgiveness, continuities. Imagination/memory and individual lives somehow connected more than we know are the promise beyond promise. Beyond. Through the closed door or open window that Richard Misner and his Anna Flood sense as they gather, again, the moly of "green, red and plum black" peppers from the abandoned Convent (305).

What a story! It is a story of stories, rupturing the polarity of Black and White through the intersecting universal polarities of male and female, heaven and earth, past and future, life and death, oblivion and memory. Mythically, Race becomes Otherness becomes Privilege becomes Identity as generative—gnostic—deep Memory. (See the schematic below for a visual representation of these structuralist triads of mythic reconciliation.) The mutual deep shame of miscegenation—Morrison's "unspeakable thing"—has been mythically recirculated into the succeeding generations of pale, creamy, ruddy, bronzed, swarthy, olive, tan, brown, and blue-black Americans: 400 years of them. Racism based on skin color—arising from whatever quarter—has been defanged through Morrison's symbolic evocation of our common humanity as men and women, our necessary humility before a transcendent Presence, and our shared history and mortality. Her mysterious, open-ended storytelling acknowledges original sin both as racism's primordial condition and—in its deep glint of a lost wholeness—as its grace-full redemption:

> "Lack of words," Richard said. "Lack of love. To lose a brother is a hard thing. To choose to lose one, well that's worse than the original shame, wouldn't you say?"..."I got a long way to go, Reverend." "You'll make it," said Richard Misner. "No doubt about it."

That is all we need to think for now. Morrison does not have to imagine the next generation for us. *We* must—as so-called White and Black slowly cease to play our self-destructive games of guilt, fear, shame, and blame and realize that these always were our truly shared *American* memories—no matter how difficult and demanding. This book is for Black Americans—but from the other side White Americans must make these our memories too. The astonishingly broad appeal of Morrison's devastated/devastating *Beloved* may show us the way forward. Perhaps that is what it means to be a Black writer, paradoxically to turn failed hopes into transcendent promise both for Blacks, who know that the future must always be forged anew, and for those who are struggling to repent of their disfiguring, imagined "Whiteness"? According to Catholic doctrine, genuine contrition is the indispensable condition of pardon, a pardon that can only come from God.

## Re-Membered Slaves

Toni Morrison is a radical revisionist, refiguring in historical fiction our racist American memory—and its many-sided valorizations and condemnations. Fearlessly bringing forward the historical record, she humanizes it by telling stories that expose the mythic scapegoating of Blacks by Whites (the myth of bestiality) and Whites by Blacks (the myth of brutality). Even deeper, she relays these parables against type, disrupting the narrative, subverting its moral lessons, confusing its voice, and resisting closure—as far from *Uncle Tom's Cabin* as you can get and still tell the same story. Finally, she strips away the moral superiority of the racial victim and, by implication, mitigates the malignity of the racist oppressor. Addressing us all from this no-man's-land between the lines and degrees of "Black" and "White," she risks everything as a Black woman writer, foreswearing the safety and sanctity of Black grievance without conceding an inch to White presumption. *How? From where?* Against expectation (as it must be), it appears that the submerged memory (*anamnesis*) of a lost gnostic wholeness, of a Presence that transcends time and change, animates her millennial hopes of a redemptive future where skin color is just that and cultural identities are free of self-righteous, self-deceiving exploitation. This is the "re-membering" her writing strives—against all partisan faction—to elicit from our primordial memories. A corruption of faithfulness that can be repaired—perhaps—if never forgiven.

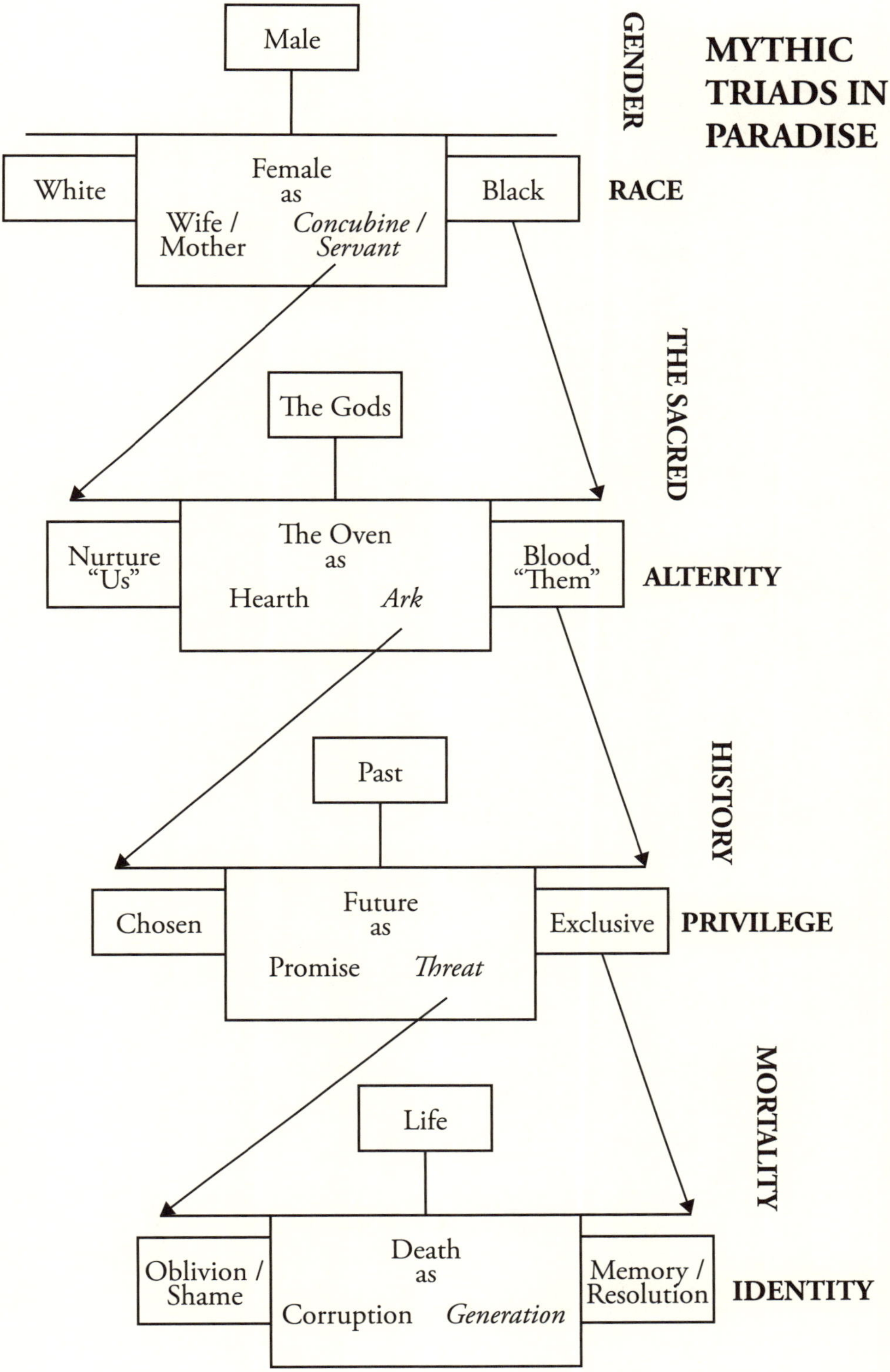
MYTHIC TRIADS IN PARADISE
GENDER
Male
White
Female as
Wife / Mother
Concubine / Servant
Black
RACE
THE SACRED
The Gods
Nurture "Us"
The Oven as
Hearth
Ark
Blood "Them"
ALTERITY
HISTORY
Past
Chosen
Future as
Promise
Threat
Exclusive
PRIVILEGE
MORTALITY
Life
Oblivion / Shame
Death as
Corruption
Generation
Memory / Resolution
IDENTITY

# Philosophical Coda

## Our Narrative Knowledge of the God of Good and Evil

*"To be human means to live as if one were not a being among beings."*
*—Emmanuel Levinas*

Who is the God for whom Malamud, O'Connor, Updike, and Morrison listen? Their common departure point is the God of Abraham, Isaac, and Jacob, the God of Moses, David, Jeremiah, Jesus, Paul, and Mohammed. This God is not just superlative but is uniquely transcendent, in St. Anselm's searching mantra: "something than which nothing greater can be conceived (*quo maius cogitari non potest*)."[1] Nothing could be added to this God that would make Him greater still; He is great beyond recounting. Paradoxically, this transcendent God of Abraham reveals Him/Her/Itself through human history and in his jealous relation to his chosen peoples and prophets: "After these things God tested Abraham, and said to him, 'Abraham!' And he said, 'Here am I.'" (Genesis 22.1) As such, this God is neither mythic archetype nor cultic idol nor philosophical abstraction. He is the living God, present, from moment to moment, place to place, person to person, to a people through their history. Thus, this God, this oxymoronic God who is both transcendent *and* present, must be—at best—"tangential," *touching our experience without entering into it.* (Imagine that God's presence touches us like a plane touches the surface of a sphere. The plane can be infinite, unlike the bounded sphere. The point of contact is, however, vanishingly small, infinitesimal.) From within the sphere of our experience, how do we register that glancing touch? A god that we could directly experience would already be an immanent god, part of the exotic furniture of the world—a pagan superior power, a superb idol. The temptation to worship idols is natural and powerful, as Moses found out. We know how to see and touch and hear them. How can we approach a God that is—at best—tangential?

---

[1] Anselm, *Proslogion,* trans. Thomas Williams (Indianapolis IN: Hackett, 1995) Ch.2.

## The God of Science and Philosophy.

Our science and philosophy must necessarily miss the mark in accounting for this God, since they search out the truths of our possible experience. As Immanuel Kant so acutely insisted, whatever lies outside of our possible perception—the noumenal as opposed to the phenomenal—is unknowable. God is literally unknowable. Yet, as Kant also insisted, we can't help but try to think of that "outside," that beyond, whatever reality ultimately is, independently of how it may "affect" us: *dinge-an-sich-selbst*. Similarly, we cannot help but think of what *we* in ourselves might be beneath the "I think" of our phenomenal experience. Who or what is doing the thinking, perceiving, theorizing, and philosophizing? The reply to Kant over the past two centuries of Western philosophy has been essentially that we should get over it. We should stop trying to think impossible thoughts. In the words of Ludwig Wittgenstein, "What is your aim in philosophy?—To shew the fly the way out of the fly bottle."[2] Philosophy should persuade us to quit butting our heads against illusory limits to our understanding. It appears that philosophy has nothing to add to understanding, except as linguistic therapy for philosophic hubris and confusion. On this "philosophic" accounting, our ordinary understanding of the world is adequate to the world, and the only real questions for debate within any historical cultural/social moment are the everyday questions of enlightened common sense and its pragmatic extension into politics, economics, technology, and education. Philosophy as the search for ultimate truth gives way to persuasion, with its rhetorics of culture, ideology, desire, and aggrandizement.[3] In the midst of all of that, "God" is just another meme to be deployed.

In the meantime, modern science has brushed aside Kant's prohibition on knowledge of a reality independent of human experience. Asking more and more esoteric questions about possible experience and empirically justifying more and more astonishing answers to those questions, science is far from common sense. Has it become the arbiter of ultimate truth? This question is at the very basis of modern science. It is the point that Galileo was forced by the Roman Inquisition to recant: his belief that the earth *really*

[2] Ludwig Wittgenstein, *Philosophical Investigations*, eds. G. E. M. Anscombe and Rush Rhees, trans. G. E. M. Anscombe (Oxford: Blackwell, 1953) §309.

[3] So, we have gone full circle, since the contest between the philosophers and the rhetoricians for the minds of the youth was Plato's central concern twenty-five centuries ago.

moves around the sun? ("*E pur si muove,*" he supposedly muttered under his breath—and spent the rest of his life under house arrest.) According to Galileo, Holy Scripture, Aristotelian/Thomistic philosophy, and common sense were all wrong about this: the sun does *not* come up in the morning. Why Galileo became such an adamant Copernican is unclear; indeed the whole two century-long shift to heliocentrism was a very murky dispute.[4] What is clear is that Galileo was the primary pioneer of a new kind of methodology in science: experimentalism. He built data sets through highly precise measurements of abstract dimensions of phenomena[5] and then tried to fit their correlations to simple mathematical formulas—and it worked. He had discovered a very powerful tool for making successful predictions beyond the range of the existing data. As Francis Bacon grasped and proclaimed, knowledge had become power—rather than insight.[6]

Is this power of prediction the same thing as truth? Because modern science relies on non-intuitive hypotheticals ("theories") and because all scientific belief is tentative (falsifiable but not provable) and historically revisable, many philosophers have tended to take an anti-realist position with respect to scientific truth. On this empiricist view, scientific theories are merely tools (instruments) for generating observable predictions (a position usually called "instrumentalism"). When predictions fail, the tools can be revised to fit the new data. Scientists, on the other hand, tend to be realists; they think the equations they guess at and the theoretical entities they dream up to model these equations are the "real" realities that (in principle) explain all the ordinary experiences of human life. At issue is the question of why modern science works so fantastically well. The instrumentalists find the answer to that question obvious, because scientists revise their equations in light of new data and with the help of heuristic models that suggest new kinds of

---

[4] For the ins and outs of it, see Thomas Kuhn, *The Copernican Revolution* (Cambridge: Harvard University Press, 1957).

[5] For example, he tried to isolate the movement of balls rolling down inclined planes from any source of friction, so that he was only measuring time and distance as they moved—as if frictionless. His crucial notion of inertia is counter to all experience and can never be observed in action, i.e., motion of a body free of any forces acting on it.

[6] "Human knowledge and human power meet in one; for where the cause is not known the effect cannot be produced. Nature to be commanded must be obeyed; and that which in contemplation is as the cause is in operation as the rule." Francis Bacon, *Novum Organum,* (Boston: Taggard & Thompson, 1863) Part I, Aphorism III.

predictions to test out. The realists retort that these theories must grab hold of key features of a hidden reality utterly independent of the human mind—the theories work too well and in such unexpected ways to be mere hacks. Realism seems to fit the situation in physics well (where the theories are, however, most bizarre)[7] and not at all in economics (where real theories are hard to find), for example. As the Nobel Prize economist Milton Friedman put it, "Truly important and significant hypotheses will be found to have 'assumptions' that are wildly inaccurate descriptive representations of reality, and, in general, the more significant the theory, the more unrealistic the assumptions."[8] At any rate, whether merely instrumental or realist in its theorizing, modern science has no need of a God in its explanations. As Pierre-Simon Laplace, the great mathematician and astronomer, reportedly replied to Napoleon when the Emperor asked where the Creator of the Universe was in Laplace's calculations: "*Sire, je n'ai pas eu besoin de cette hypothèse*" ("Sire, I have no need of that hypothesis").

## The God of Testimony.

We seem to have painted ourselves very shortly into a corner. If science and philosophy neither can find nor need a transcendent God, if—at best—God is vanishingly present to us in our direct experience, then what is left to say? But a lot has already been said, by Abraham and his descendants, story after story after story. The God of Abraham, Isaac, and Jacob, the God of Moses, David, Jeremiah, Jesus, Paul, and Mohammed is not the theologians' God. He is the God of the Torah, the Tanakh, the Talmud, the Old and New Testaments, the Qur'an and hadith. Story after story after story he is God as metaphor, symbol, oral and written tradition, apocrypha, folk tales. He is the God of the stories of a Malamud, an O'Connor, an Updike, a Morrison.[9] To admit this is not to give up the game; it is to seize the advantage.

---

[7] However, see Owen Barfield's fascinating attempt to flip the issue by exposing scientific bad faith or broken-backed thinking, which I briefly discuss below.

[8] Milton Friedman, "The Methodology of Positive Economics," *Essays in Positive Economics* (Chicago: University of Chicago Press, 1966) 14.

[9] As Emmanuel Levinas affirms, "I think that across all literature the human face speaks—or stammers, or gives itself a countenance, or struggles with its caricature." Emmanuel Levinas, "Ethics and Spirit," *Difficult Freedom: Essays on Judaism*, trans. Seán Hand (Baltimore: The Johns Hopkins University Press, 1990) 117.

There are ways to attend to reality other than the scientific or the philosophic or the theological. As Owen Barfield has suggestively argued, the scientific and philosophic seem themselves to be derivative from the poetic.[10] Language, as it emerged evolutionarily, created increasingly complex ways of knowing our world and ourselves. Contrary to the exploded positivist presumptions that experience comes to us parceled up as perspicacious simples (sense data, sense impressions),[11] articulable experience began—as it does for all of us as babes—with bewilderingly amorphous and ambiguous apprehensions (Kant's "manifold of intuitions"), as much felt as perceived, the dawn of consciousness. Survival was enhanced by being able to direct attention with gestures and sounds to aspects of communally shared awareness, where our desires, fears, pains, and pleasures—and the sensations that evoke them—overlap with others' feelings and sensations. Survival was further enhanced as these primitive words were poetically stretched to project resemblances, connections, and extensions between or within or beyond aspects of experience. Broadly speaking, this process of specification/connection was poetic, metaphorical: "*any* specifically *new* use of a word or phrase is really a metaphor, since it attempts to rouse cognition of the unknown by suggestion from the known."[12]

In the fullness of time, as these useful metaphorical extensions became literalized, they were available for definition and systematization, as abstract ideas (itself a metaphorical extension). In a cunning irony, the logicist impulse to manipulate these abstracted tokens of enhanced consciousness gave rise to the inherent skepticism of the Sophists, to the dialectical questioning

---

[10] Barfield introduces this idea in the midst of a complicated analysis of the force of "poetic diction," what poetry does to us as we read it and how it does it. But, his point is much broader. As I will briefly discuss below, he argues that metaphor is essentially the basis on which all language develops as a form of directed, articulated consciousness.

[11] For classic takedowns of foundational empiricism see Wilfred Sellars, "Empiricism and the Philosophy of Mind," *Minnesota Studies in Philosophy of Science, Vol. I*, eds. Herbert Feigl and Michael Scriven (Minneapolis: University of Minneapolis Press, 1956) or J. L. Austin, *Sense and Sensibilia* (Oxford: Clarendon, 1962).

[12] Owen Barfield, *Poetic Diction: A Study In Meaning* (Middletown CN: Wesleyan University Press, 1973) 106. The example Barfield offers as "the lowest common measure of our subject" is a Pidgin English "poetic" description of a three-masted screw steamer with two funnels: "Thlee-piecee bamboo, two-piecee puff-puff, walk inside, no-can-see" ibid., 35–36.

of a Socrates, to the speculations and arguments of Plato, Aristotle, Euclid, Galileo, Locke, Newton, Hume, Planck, Wittgenstein, and Ryle. Modern science, according to Barfield's critique, has tended to confuse the abstracted linguistic tokens of our evolving consciousness of reality with Reality itself, independently of our consciousness. On the one hand, these theorized creations of our own minds are taken as miraculously describing the mysterious unrepresentable behind all experience and all phenomena (e.g., quantum waves and the Krebs cycle), and, on the other hand, our own participation in our representations of Reality is dismissed as the mere effect of these theorized indiscernibles on our senses and minds. Then, in a backlash beyond mere irony, our own existence as centers of consciousness and our own world's existence as what we perceive and imagine (our "figurations" of reality, as Barfield calls them), are dismissed as mere illusions within this "mechanomorphic" universe.[13] And, of course, our consciousness of God is the first "illusion" to go.

In spite of Kant's most scrupulous efforts, post-critical scientists and fellow-traveling philosophers[14] fetishize the unrepresentable and then dismiss the conscious soul (and its tangential knowledge of God) as mere idolatry, "the dogma of the Ghost in the Machine," in Gilbert Ryles's formulation.[15] But with Barfield, we can recall that our linguistic knowledge, our expanding knowledge *through the poetic word*, is originally tangential, a metaphor rather

---

[13] Barfield examines the history of this scientific/philosophic conviction of our own nonexistence in *Saving the Appearances: A Study in Idolatry* (Middletown CN: Wesleyan University Press, 1988): "To the extent therefore that the phenomena are experienced as a machine, they are believed to exist independently of man, not to be participated and therefore not to be in the nature of representations,...[depriving] the phenomena of those last representational overtones—'last enchantments', as Matthew Arnold called them—which still informed them in the Middle Ages, and [eliminating] from them the last traces of original participation." Ibid., 51–52.

[14] For brilliant introductions to the materialist philosophy of cognitive science, see Daniel Dennett, *Consciousness Explained* (Boston: Little, Brown and Company, 1991) or Paul and Patricia Churchland, *On the Contrary: Critical Essays 1987–1997* (Cambridge: MIT University Press, 1998). Dennett's *Breaking the Spell: Religion as a Natural Phenomenon* (New York: Viking Penguin, 2006) made him a leading "New Atheist," along with Sam Harris, Richard Dawkins, and Christopher Hitchens.

[15] Gilbert Ryle, *The Concept of Mind* (New York: Barnes & Noble, 1949) 15–16. Ryle fetishizes observable behaviors, a kind of halfway house on the way to a more fundamental materialism.

than a literalism: "a cognition of the unknown by suggestion from the known." In this, listening in our experience for the transcendent word of God is no more or less metaphorical than any other complex apprehension—it just has further to jump and less to go on. The question should be, "What is the metaphor for the divine?" What does it mean to listen for something that will not show itself in our experience? The Word of God *is* that metaphor. What does it mean to listen for the Word of God?

Barfield was speaking of the evolution of linguistic consciousness (and imagining its further and future evolution), but language itself as a medium of communication always grasps what reaches beyond the possible experience of the subject. It is through and through symbolic. It is what Walker Percy, following C. S. Pierce, called "the Delta factor," a triad of person, world, and word where the word transforms organism into "person" and physical environment into "world" (the Helen Keller moment, Percy called it).[16] The word is neither an element of the physical environment (although for communication purposes we have devised various systems of physical signs (languages) to stand in for concepts) nor is it a subjective state of the organism (although the capacity for conceptual thinking is an emergent property of neural networks of sufficient complexity and is originally applied to our subjective sensations and feelings as part of the world: "red," "hungry," "mama"). Instead, the word refers *to* the world *for* an agent. In short, it functions symbolically or intentionally—it points beyond its material basis.[17] The things of this

---

[16] At the age of six, as Miss Anne Sullivan "spelled" the word "w-a-t-e-r" into one of her hands while holding the other hand under a spout of well-water, Helen Keller—deaf and blind from an unknown fever from the age of nineteen months—grasped the mystery of language: "I knew then that 'w-a-t-e-r' meant the wonderful cool something that was flowing over my hand. That living word awakened my soul, gave it light, hope, joy, set it free!" Walker Percy, *The Message in the Bottle* (New York: Farrar, Straus and Giroux, 1975) 33–39.

[17] The great philosopher of science, Karl Popper, used a homely example to illustrate the separate and objective reality of this "World 3" of truths, proofs, theories, and observations communicable through language. He says, suppose all of human technical knowhow and scientific knowledge was somehow wiped from our memories. It would take untold generations to begin to recover it piecemeal by guesses, trial, and error. But if the libraries of the world were still left intact and we could read, then in relatively no time at all we could recapture and duplicate our most advanced knowledge. The knowledge is there in the concepts, not in our brains, and is there independently of whether or not *we* can decipher the signs in which they are inscribed. English, German, Chinese doesn't alter the concepts. Karl Popper,

world are present to us both in our experience (felt and seen and tasted, etc.) *and* symbolically (as "satiny" or "red" or "sweet," for example).[18] The transcendent God is present to us *only* symbolically. The Word of God defines us; we do not define it. So, how do we approach it?

Pierce and Percy take us a step beyond Barfield but they are still too close to Kant and his *a priori* categories of the understanding, too focused on the static moment (the Helen Keller moment) of the apprehension—the gathering in—of what is said. It is Levinas who pushes us back to whatever has already passed in all apprehensions of the Said, which is the *Saying*. The Saying is the orientation to the Other in the welling-up of speech, the desire to communicate, make contact, be heard.[19] He calls it a kind of wakefulness or attention to the other as Other, a proto-symbolism. In the Saying, we are exposed to the Other before we have a chance to gather ourselves in expression of our *conatus essendi*, our struggle to be, as Spinoza called it.[20] Thus, we are exposed in the face of the Other before we can conceptually capture or technologically manipulate or politically master the Other: "Language as *saying* is an ethical openness to the other; as that which is *said*—reduced to a fixed identity or synchronized presence—it is an ontological closure to the other."[21] Levinas sees in this radical vulnerability of the disarmed self the prophetic trace of an infinite height beyond being: "For ethics, it is only in the infinite relation with the other that God passes (*se passé*), that traces of God

*Objective Knowledge: An Evolutionary Approach* (New York: Oxford University Press, 1975).

[18] Even words that seem purely symbolic and made up, such as "neutrino" or "infinite," must find some purchase either in our remote experience or in some logical necessity if they are to have a definite meaning. The positivists were right in this.

[19] As Wittgenstein made clear there can be no private language, a language for my ears only. Language always has sociality at its basis. Ludwig Wittgenstein, *Philosophical Investigations*, §§244–271.

[20] "Each thing, as far as it can by its own power, strives to persevere in its being." Baruch Spinoza, *The Ethics*, Part III, Postulate 6, in *A Spinoza Reader*, ed. and trans. Edwin Curley (Princeton: Princeton University Press, 1994) 159.

[21] Richard Kearney, "Dialogue with Emmanuel Levinas," *Face to Face with Levinas*, ed. Richard Cohen (Albany NY: State University of New York Press, 1986) 31.

are to be found."[22] If, as Heidegger said, "Language is the house of being,"[23] then in the priority of Saying to the Said, our ethical responsiveness to the Other is more primordial than Being. The philosophic dream of an adequation of thought and Reality, the world as a Totality, betrays the human and alienates God. In the trace of God's having been, in our preliminary (always, already) awareness of His judgment, the presentedness or disclosiveness of Being itself is put under judgment—the Being of beings is put under judgment. Another name for this judgment is "time," real time or diachrony, where responsibility comes from a past that is not mine and extends to a future beyond my mortality, the trace of the sacred. Levinas presses on us (he declines to call it preaching) "the necessity to think time in the devotion of a theology without theodicy....Contrary to a religion that feeds on representations, it does not begin with a promise. Is it necessary to again recognize in it the difficult piety—all the certainties and personal risks—of the twentieth century, after the horrors of its genocides and its holocaust?"[24]

Just as hearing the ordinary word transforms the organism into a person, *listening* for the Word of God transforms persons into spiritual seekers (ensouled beings) with a destiny beyond the actions and satisfactions of this world. In Levinas's gloss on Abraham's "Here am I,"

> When in the presence of the Other, I say "Here I am!", this "Here I am!" is the place through which the Infinite enters into language, but without giving itself to be seen. Since it is not thematized, in any case originally, it does not appear....Thus, in the "Here I am!" of the approach of the Other, the Infinite does not show itself. How then does it take on meaning? I will say that the subject who says "Here I am!" *testifies* to the Infinite. It is through this testimony, whose truth is not the truth of representation or perception, that the revelation occurs. It is through this testimony that the very glory of the Infinite glorifies

---

[22] Ibid., 29.

[23] Martin Heidegger, "Letter on Humanism," *Pathmarks*, ed. W. McNeill, trans. F. A. Capuzzi, (Cambridge: Cambridge University Press, 1998) 145. Originally published in 1947.

[24] Emmanuel Levinas, *Time and the Other*, trans. Richard Cohen (Pittsburgh PA: Duquesne University Press, 1987) 120.

> *itself.* The term "glory" does not belong to the language of contemplation.[25]

Kant's Categorical Imperative captures the essence of this transformation: "Act in such a way that you treat humanity, whether in your own person or in the person of any other, never merely as a means to an end, but always at the same time as an end."[26] We are more than freely willing agents; we are ends in ourselves. The Other is not simply a means to my happiness. Kant saw clearly that our intrinsic value is not contingent on this world and cannot be explained in terms of this world. Nevertheless, he tried heroically to derive this ultimacy from reason as autonomous law-giver together with metaphysical postulates of "God" and "immortality."[27] These postulates of practical reason or ethical presumptions have no empirical content, so the understanding can neither affirm nor deny them. As Kant (proudly? reluctantly?) proclaimed, "I have therefore found it necessary to deny knowledge, in order to make room for faith."[28] But faith is not simply a rather hollow belief; it is a responsiveness and a hope. Kant is right that we cannot know/experience God; he is right that we cannot derive our ethical stature from what we can know/experience; he is right that faith is required but his notion of faith is simply a weak shadow of empirical belief: "postulates." The faith required is testimony; it is listening for God's transformative Word: "Here I am!"

## Casting Out the Idols.

Remarkably, the children of Abraham—desert wanderers and marginal exiles—grasped what Kant could not. The story of God's presence *is* God's

---

[25] Levinas, *Ethics and Infinity*, 106–107.

[26] Immanuel Kant, *Grounding for the Metaphysics of Morals*, trans. James Ellington (Indianapolis IN: Hackett, 1993) 36.

[27] Kant introduces these postulates to make the manifest injustice of the world come out right—to vindicate acting in accord with the Categorical Imperative. For him, ethics requires a God who can fix things, fix Being itself for us, according to what we deserve, eventually, at the end of time. As Levinas helps us see, this is not an expression of piety but a rationale for its superfluity, for the superfluity of testimony.

[28] Immanuel Kant, *Critique of Pure Reason*, trans. Norman Kemp Smith (London: Macmillan, 1933) 29.

presence—as testimony, not representation.[29] For Jews, Christians, and Muslims, God's transcendent presence is mediated through the word. He is uniquely a God of the Book. How can God be made present through words? Words must become words for the sacred, words for what transcends words, words at their limits gesturing toward the liminal, at a tangent to the transcendent. The first step toward testimony must be to separate it from representation. We must first separate the idols in these stories from testimony to the living God. The Tanakh or Old Testament shows us the way.

If we begin at the Beginning[30] or *Genesis* of the Word of God, we are presented with three different narratives of God's presence. Two of them aim to describe "God" as representation, as superb idol. The third helps us understand that we cannot understand God; we can only testify to the difficulty of a piety that judges us. What are these three narratives? First, there is the story of a *metaphysical* God, Creator and Sustainer of everything that exists under the heavens and on the earth—present through his handiwork from the starry heavens above to the monsters of the deep. He is a leftover hypothesis from the mythic prescientific age. Second, there is the story of an *ideological* God, Lord and Master of every living thing—present in his commands and covenants, rewards and punishments, the fates of nations. He is an

---

[29] In the famous Hasidic tale shared by Elie Wiesel, the Baal Shem Tov could avert misfortune for the Jews by retiring to a special place in the forest to meditate, light a fire, and say a special prayer—and the miracle would be accomplished. With each succeeding generation of his disciples, a piece of this ritual was lost, but the miracles were still accomplished. Finally, it fell to Rabbi Israel of Rizhin to avert disaster. Sitting in his armchair, he confessed to God that he was unable to find the place in the forest or light the fire or say the prayer: "All I can do is tell the story, and this must be sufficient. And it was sufficient. For God made man because he loves stories." Elie Wiesel, *The Gates of the Forest*, (New York: Holt, Rinehart and Winston, 1995) vi–ix.

[30] More about how you begin the Beginning below. Kant famously argued that the competing ideas of infinite preexistence and of a finite beginning of things are equally plausible to reason because they are absolutely unknowable—not even describable without self-contradiction. This Kantian "antimony of reason" is analogous to narrative amphiboly, the illusion of a beginning and an ending when beginning and ending are also simply events in a series of events (which in turn are merely meaningless "moments" without beginnings and endings to connect them). In the analysis I adapted from Erich Auerbach (see "An Interpretive Strategy" above, pp. 13–15) the question is does a story exploit this amphiboly or conceal it?

atavistic relic of the warrior-priest, god-king regimes of ancient agrarian civilizations. Finally, there is the story of an *ethical* God, Judge and Redeemer of mankind—present in the contest between good and evil in every human breast, "original sin." This is the divine spark that makes humans reach for spiritual humanity and makes human life significant in an otherwise indifferent universe. Tellingly, these three Biblical narratives are already set at tension with one another in Genesis.

The ideological God seems to emerge naturally from the metaphysical God—and both are familiar from other religious traditions: God as Creator, God as Lord, Lord God Almighty. God made the world; it is his to command. The insistence on monotheism in this tradition sets this essentially patriarchal, tribal God apart. There are no other gods, just false idols: "You shall have no other gods before me." Worship me, follow my commandments, and I will keep my promise to you. Go whoring after other gods, take my name in vain, and I will punish you. From this metaphysical and ideological perspective, everything hinges on God as the sole creator, which is the very point that the modern world, particularly modern science, doubts. Moreover, this theological framework raises a deeply significant question. If God as Maker and Ruler were in charge of it all, then why would there be so much cruelty, disaster, and death? Where is the Good in all of this? The statement of the problem of evil goes back, according to David Hume, all the way to Epicurus (341–270 BCE): An all-powerful, all-knowing, and morally perfect God would prevent evil. Evil exists. Therefore, God does not.[31] Traditional theodicies, or justifications of God, seek either to show that an omnipotent God is somehow compatible with the existence of evil or that evil, per se, does not truly exist in God's world. Levinas calls this out as blasphemy. The sacred exists in human life through *the acknowledgement of the incomprehensibility of evil.* The fundamental metaphysical question is not Leibniz's ontological question: "Why is there something rather than nothing?" It is the normative question: "Why is there evil rather than good?"[32]

In Genesis, this question reveals a stark tension between God as Creator Lord and God as Judge. An inexplicable seam runs through Genesis and

[31] David Hume, *Dialogues Concerning Natural Religion*, ed. Nelson Pike (Indianapolis IN: Bobbs-Merrill Company, 1970) 88.

[32] Emmanuel Levinas, "Transcendence and Evil," *Collected Philosophical Papers*, trans. Alphonso Lingis (Dordrecht: Martinus Nijhoff, 1987) 182.

much of the Old and New Testament. On the one side are the awe and diffidence owed the Lord God Almighty, with all the disappointments, departures, disasters, and restorations that human culture and psychology—our creatureliness—intrude on this supernaturally commanded allegiance.[33] On the other side is our accountability—in spite of our creatureliness—for our actions in this world. On the one side it is all on God—and our obedience. On the other side it is all on us—and our choice. As the serpent said, "You will be like God knowing good and evil."[34] If we can choose good knowing it to be good, we can also choose evil knowing it is evil. The terror and exaltation this introduces into God's Creation gives the Bible its theological depth and imbues belief in the biblical God with existential purpose. The Word of God preserves and deepens our knowledge of good and evil, our sacred awareness of a transcendent judgment shaping the meaning of our life stories, of each soul, each family, each community, each people and nation. Let us look a little deeper.

## God as Creator.

Genesis actually begins with the sacred word that gives it its title (*Bereshit*), in the Hebrew text: "*Bereshit bara elohim et hashamayim ve'et ha'aretz.*" As Gabriel Josipivici points out, the phrase seems intentionally ambiguous in its syntax.[35] *Bereshit* can mean either "In the beginning" or "When." Either "In the beginning God created the heavens and the earth. And the earth was *tohu* and *bohu*; and darkness was on the face of the deep." Or "When God set about to create heaven and earth—the world being then *tohu* and *bohu* with darkness over the seas...." The former reading is radical creation *ex nihilo*, with nothing to limit or precede God's powers. The latter reading is, by

[33] The dominion of God is echoed in the dominion of man over every other living thing (Genesis 1.28). Not to be flippant, but as God is to man, so is man to dog. Creaturely impulses are always more of a problem to the Master than to the creature.

[34] God as Creator and Lord raises the specter of God's own ability to choose evil. Baruch Spinoza's pantheistic theodicy, for example, walks around this demonic threat by substituting necessity for God's unaccountable desire to create the good and by making all evil disappear except in men's limited perception.

[35] Gabriel Josipovici, *The Book of God: A Response to the Bible* (New Haven/London: Yale University Press, 1988) 53–59.

contrast, consonant with other ancient Near East creation stories; so, the Akkadian *Enuma Elish* begins "When on high the heaven had not (yet) been named and below the firm ground had not (yet) been given a name, when primeaval Apsu, their begetter, and Mummu-Tiamat who gave them all birth, still mingled their waters,...then the gods were created in their midst." Either creation out of nothing or mythic cosmogony. But, in fact, the ancient Hebrew reads most literally: "At the beginning of [*sic*] created God the heaven and the earth and the earth was *tohu* and *bohu* and darkness on the face of the deep." How to begin with the presence of God in a word? Josipivici argues that the genius of the Hebrew Bible is to start neither with the incomprehensible "out of nothing" nor with the too easily familiar mythic genealogy, but with an ambiguity that is open to both—because the point is to begin, to break the silence, to start the book, to begin to listen for the word of God. How to start? By starting: *Bereshit.* The Hebrew Bible is neither a theory nor a myth. It is listening for God's presence in the word. We start with listening, not with hearing—an ambiguous beginning is an open opening.

But, indeed, something does precede God's creative act—there is more to the story than meets the eye. "And God said, 'Let there be light' and there was light. God saw that the light was good." The Good is not created—it is recognized. The metaphysical God presumes the ethical God. It is not that God called the light "good," and thereby it became good. If so, then he could have as easily called it "bad," and it would become bad. Moreover, if the goodness of the light were simply a matter of God's creative will, then he could at some later time call it bad and it would be bad. As God's creative action reaches its climax with the creation of Adam and Eve, this presumption of the priority of the ethical God to the metaphysical God is confirmed. In the Garden stands the Tree of the Knowledge of Good and Evil. It is this knowledge that ultimately distinguishes the Creator from his creation. As the serpent promised Eve, "For God knows that when you eat of it your eyes will be opened, and you will be like God, knowing good and evil." It is not the exercise of power and authority but unfolding, difficult, confounding self-knowledge as sinners that characterizes the sacred in human life.

## God as Ruler.

In creating humans, God goes beyond blessing them. He gives them dominion over all living things. This authority is explicitly similar to God's own authority—in His image. (In giving birth to Cain, Eve claims similarity as well as a creator, "She said, 'I have a created a man, just as the Lord did.'") The command not to eat of the fruit of the tree of the knowledge of good and evil is the first assertion of a hierarchy of authority. Just as man is to rule the living creation, man is to obey God. Ruling is a harder job than creating, however. Eve and Adam disobey—*not* "good." The serpent and Eve's offspring become enemies. The ground is cursed and will yield its fruits only with Adam's labor. Adam shall really rule only over his wife. And Adam and Eve are banished and driven out of the garden.

The fatal struggle for God's favor between Cain the sedentary farmer and Abel the nomadic shepherd sets the stage for God's invidious assertion of power. His favorites are hedged about with promises and covenants. As sole survivors of God's ethnic cleansing, Noah and his sons are given fearful power over every creature on earth and a promise never again to blot out the earth in flood. Out of an insult to his filial authority, Noah in his turn curses the sons of his son Ham and condemns them to slavery. In their subsequent flourishing, the clans of Noah get above themselves and propose to build a city and a sky-topping tower. God divides them and scatters them abroad in a fateful disunity whose violence we are still reaping today. And then, for no discernable reason (which may well be the point), the Lord tells Abram—a refugee with his father recently emigrated from Ur in Mesopotamia to Harran in Turkey—to leave Harran with his barren wife and his nephew in tow to "go to the land that I will show you. And I will make you into a great nation." Arriving in Canaan, God gives the Canaanites' land to Abram and his descendants. The promise will be a long time coming to fruition and not until Abram's willingness to obey had been put to the ultimate test. When Abram was already one hundred years old and Sarai, his wife, was ninety, God promises him a son, with whom He will have an everlasting covenant for all generations. In token of Abram's fealty, he must accept a new name—Abraham, Father of a Multitude—and be branded in the flesh with God's mark: circumcision. In due time the son, Isaac, is born. Testing Abraham, God says, "Take your son, your darling, whom you love, Isaac, and go to the land of Moriah, and burn him there as a sacrifice on one of the hills that I will show you." Not until the knife is raised to slit his son's throat does God relent: "Now I know how deeply you revere God, since you have not withheld your son, your darling, from me." Ideologically, God's purposes override human solidarity and decency.

## God as Judge.

No one has probed more deeply into the tension between this authoritarian God and the God who knows good and evil than Søren Kierkegaard. In *Fear and Trembling*, Kierkegaard asks whether Abraham is ethically justified to sacrifice his son at God's command? A father's highest duty is to love and protect his son. If Abraham is willing to violate this duty in order to maintain his special relation to God, then he is little better than a murderer. In that case, his egoism would tempt him to see himself as superior to the ordinary laws of filial piety. In Kierkegaard's language, he would be asserting his particularity over against the universal—just as does every ordinary outlaw and scoundrel ("these laws that apply to everyone else don't apply to *me*"). Nor is Abraham an Agamemnon, sacrificing—in pain and anguish—his daughter Iphigenia in order to save his people, redeem the honor of his household, and reconcile angry deities. Agamemnon's kingly tragedy is the highest expression of the universal, sacrificing the personal and particular for a higher duty as king, a duty that even Iphigenia might recognize. Perhaps, Kierkegaard asks, Abraham somehow has an absolute duty toward God that altogether sets aside the universal, sets aside the ordinary demands of loyalty, love, justice, truth, and honor, a "teleological suspension of the ethical?" Every attempt to make such an absolute duty intelligible must fail, first because the desire on the part of Abraham to make it intelligible would be hypocritical and a mere temptation (a desire to sneak the inexcusable back into the acceptable universal), second because "intelligibility" is mediated through the universal, the shared values and meanings of a community.[36] In this extremity, the God who commands and the God who knows good and evil are placed at dialectical—but irreconcilable—odds.

Within the Bible, this disconnection between God as Maker and Ruler and God as Righteous Judge is descried most pungently by Job on his dung heap. The *Book of Job* is one of the striking anomalies within the Old

---

[36] "Humanly speaking, he is crazy and cannot make himself intelligible to anyone. And yet it is the mildest expression to say that he is crazy. If he is not supposed to be that, then he is a hypocrite, and the higher he climbs on this [solitary] path, the more dreadful a hypocrite he is." Søren Kierkegaard, *Fear and Trembling: A Dialectical Lyric*, trans. Walter Lowrie (Garden City NY: Doubleday, 1954) 86.

Testament.[37] Who wrote it, when? The prose frame tale of Job in his household and God in his heaven with Ha-Satan, "The Accusing Angel," ranging about the earth seems ancient legend. The poetry of the central dialogue between Job and his so-called comforters—and ultimately between God himself and Job—contains some of richest and most variable language in the Bible. Job is not a Jew. Perhaps the author of *Job* was also a Gentile? Like that other extraordinarily anomalous canonical book *Ecclesiastes*, the *Book of Job* offers a theological perspective that makes nonsense of human life. Job is guiltless. He fears God and lives in anxiety at the possibility that he or his sons might sin inadvertently. When God brags on him as his obedient servant, Satan proposes a test even more severe than Abraham's. *Take away all that he has and he will curse you.* This will be a test that Job wins only by losing. His friends come to console him in his destitution and agony and stay to become his accusers. *Surely you have sinned somehow; you insult God and us by insisting on your innocence.* His wife tells him, *Curse God and die; there is nothing left to live for.* Now it is endings that crucially matter. Can there be an end that truly ends this farcical tragedy? Alone—a speck in the universe—Job cries out: *Tell me where I have sinned.* If he is in the right, then God is in the wrong. But the God that answers him from the whirlwind is the metaphysical God, the Maker of everything. *Can you pull up Leviathan on a fishhook? You are nothing, I am everything.* In that moment of presence, Job shuts his mouth. The question of guilt and innocence disappears before the majesty of God and his inconceivable Creation. For us, this ending is astoundingly insufficient—ethics reduced to rubble. Job's restoration in the epilogue is patently insufficient morally to replace the lost children and the lost security of his righteousness. Of Job's thoughts, we learn nothing more. God has silenced him metaphysically, leaving all his ethical questions silently resounding—even more so when God admits that Job's accusers were wrong in their insistence on his guilt. We are disappointed by this oriental Potentate and his whims, like the three rabbis at Auschwitz who put G-d on trial—and found Him *chayav* or "owing us something." In spite of our impulses to make this

[37] Robert Gordis goes so far as to claim that the Book of Job is without parallel: "The greatness of Job is heightened by the fact that it belongs to a unique literary genre, without parallel before or since its composition. It is literally the only book of its kind." *The Book of God and Man: A Study of Job* (Chicago/London: University of Chicago Press, 1978) 4.

come out right somehow, we are left in tension, faced with a truly ultimate question, *from whence can even God the Lord and Creator be judged?*

Friedrich Nietzsche was the first philosopher to grasp just how extraordinary a leap the ancient Jews had made beyond "natural morality" in encountering this God of Judgment. Natural morality, according to Nietzsche, is the tablet of virtues and goods prized by the superior human animal, superior by nature to other animals and to other men. Ancient Greece, with its implacable gods and tragic honor, is his touchstone for this aristocracy of mind and spirit. Superb instincts and traditions of excellence, together with a huge appetite for risk and mastery, elicited the exceptional, the brilliantly careless, the heroic. Alcibiades the Beautiful is his exemplar—he never counts the social cost of his overflowing exuberance, any more than nature counts its overflowing creation and destruction. Nature is going nowhere, no more than man is. The ability to embrace this profligate life energy, Nietzsche thinks, is the mark of the superior spirit, a nihilism that is *amor fati*, a love of necessity. His criticism of modern "degenerate" European herd morality[38] (and the philosophers like Immanuel Kant who attempt to rationalize it) has several strands to it—suffice it to say, he claims that it turns natural morality on its head. The natural good (predatory mastery) becomes evil exploitation and the natural bad (weakness and deficiency) becomes saintly restraint—he calls it a slave morality: the masters (the arrogant and self-willed) are "evil"; the slaves (the meek and obedient) are "good." His key point is it all began with the Jews ("natural slaves" according to Tacitus according to Nietzsche): "What Europe owes to the Jews? Many things, good and bad, and above all one thing that is both of the best and the worst: the grand style in morality, the terribleness and majesty of infinite demands, infinite meanings, the whole romanticism of and sublimity of moral questionabilities."[39]

---

[38] As much as he despises its final expression in the tepid Protestant Christianity of Northern Europe and Germany, he recognizes that the 2,500 years of its evolution from Socrates/Plato and Jesus/Paul/Augustine/Aquinas ("Christianity is Platonism for 'the people'") accomplished an immense deepening of human thinking. Friedrich Nietzsche, *Beyond Good and Evil: Prelude to a Philosophy of the Future*, trans. Walter Kaufmann (New York: Random House, 1966) 3. Thus, Nietzsche hypothesizes that the decay and death of Christian dogmatism offers an opportunity for yet another spiritual evolution, *amor fati with philosophic self-consciousness*, the *Übermensch* who can live joyously and honestly in a meaningless world without being seduced by the noble Platonic lies of a Kingdom of Heaven where purity of spirit embraces the sovereignty of the good.

[39] Ibid., 185.

## Original Sin.

In a world that is arbitrarily determined by a multitude of contending energies, wills, and perspectives, the Jews encountered a beyond that was absolutely unconditioned, a beyond that judged kings and pharaohs and even the gods, even the Lord God Almighty Himself. Nietzsche's metaphysical perspectivism[40] required that this be merely a philosophic fiction, as he considered even logic to be ("measuring reality against the purely invented world of the unconditional and self-identical.)"[41] But, following Levinas's rethinking of our philosophic and religious traditions, the children of Abraham encountered God *not* just as a necessary idea or preeminent dogma or ultimate reality, but as a primordial accountability, as a personal responsibility and fraught capacity for action that foreshadows the world and its will to power, *as original sin.* The issue is not one of metaphysics or faith; it is one of ethics and culpability. The God who can be present to us in this era of disenchantment is the God of Judgment. When we set aside the metaphysical mumbo-jumbo ("Creator") and the ideological hocus-pocus ("Lord"), we are left with the unique human capacity for sin, for willing evil because it is evil (an action already so incomprehensible that Plato declared it literally inconceivable). In our generations, the Holocaust (as the most unspeakable atrocity of all the wars and genocides of the modern era) stands for that absurd malignity.

Levinas helps us grasp the revolutionary import of the atemporal priority of ethics to metaphysics, of truly originating sin. He accepts Nietzsche's critique of Christianity and strips Christianity of its Platonism to recuperate the wisdom of Judaism, a prophetic wisdom he thinks is needed now more than ever. Western philosophy begins with the Greeks, with visions of Being, what it is really to exist and show forth, and of Reason as the ideal capacity to

---

[40] As Arthur Danto summarizes this "perspectivism" (quoting and translating from Nietzsche's unpublished notes, as indicated below) "There are *only* rival interpretations: 'There are no facts [*Tatsachen*], only interpretations.' And accordingly no *world in itself* apart from some interpretation—'As though there would be a world left over once we subtracted the perspectival!' We cannot even speak of these interpretations as 'distorting' reality, for there is nothing that counts as a veridical interpretation relative to which a given interpretation could distort: or *every* interpretation is a distortion, except that there is nothing for it to be a distortion of." *Nietzsche as Philosopher* (New York: Macmillan, 1965) 76–77.

[41] Nietzsche, *Beyond Good and Evil*, 12.

understand the totality of all beings.[42] Within this vision, a persistent challenge has been to find a metaphysical foundation for a rational ethics, for morality that has a universal rationale. From Plato to Kant, these brilliant efforts have failed. Following Hume's clear-eyed skepticism, contemporary philosophy reduces morality to sentiment, utility, or evolutionary advantage. Marx, Nietzsche, and Freud had already exposed its genealogies in disguised class privilege, slavish resentment, and repressed patricide, the secret bad faith that makes ethics just a covert assertion of the will to power. After the Holocaust, surely we all can see the hollowness of the pious hope that justice is built into the world,[43] just as, in this present moment, the brutal contest between Western protectors of individualistic human rights and radical Islamic jihadists mocks the notion of righteousness.[44]

As Levinas opens the question in his Preface to *Totality and Infinity*,

> Does not lucidity, the mind's openness upon the true, consist in catching sight of the permanent possibility of war? The state of war suspends morality; it divests the eternal institutions and obligations of their eternity and rescinds ad interim the unconditional imperatives;...it renders morality derisory. The art of foreseeing war and winning it by every means—politics—is henceforth enjoined as the very exercise of reason. Politics is opposed to morality, as philosophy to naïveté.[45]

Agreeing with Nietzsche that being *is* war, the totality of "Individuals...reduced to being bearers of forces that command them unbeknown to

[42] "Perhaps the most essential distinguishing feature of the language of Greek philosophy was its equation of truth with an *intelligibility of presence*. By this I mean an intelligibility that considers truth to be that which is present or copresent, that which can be gathered or synchronized into a totality that we would call the world or cosmos." Kearney, "Dialogue with Emmanuel Levinas," 19.

[43] Random murder trumps the heart's desire: "The arc of the moral universe is long but it bends toward justice," Martin Luther King, Jr. proclaimed in 1967—paraphrasing a sermon by the abolitionist Theodore Parker in 1853—seven months before King was assassinated in Memphis.

[44] In one of his essays on Judaism, Levinas exclaims, "The European moral conscience did exist! It flourished in that happy period in which centuries of Christian and philosophic civilization had not yet revealed, in the Hitlerian adventure, the fragility of their works." "Ethics and Spirit," 5.

[45] Levinas, *Totality and Infinity*, 21–23. The following quotations from *Totality and Infinity* are from these pages.

themselves," Levinas looks instead to a messianic diachrony[46]—a Jewish wisdom to supplement Greek wisdom—as a relationship with "*a surplus always exterior to the totality*." He calls this rupture of totality a "relation with the infinity of being which exceeds the totality,...the possibility of a *signification without a context*." This possibility of a "signification without a context" eludes Nietzsche's perspectivism and thereby his nihilism—without falling back into Platonism and its hierarchy of Being.

How is it possible for us to refer to something when we have no idea where or what we are (without a context—without a metaphysics or an ideology)? Only if it breaks up our solitude by referring *to us*: "One looks at a look."[47] At its most elemental, according to Levinas, my being-for-the-Other is "always already," that is, my consciousness of myself as a will to power and unique perspective among others dawns in the face of the Other and its resistance to possession and my consequent temptation to murder, "the temptation of absolute negation": "To awaken to a face is already to hear 'You shall not kill', and to hear 'You shall not kill' is to hear 'Social justice.'"[48] The unconditional heteronomy that conditions my derivative autonomy means I am primordially responsible for my capacity to murder—*I find myself defined prior to any action or intention in the world as a potential murderer*: "The Other counts as an interlocutor prior even to being known." My autonomy—my will to power—is null and void except in a social context, a context that holds me endlessly responsible for my neighbor. This finally is the answer to Kant. Ethics is not the product of my autonomy as a rational will (within the cogency of a merely postulated sacred scene of action); it is the accusation of the Other actually before me prior to my willing: original sin—sacral from before the beginning of beginning—the ultimate narrative amphiboly. In our

---

[46] The Messiah has come this very day. It all waits on us now—and our repentance. We don't have to wait on a new prophet—a new generation—a new politics—a new philosophy—a new dialectical reconciliation—a new genome—a new divine dispensation—a renewed time. It is simply infantile at this stage of human history to insist we're not ready yet to shoulder our responsibilities for our neighbor (maybe tomorrow after I get a raise?): "Salvation does not stand as an end to History, or act as its conclusion. It remains *at every moment* possible." Emmanuel Levinas, "Messianic Texts," *Difficult Freedom: Essays on Judaism*, trans. Seán Hand (Baltimore: The Johns Hopkins University Press, 1990) 84.

[47] Levinas "Ethics and Spirit," 8–9. The following quotations from "Ethics and Spirit" are from these pages.

[48] He continues, "And everything I can hear coming from God or going to God, Who is invisible, must have come to me via the one, unique voice."

tangential knowledge of God, we must live as if we are already in the midst of a cosmic story, our lives testimony to its judgment on us.[49] Don't we—and Nietzsche too(!)—already know this, however much we may try to evade, dull, or resist it? Don't we?

[49] Nietzsche's active nihilism seems here to be a frantic and neurotic attempt to evade this judgment, perhaps both because he felt it so acutely and because he was unable clearly to distinguish his "active" nihilism from the "passive" nihilism of Romantic *Weltschmerz.* See Gianni Vattimo, "Nihilism: Reactive and Passive," *Nietzsche and the Rhetoric of Nihilism,* eds. Tom Darby, Bela Egyed, and Ben Jones (Ottawa: Carleton University Press, 1989) 15–21.

# Selected Bibliography

This meditation, long in gestation, is rich in suggested reading and expansive illustrations. Accordingly, I have restricted this working bibliography to texts and authors that are most immediately probative for the claims I make herein. In every case, adequate documentation exists in the footnotes to access the broader "aura" of my thought, as desired. But you'll have to read the footnotes to get all of it.

## General


Anselm. *Proslogion, with the Replies of Gaunilo and Anselm.* Translated by Thomas Williams. Indianapolis IN: Hackett Publishing Company, Inc., 1995.

Auerbach, Erich. *Mimesis: The Representation of Reality in Western Literature.* Translated by Willard Trask. Princeton: Princeton University Press, 1953.

Bacon, Francis. *Novum Organum.* Boston: Taggard & Thompson, 1863.

Barfield, Owen. *Poetic Diction: A Study In Meaning.* Middletown CN: Wesleyan University Press, 1973.

———. *Saving the Appearances: A Study in Idolatry.* Middletown CN: Wesleyan University Press, 1988.

Bloom, Harold. "Inescapable Poe." *New York Review of Books* 31.15 (1984) www.nybooks.com/articles/1984/10/11/inescapable-poe/.

Booth, Wayne. *The Rhetoric of Fiction,* 2nd ed. Chicago: University of Chicago Press, 1983.

Brooks, Peter. *Reading for the Plot: Design and Intention in Narrative.* Cambridge: Harvard University Press, 1992.

Browne, Jackson. "Running on Empty." Asylum Records, 1977.

Calvin, John. *Brief Instruction for Arming All the Good Faithful Against the Errors of the Common Sect of the Anabaptists,* 1549. www.truecovenanter.com/calvin/calvin_against_anabaptists.htm.

Cohen, Leonard. "Anthem." *Columbia Records*, 1992.

Cohen, Michael. "Paul Laurence Dunbar and the Genres of Dialect." *African American Review* 41.2 (2007).

Crossan, John Dominic. *The Power of Parable.* San Francisco: Harper One, 2012.

Danto, Arthur. *Nietzsche as Philosopher.* New York: Macmillan, 1965.

Davie, Grace. "Believing without Belonging: Is This the Future of Religion in Britain?" *Social Compass* 37.4 (1990): 455-469.

DuBois, W.E.B. *Dusk of Dawn: An Essay Toward an Autobiography of a Race Concept.* New York: Schocken Books, 1968.

———. "On Being Ashamed of Oneself: An Essay on Race Pride." *Crisis* 40 (9 September 1933).

———. *The Souls of Black Folk*. Boston: Bedford Books, 1997.

Eliade, Mircea. *The Myth of the Eternal Return: Cosmos and History*. Translated by Willard R. Trask. Princeton: Princeton University Press, 1971.

———. *The Sacred and the Profane: The Nature of Religion*. Translated by Willard R. Trask. New York: Harper Torchbooks, 1961.

Emerson, Ralph Waldo. "The American Scholar." *Essays and English Traits*. The Harvard Classics, Vol.5. New York: P.F. Collier & Son, 1909.

Everette, Anna. "'I Want The Same Things Other People Enjoy': The Black Press and the Classic Hollywood Studio System, 1930-40." *Spectator* 17.1 (1996). cinema.usc.edu/assets/099/15965.pdf.

Durkheim, Emile. *The Elementary Forms of Religious Life*. Edited by Mark S. Cladis. Translated by Carol Cosman. Oxford: Oxford University Press, 2001.

Friedman, Milton. "The Methodology of Positive Economics." *Essays in Positive Economics*. Chicago: University of Chicago Press, 1966.

Gates, Jr., Henry Louis. *The Signifying Monkey: A Theory of African-American Literary Criticism*. New York: Oxford University Press, 1988.

Gellner, Ernest. *Plough, Sword and Book: The Structure of Human History*. Chicago: University of Chicago Press, 1988.

Goldberg, Jonah. *The Suicide of the West: How the Rebirth of Tribalism, Populism, Nationalism, and Identity Politics Is Destroying American Democracy*. New York: Random House, 2018.

Gordis, Robert. *The Book of God and Man: A Study of Job*. Chicago/London: University of Chicago Press, 1978.

*Hedgehog Review: After Secularization* 8:1/2 (Spring/Summer 2006).

Heidegger, Martin. "Letter on Humanism." *Pathmarks*. Edited by W. McNeill. Translated by F. A. Capuzzi. Cambridge: Cambridge University Press, 1998.

Hruska, Anne. "Love and Slavery: Serfdom, Emancipation, and Family in Tolstoy's Fiction." *The Russian Review* 66.4 (2007).

Hume, David. *Dialogues Concerning Natural Religion*. Edited by Nelson Pike. Indianapolis IN: Bobbs-Merrill Company, 1970.

Jackson, Kevin. "The Great Bad Writer." *Prospect: The Leading Magazine of Ideas* (March 2012).

Jaspers, Karl. *The Origin and Goal of History*. New Haven CN: Yale University Press, 1953.

Josipovici, Gabriel. *The Book of God: A Response to the Bible*. New Haven/London: Yale University Press, 1988.

Kant, Immanuel, *Critique of Pure Reason*. Translated by Norman Kemp Smith. London: Macmillan, 1933.

———. *Grounding for the Metaphysics of Morals*. Translated by James Ellington. Indianapolis IN: Hackett Publishing Company, Inc., 1993.

Kearney, Richard. "Dialogue with Emmanuel Levinas." *Face to Face with Levinas*. Edited by Richard Cohen. Albany NY: State University of New York Press, 1986.

———. "Narrative Imagination: Between Ethics and Poetics." *Philosophy and Social Criticism* 21.5/6 (1995).

Keats, John. *The Complete Poetical Works and Letters of John Keats*. Edited by Horace E. Scudder. Boston: Houghton, Mifflin and Company, 1899.

———. *The Letters of John Keats, 1814-1821*. Edited by Hyder Edward Rollins. Cambridge: Cambridge University Press, 1958.

Kiberd, Declan. "Anglo-Irish Attitudes." *Field Day Pamphlet, No. 6* (1984).

Kierkegaard, Søren. *Concluding Unscientific Postscript*. Translated by David Swenson and Walter Lowrie. Princeton: Princeton University Press, 1941.

———. *Fear and Trembling: A Dialectical Lyric*. Translated by Walter Lowrie. Garden City, NY: Doubleday, 1954.

Leach, Edmund and D. Alan Aycock. *Structuralist Interpretations of Biblical Myth*. Cambridge: Cambridge University Press, 1983.

Levinas, Emmanuel. "Diachrony and Representation." *Time and the Other and Additional Essays*. Translated by Richard A. Cohen. Pittsburgh: Duquense University Press, 1987.

———. *Ethics and Infinity: Conversations with Philippe Nemo*. Translated by Richard Cohen. Pittsburgh PA: Duquesne University Press, 1987.

———. "Ethics and Spirit." *Difficult Freedom: Essays on Judaism*. Translated by Seán Hand. Baltimore: The Johns Hopkins University Press, 1990.

———. "Messianic Texts." *Difficult Freedom: Essays on Judaism*. Translated by Seán Hand. Baltimore: The Johns Hopkins University Press, 1990.

———. *Otherwise than Being or Beyond Essence*. Translated by Alphonso Lingis. The Hague: Martinus Nijhoff Publishers, 1981.

———. "Philosophy and the Idea of Infinity." *Collected Philosophical Papers*. Translated by Alphonso Lingis. Dordrecht: Nijhoff, 1987.

———. *Time and the Other*. Translated by Richard Cohen. Pittsburgh PA: Duquesne University Press, 1987.

———. *Totality and Infinity: An Essay on Exteriority*. Translated by Alphonso Lingis. Pittsburgh: Duquesne University Press, 1969.

———. "Transcendence and Evil." *Collected Philosophical Papers*. Translated by Alphonso Lingis. Dordrecht: Martinus Nijhoff, 1987.

Lévi-Strauss, Claude. *The Savage Mind*. Translated by George Weidenfield. Chicago: University of Chicago Press, 1962.

———. *Structural Anthropology*. Translated by Claire Jacobson and Brooke Grindfest Schoepf. New York: Basic Books, 1963.

Marchisio, Roberto and Maurizo Pisati. "Belonging without Believing: Catholics in Contemporary Italy." *Journal of Modern Italian Studies* 4.2 (1999): 236-255.

Nietzsche, Friedrich. B*eyond Good and Evil: Prelude to a Philosophy of the Future*. Translated by Walter Kaufmann. New York: Random House, 1966.

———. *The Wanderer and his Shadow*. Translated by R.J. Hollingdale. Cambridge: Cambridge University Press, 1996.

Otto, Rudolph. *The Idea of the Holy*. Translated by John W. Harvey. Oxford: Oxford University Press, 1958.

Pagels, Elaine. "From Jesus to Christ." *Frontline* www.pbs.org/wgbh/pages/frontline/shows/religion/maps/primary/thunder.

Parks, Tim. "In Search of Authenticity," *New York Review of Books* (4 February 2015). www.nybooks.com/daily/2015/02/04/novels-search-authenticity/.

Pew Research Center. "America's Changing Religious Landscape." (12 May 2015).

Percy, Walker. *The Message in the Bottle.* New York: Farrar, Straus, and Giroux, 1975.

Poe, Edgar Allan. "The Philosophy of Composition." *Graham's Magazine* 28.4 (1846).

Popper, Karl. *Objective Knowledge: An Evolutionary Approach*. New York: Oxford University Press, 1975.

Prine, John. "Angel from Montgomery." www.lyrics.com/lyric/2853521. (1971).

Ricoeur, Paul and Richard Kearney. "Myth as the Bearer of Possible Worlds." *The Crane Bag* 2.1/2 (1978).

Robinson, Marilynn. "On Edgar Allen Poe." *New York Review of Books* 62.2 (2015). www.nybooks.com/articles/2015/02/05/edgar-allan-poe/.

Rorty, Richard. "Pragmatism, Pluralism and Postmodernism." *Philosophy and Social Hope*. London: Penguin Books, 1999.

Ryle, Gilbert. *The Concept of Mind.* New York: Barnes & Noble, 1949.

Scott, Jr., Nathan A. *Negative Capability: Studies in the New Literature and the Religious Situation.* New Haven CN: Yale University Press, 1969.

Shakespeare, William. *As You Like It*, 1598.

Sophocles, *The Three Theban Plays*, Translated by Robert Fagles. New York: Viking Penguin, 1982.

Taylor, Charles. *A Secular Age*. Cambridge: Harvard University Press, 2007.

"Thunder, Perfect Mind." Translated by George MacRae. *The Nag Hammadi Library*, 2009. www.gnosis.org/naghamm/thunder.

Tillyard E.M.W. and C.S. Lewis, *The Personal Heresy: A Controversy*. Oxford: Oxford University Press, 1939.

Unger, Roberto. "The Critical Legal Studies Movement." *Harvard Law Review* 96 (1983).

United States Holocaust Memorial Museum, "Protocols of the Elders of Zion," *Holocaust Encyclopedia*, www.ushmm.org/wlc/en/article.php?ModuleId=10007058

Vattimo, Gianni. "Nihilism: Reactive and Passive." *Nietzsche and the Rhetoric of Nihilism*. Edited by Tom Darby, Bela Egyed, and Ben Jones. Ottawa: Carleton University Press, 1989.

Watt, Ian. *The Rise of the Novel.* Berkeley: University of California Press, 1957.

Weber, Max. "Science as a Vocation." *Max Weber: Essays in Sociology*. Edited by Hans Gerth and C. Wright Mills. London: Routledge & Kegan Paul, 1948.

Weston, Jessie Laidlay. *The Quest of the Holy Grail.* London: G. Bell, 1913.

Wimsatt, Jr., W.K. and Monroe Beardsley. "The Intentional Fallacy." *Sewanee Review* 54 (1946): 468-488.

Wittgenstein, Ludwig. *Philosophical Investigations*. Edited by G.E.M. Anscombe and Rush Rhees. Translated by G.E.M. Anscombe. Oxford: Blackwell, 1953.

## Malamud

*Bernard Malamud: A Collection of Critical Essays*. Edited by Leslie A. Field and Joyce W. Field. London: Prentice-Hall, 1975.

*Bernard Malamud and the Critics*. Edited by Leslie A Field and Joyce W. Field. New York: New York University Press, 1970.

*Bernard Malamud, Modern Critical Views*. Edited by Harold Bloom. New York: Chelsea House Publishers, 1986.

Bilik, Dorothy Seidman. *Immigrant-Survivors: Post-Holocaust Consciousness in Recent Jewish American Fiction*. Middletown: Wesleyan University Press, 1981.

Brown, Peter C. "Negative Capability and the Mystery of Hope in Malamud's 'The First Seven Years.'" *Religion & Literature* 29.1 (1997): 63-94.

Cohen, Sandy. *Bernard Malamud and the Trial by Love*. Amsterdam: Rodopi, 1974.

*Critical Essays on Bernard Malamud*, Edited by Joel Salzberg. Boston: G.K. Hall & Co, 1987.

Davis, Phillip. *Bernard Malamud: A Writer's Life*. Oxford: Oxford University Press, 2007.

Ducharme, Robert. *Art and Idea in the Novels of Bernard Malamud: Toward The Fixer*. The Hague: Mouton, 1974.

Hassan, Ihab. *Radical Innocence: Studies in the Contemporary American Novel*. Princeton: Princeton University Press, 1961.

Helterman, Jeffrey. *Understanding Bernard Malamud*. Columbia: University of South Carolina Press, 1985.

Hershinow Shelton. *Bernard Malamud*. New York: Ungar, 1980.

Kermode, Frank. *Continuities*. London: Routledge, 1968.

Klein, Marcus. *After Alienation: American Novels in Mid-Century*. Cleveland: World, 1965.

Malamud, Bernard. *The Complete Stories*. Edited by Robert Giroux. New York: Farrar, Straus and Giroux, 1997.

———. *The Natural*. New York: Farrar, 1952.

Richman, Sidney. *Bernard Malamud*. New York: Twayne, 1966.

Smith, Janna Malamud. *My Father Is A Book*. Boston: Houghton Mifflin Co., 2006.

Solotaroff, Robert. *Bernard Malamud: A Study of the Short Fiction*. Boston: Twayne, 1989.

Stern, Daniel. "The Art of Fiction, Bernard Malamud No. 52." *The Paris Review* 61 (1975). www.theparisreview.org/interviews/3869/bernard-malamud-the-art-of-fiction-no-52-bernard-malamud.

Wisse, Ruth R. *The Modern Jewish Canon*. New York: The Free Press, 2000.

## O'Connor

Coffey, Warren. "Flannery O'Connor." *Commentary* (November 1965), www.commentarymagazine.com/articles/flannery-oconnor/.

Fike, Matthew. "The Timothy Allusion in 'A Good Man Is Hard to Find.'" *Renascence: Essays on Value in Literature* 52.4 (Summer 2000): 311-19.

Gentry, Marshall Bruce. *Flannery O'Connor's Religion of the Grotesque*. Jackson, MS: University Press of Mississippi, 1986.

Gooch, Brad. *Flannery: A Life of Flannery O'Connor*. New York: Little, Brown, 2009.

Hawkes, John. "Flannery O'Connor's Devil." *Suwanee Review* 70.3 (1962).

Niederauer, George. "Flannery O'Connor's Religious Vision." *America, The Jesuit Review* (2007). www.americamagazine.org/issue/639/article/flannery-oconnors-religious-vision.

O'Connor, Flannery. *O'Connor: Collected Work*, Edited by Sally Fitzgerald. New York: Library of America, 1988.

———. *The Complete Stories*. Introduction by Robert Giroux. New York: Farrar, Straus, & Giroux, 1972.

———. *Letters of Flannery O'Connor: The Habit of Being*. Edited by Sally Fitzgerald. New York: Farrar, Straus, & Giroux, 1979.

———. *Mystery and Manners: Occasional Prose*. Edited by Sally Fitzgerald and Robert Fitzgerald. New York: Farrar, Straus, & Giroux, 1969.

O'Neil, Joseph. "Touched by Evil." *The Atlantic* (June 2009). www.theatlantic.com/magazine/archive/2009/06/touched-by-evil/307422/.

## Updike

Baddiel, Adam. "Suburban Legend," *NewStatesman* (2 May 2014) www.newstatesman.com/2014/04/judging-john-updike.

Barnes, Julian. "Running Away." *The Guardian* (16 October 2009). www.theguardian.com/books/2009/oct/17/julian-barnes-john-updike-rabbit.

Batchelor, Bob. *John Updike: A Critical Biography*. Santa Barbara, CA: Praeger, 2013.

Begley, Adam. *Updike*. New York: HarperCollins, 2014.

Bloom, Harold. *John Updike*. New York: Chelsea House, 1987.

Deresiewicz, William. "'A Great Symphony of American Junk': What David Foster Wallace misunderstood about John Updike." *The New Republic* (8 September 2014). newrepublic.com/article/119200/updike-reviewed-william-deresiewicz.

Detweiler, Robert. *John Updike*. Boston: Twayne,1984.

Farmer, Michial. "On Updike: An Interview with Michial Farmer on Updike in the Contemporary Moment." *Former People* (8 April 2017). formerpeople.wordpress.com/2017/04/08/on-updike-an-interview-with-michial-farmer-on-updike-in-the-contemporary-moment/.

*John Updike and Religion: The Sense of the Sacred and the Motions of Grace*. Edited by James Yerkes. Grand Rapids, Michigan: William B. Eerdmans, 1999.

McEwan, Ian. "On John Updike." *New York Review of Books* (12 March 2009).

Ricks, Christopher. "Flopsy Bunny." *New York Review of Books* (16 December 1971).

Siegel, Lee. "Writing Off Updike." *The Daily Beast* (1 February 2009). www.thedailybeast.com.

Ulin, David. "For better or worse, John Updike produced a nearly endless stream of work." *Los Angeles Times* (27 January 2009).

Updike, John. *The Early Stories, 1953-1975*. New York: Knopf, 2003.

———. *Endpoint*. New York: Alfred A. Knopf, 2009.

———. *Higher Gossip: Essays and Criticism*. New York: Alfred A. Knopf, 2011.

———. "John Updike, The Art of Fiction No.43." Interviewed by Charles Thomas Samuels. *Paris Review* (Winter 1968).

———. *Licks of Love*. New York: Random House, 2000.

———. "On The Sidewalk (After Reading, at Long Last, *On the Road*, by Jack Kerouac)." *The New Yorker* (25 February 1959).

———. *Picked-Up Pieces*. New York: Random House, 1975.

———. "Pigeon Feathers." *The New Yorker* (19 August 1961), www.newyorker.com/magazine/1961/08/19/pigeon-feathers.

———. *Rabbit Angstrom: A Tetralogy*. New York: Knopf, 1995

———. *Self-Consciousness: Memoirs*. New York: Random House, 1989.

Wallace, David Foster. "John Updike, Champion Literary Phallocrat, Drops One; Is This Finally the End for Magnificent Narcissists?" *The New York Observer* (13 October 1997). observer.com/1997/10/john-updike-champion-literary-phallocrat-drops-one-is-this-finally-the-end-for-magnificent-narcissists/

Wood, James. "Gossip in Gilt." *London Review of Books* 23 (19 April 2001).

## Morrison

Als, Hilton. "Ghosts in the House: How Toni Morrison fostered a generation of black writers." *The New Yorker* (27 October 2003). www.newyorker.com/magazine/2003/10/27/ghosts-in-the-house.

Blatt, Ben. "Toni Morrison Is More Hemingway than Hemingway Himself." *Literary Hub* (17 March 2017).

Crouch, Stanley. "Literary Conjure Woman." *The New Republic* (19 October 1987).

Dreifus, Claudia. "Chloe Wofford Talks About Toni Morrison." *New York Times Book Review* (11 September 1994).

Ghansah, Rachel Kaadzi. "What Toni Morrison Saw." *New York Times Magazine* (12 April 2015).

Joyner, Louisa. *Toni Morrison, the Essential Guide*. London: Vintage, 2003.

Kakutani, Michiko. "'Paradise': Worthy Women, Unredeemable Men." *New York Times* (6 January 1998). www.movies2.nytimes.com/books/98/01/04/daily/morrison-book-review-art.html.

Leve, Ariel. "Toni Morrison on Love, Loss, and Modernity." *The Telegraph* [UK] (17 July 2012).

Mitchell, Koritha. "Belief and Performance, Morrison and Me." *Toni Morrison: Forty Years in the Clearing*. Edited by Carmen Gillespie. Lewisburg PA: Bucknell University Press, 2012).

Morrison, Toni. *Beloved*. New York: Vintage, 2004.

———. *The Bluest Eye*. New York: Washington Square Press, 1970.

———. *Conversations with Toni Morrison*. Edited by Danielle Taylor-Guthrie. Jackson, MS: University Press of Mississippi, 1994.

———. "Home." *The House That Race Built*. Edited by Wahneema Lubiano. New York: Pantheon, 1997.

———. "'I Regret Everything': Toni Morrison Looks Back on her Personal Life." *Fresh Air* (24 August 2015). ///F:/Book/Morrison/'I Regret Everything'%20 Toni Morrison Looks Back On Her Personal Life%20%20 NPR.htm.

———. *Jazz*. New York: Vintage, 2004.

———. *Paradise*. New York: Vintage, 2014.

———. *The Origin of Others*. Cambridge: Harvard University Press, 2017.

———. *Playing in the Dark: Whiteness and the Literary Imagination*. New York: Random House, 1992.

———. "Unspeakable Things Unspoken: The Afro-American Presence in American Literature." *The Tanner Lectures at the University of Michigan* (7 October 1988). tannerlectures.utah.edu/_documents/a-to-z/m/morrison90.pdf.

———. *What Moves at the Margin: Selected Nonfiction*. Edited by Carolyn C. Denard. Jackson MS: University Press of Mississippi, 2008.

Roynon, Tessa. "The Africanness of Classicism in the Work of Toni Morrison." *African Athena: New Agendas*. Edited by Daniel Orrells et al. Oxford: Oxford University Press, 2011.

———. *The Cambridge Introduction to Toni Morrison*. Cambridge: Cambridge University Press, 2013.

Schappell, Elissa."Toni Morrison, The Art of Fiction No. 134." *The Paris Review* 128 \(1993). www.theparisreview.org/interviews/1888/toni-morrison-the-art-of-fiction-no-134-toni-morrison.

*Toni Morrison and the Bible*. Edited by Shirley Stave. New York: Peter Lang, 2006.

*Toni Morrison: Critical Perspectives Past and Present.* Edited by Henry Louis Gates, Jr. and K.A. Appiah. New York: Amistad Press, 1993.

*Unflinching Gaze: Morrison and Faulkner Re-Envisioned.* Edited by Carol Kolmerten et al. Jackson: University Press of Mississippi, 1997.

Wood, James. "Toni Morrison's False Magic." *The Broken Estate: Essays on Literature and Belief.* New York: Random House, 1999.

Young, John. "Toni Morrison, Oprah Winfrey, and Postmodern Popular Audiences." *African American Review* 35.2 (2001).

# Index

The table of contents makes patent the regime of references to the fictions by the four primary authors discussed. This index is accordingly restricted to references to critical, theological, and philosophical perspectives brought to bear on the interpretation of these authors and their works